MOON OVER MARRAKECH

MOON OVER MARRAKECH

A MEMOIR OF LOVING
TOO DEEPLY
IN A FOREIGN LAND

NAZNEEN SHEIKH

author of *Tea and Pomegranates*

Cormorant Books

Canada Council   Conseil des Arts
for the Arts   du Canada

The publisher gratefully acknowledges the support of the Canada Council for the Arts
and the Ontario Arts Council for its publishing program. We acknowledge the
financial support of the Government of Canada through the Book Publishing
Industry Development Program (BPIDP) for our publishing activities.

Printed and bound in Canada

Library and Archives Canada Cataloguing in Publication

Sheikh, Nazneen
Moon over Marrakech / Nazneen Sheikh.

ISBN 978-1-897151-71-6

1. Sheikh, Nazneen. 2. Sheikh, Nazneen — Marriage.
3. Manic-depressive persons — Family relationships — Canada.
4. Marrakech (Morocco) — Biography. 5. Toronto (Ont.) — Biography.
6. Authors, Canadian (English)—20th century — Biography. I. Title.

PS8587.H379Z53 2010   C813'.54   C2009-906867-2

Cover design: Angel Guerra/Archetype
Text design: Tannice Goddard, Soul Oasis Networking
Printer: Transcontinental

CORMORANT BOOKS INC.
215 SPADINA AVENUE, STUDIO 230, TORONTO, ON CANADA M5T 2C7
www.cormorantbooks.com

FSC

Mixed Sources
Product group from well-managed
forests, controlled sources and
recycled wood or fiber

Cert no. SW-COC-000952
www.fsc.org
© 1996 Forest Stewardship Council

FOR DRISS MOUSSOUI
True hero of the Maghrib

There will be time, there will be time
To prepare a face to meet the faces that you meet;
There will be time to murder and create,
And time for all the works and days of hands
That lift and drop a question on your plate;
Time for you and time for me,
And time yet for a hundred indecisions,
And for a hundred visions and revisions,
Before the taking of a toast and tea.

T. S. ELLIOT, FROM "THE LOVE SONG OF J. ALFRED PRUFROCK"

CHAPTER I

TORONTO, MARCH 2007

MY FRIENDS ARE SHOCKED BY my predicament. An illegal wedding in Morocco, my brutal exploitation by a man for whom I almost gave up my life in Toronto. My current financial woes are difficult enough. What really puzzles me are items of missing jewellery, curious items of lingerie, a missing rare first edition — Tavernier's *Travels in India* with its antique maps — and an art folio of expensive prints. When my cartons arrived in Toronto, I found that even a collection of photographs along with the negatives, and bills from the wedding caterer in Morocco had also disappeared. However, everyone seems to be relieved that I have returned home.

I am standing before the wall of glass windows looking at the Rosedale Valley Ravine. Snow covers the trees, bending them out of shape, and the morning light is a band of grey. The skidding line of cars on the street below moves in a stop and start pattern, their overworked exhausts shrouding them in white fog. The complete absence of colour outside reflects my internal state as well. I have always associated colour with the movement of life and at this moment, I feel like a bird whose flight has been arrested mid-air. I hover between two worlds, unable to land safely in either one.

Although I am familiar with the capricious vagaries of April in Toronto, I have no sense of ownership or familiarity. My disconnected state brings relief only in the type of anonymity I have created on my return. My sole focus in life is the recovery of my fractured arm and gathering fragments of a life I discarded last year. I am not even certain if this life will suit me, so both tasks remain daunting.

Behind me, the new apartment close to my old neighbourhood displays all the Moroccan furnishings I designed, acquired, and shipped back. This is a home that vividly exhibited another history just as my old home, the Endhouse, did. In the bedroom, the bed from Casablanca lies flanked by the metal-embossed night tables, ivory camel-skin lamps banded with strips of metal, and a long chest of drawers draped in hammered metal. The treasures of the craftsmen of Marrakech have followed me to Canada.

I still sleep on "my" side of the bed because the other side is like the edge of an abyss. There are moments when I think I should get rid of everything Moroccan in my home but I am tired of buying and discarding furniture. When the container arrived and the cartons were unpacked, there was an odour of leather, wood, and musk I was unable to get rid of for days. The scent of Marrakech roses, dusty environs, golden sunlight, and steaming "Tajines" seemed trapped into the seams of fabrics and stitched into the lining of my soul.

But I view them coldly now and halt the roll of nostalgia with a barricade of newly acquired resistance. When a framed photograph of Khadim rolled out of the packing material, I immediately turned it on its face. Although I have organized the spacious apartment with my customary flair, down to having it painted in the rose-tinted terracotta hue of Marrakech, I have no interest in it whatsoever.

This is the fourth home I have created in nine months. I have faultlessly brought back with me an emotionally perilous ambience and its exotic flavour enchants my friends, but mocks me daily. I have a twelve-month plan for survival and beyond that, I have no other life plan.

I rejoined a health club nearby where all the exercise equipment is spread out. On the first day I go to it, I look at the weight machines and do not permit my accident at the health club in Marrakech to discourage me. It reminds me of my father placing me back on the horse I had fallen off as a child. My arm was released from its cast yesterday and I am learning not to hate the long scar, which stretches from the middle of the forearm to the elbow.

There are two metal plates in this arm, which the surgeon in Marrakech inserted, and I believe that a foreign substance has entered my body forever. This limb is suspect and unreliable. I pretend it does not exist.

To my surprise, my body exerts its own will and within weeks I develop my muscle tone and the injured arm regains all its former strength. Each month when I march into the Orthopaedic wing of the hospital and look at the new set of X-rays, I become conscious that both the gap on the fractured bone and the rip in my shredded psyche are closing.

The grotesque eight-month experience has altered my perception of the predictability of my previous life. There are times when I question whether the frequent and relentless challenge to my survival skills has introduced a new reflex into my behaviour. Will the grid of my innate personality become unfamiliar? My decision to trade a thriving metropolis for a picturesque small town in North Africa transformed me into a precarious acrobat balanced over the charm of a city's rose-coloured antiquity and seared by the flame of failed promises.

Had I yearned for an organic solution to my technology-riddled society and chosen a partner who appeared to reincarnate a fabled mythology? Had I simply projected my vision fuelled by a powerful imagination on an unworthy ally whose utterances were simply a hashish dream?

BEFORE I LEFT MARRAKECH, I only telephoned one person to say goodbye. She was a distinguished author in Rabat.

"You are leaving?" said Fatema.

"Yes," I reply. "I think Marrakech was simply a dream and the man who brought me here has disappeared. I am going home. I have had an operation and I want my own medical system."

"But it was your dream."

"No, I always believed he shared it with me."

"Rubbish. It was always your dream. He was an opportunist. He just walked into your dream."

I am close to tears. "I think it is more than that, I have a history with Marrakech. I felt it was my city."

"Of course Marrakech will always be your home. Finish the book and come back for a holiday whenever you want," she says briskly.

These are days when I turn inwards. I examine my spiritual identification with Khadim. My best tool for this exercise is pragmatism. I spend days mulling over it and realize that what he practised is not the faith I was raised in. It is the Malakite interpretation of Islam practiced in Morocco, mired in dogmatic absolutism. Lurking beneath his urbane and thinly lacquered French patina was the ferocity of a tribal code that confined women to locked homes, exercised a rapacious control over their personal assets and mobility, and then sought absolution through prayer. His daily devotion in the form of prayer is tainted, and his behaviour is both godless and suspect.

I am now able rationally to disentangle the skeins of eroticism from spiritualism and examine the guilt-ridden crevices of my own life. I have been raised by liberal Muslim parents who did not pray five times a day. I married out of my faith and only retained a symbolic association with the faith practised by my parents. Through Khadim, I intended to reclaim a spirituality that I mistakenly thought had been repressed for years. It was an unpredictable life journey and I was unable to recognize hazard when it bludgeoned me under the guise of romance. Yet the tip of North West Africa, like the handle of a Berber dagger, was plunged into me and now I must endure. Outwardly, I embrace the flow of my sane and familiar civil society but inwardly my life is marked by the solitude of a misplaced warrior. These are emotions I cannot reveal, as I do not wish to be perceived as a victim. I intend to convert misadventure into a survival skill of sorts and am repelled by the notion that I am diminished.

Although my study was assembled within hours with the writing desk and all my familiar items, I only enter it to lie on the couch and watch television at night. Sometimes I glance at the computer lying with its lid closed but am aware that I am not ready to start. It is as though white paint has been poured over a series of vivid paintings. There is nothing to see, so there is nothing to describe and I have convinced myself that I have lost my ability to write. A long-standing devotee of the full moon, I watch it one night coming home from a party. I park my car and gaze up at the night for a few seconds and when I return home I walk into the study and open the black fabric book bag lying at the corner of the desk.

It contains two manuscripts in separate folders and my journal. I have not opened this bag for three months. The bag was packed in Marrakech in a small carton. I labelled it with my left hand as the right was in the sling. I scrolled the Arabic word "Kitab," which means book, and in that largely traumatized condition, post surgery, I hoped that the ship sailing from Casablanca to Montreal would capsize en route.

I now pull open the sturdy Velcro fastening and discover that the notebook with the maroon spine is missing. It was stolen by the only person who knew of its existence, location, and contents. My outrage at Khadim, followed by a searing anger, makes me hurl the bag across the room where the folders open and an avalanche of paper spills around my desk. I pick up my car keys and head for the lakeshore at the foot of the city. Here, I drive west along the boulevard and reach a familiar spot. I stand by the edge of the dark water of Lake Ontario with the skyline of my powerful city behind me. Cesar's incommunicable spirit floats across the water and the first ray of light enters my consciousness.

This is the miracle that I am hoping for. The writer in me resurfaces.

The next morning when I wake up, I call a deeply respected friend, Margaret Atwood. We meet at a neighbourhood café. She walks in bundled in a black winter jacket, her face framed in a halo of silky white curls. She embraces me and tells me that I still carry the Moroccan sun on my face. I gaze at her, pressing back the tears that threaten to spill out at her display of gentleness.

"I think I am ready to start work on my long abandoned book," I say.

What follows is a brisk conversation about publishers and agents and my ability to deliver the manuscript in the next six months. She is familiar with the details of my experience in Marrakech and, before leaving, tells me that under no circumstances am I to return to the country that has brutalized me.

"It's not in the cards —" I reply vaguely, looking away.

"Look into my eyes and repeat that you will not return," Margaret's gaze pins me down.

"I will never return to Marrakech," I chant like an obedient child.

FIVE DAYS BEFORE MY BIRTHDAY in June, the telephone rings early in the morning.

"Hello. Hello. How are you?" Khadim's low-pitched voice rolls out of the receiver.

The line disconnects immediately. It is 6 a.m. and I sit up in bed wide-awake. I dial the number in Marrakech that I know by heart. The telephone is answered at the first ring.

"Hello," I say.

"I was coming to surprise you for your birthday but I have just received a summons from the Ministry of Tourism in Rabat. What have you told them?"

"The Moroccan ambassador in Canada has forwarded a complaint about your behaviour," I inform him.

"Send them a fax." His tone is cajoling, familiar, and ultimately confident. "Tell them this is personal and not professional."

"Did you know I broke my arm?" I ask, stunned at the conversation.

"Darling, I was not in Marrakech. I went to France, I had an operation."

The stench of his lie rises from the coastline of Morocco and floats across the Atlantic to swirl around my bed in Toronto. I replace the receiver and leave my bedroom distraught that the power in his voice has re-awakened every dormant sentiment I discarded five months ago. I make coffee, measuring both the powder and the betrayal orchestrated by my heart.

His use of the word "darling" is sweeter than the honey I am adding to my coffee. It immediately plunges me back into the nights in Marrakech when the full moon conspired to turn a city into an unparalleled dreamscape and I felt as though love would never let me go. As the caffeine wakes me up, the warrior within me steps out, and I am fully conscious that the call is a beckoning of sorts. The destination, as in all mythologies, is to a serpent's lair.

The telephone calls continue for four weeks. I am now practising the art of deception and my teacher is Khadim. My objective is that under the guise of a recently severed link I may be able to lead Khadim to a comfort zone where he reveals himself utterly. Although the shadow of his dishonesty emerges in each bizarre conversation where he claims not to have been in Marrakech when I had my accident, yet I still seek the confirmation of his betrayal and abandonment. I hear daily his complaints: that the grind of Moroccan investigative bureaucracy, spearheaded by an ambassador, will jeopardize his ability to practise his profession, and restrict his ability to travel and join me. His mother is on her deathbed. He is unable to sleep in my absence, he misses me terribly, and his life has become a nightmare.

"What have you done with my journal?"

"Darling, I swear to you I have never seen it," he lies with passion. "Step by step I will settle everything and you must tell them that."

At the end of four weeks on a clear day in July, I send him a four-line fax stating that his verbal assurance to settle matters between us fills me with hope. I never hear from him again and when I call, he never answers. This revelation of his motives finally confirms what I have known for a long time and never fully accepted.

All the theft of my personal items in Marrakech was conducted by the man who boasted that he could make things appear and disappear. He also removed the entire paper trail that could incriminate him, down to the magnifying glass in my study with which he forged my signature on my cheques.

"I DO NOT NEED TO SEE you again," says the smiling young doctor.

"What about the steel plates?" I ask.

"They stay in forever. We would have to open your arm again to remove them. It is not advisable," he replies firmly.

"Can I play tennis now?"

"Yes. You have amazing recuperative powers." He shakes my hand.

"Good genes." I smile at him, and walk away.

The two thin incision lines on my arm begin to fade. However, the longer one on the top rises in a point and then flows down again. It resembles a sand dune, I think, wondering if the Moroccan surgeon had tattooed my favourite landscape with some intimate knowledge of who I was.

Had I not broken my arm I might still be trapped in a diabolical existence ruled by the games of magic. Life, nuanced by a shoddy illusionist's penchant for smoke and mirrors. To survive, I must immediately discard a life history that has only usurped one year from my life. I also feel a rush of anger for the foreign elements in my arm.

Phrases, sentences, and chapters mark the passage of my life now as I begin writing. Masses of paper accumulate on my desk as I edit words I wrote fifteen years ago. The outline of my book becomes redefined, and my confidence increases. I open my home, entertain my friends, and even cook Moroccan cuisine for them. It is as though I have lived in a foreign country for a while and learned new things. Khadim's name or any reference to him never comes up. Every photograph or object associated with him lies in the basement locker of the condominium building. Sometimes I speak to my British friends in Marrakech to find out how they are faring. It is a friendship nurtured on both sides. Our countries are irrelevant.

They are in Canada and have come to visit me.

"You look wonderful and happy," says Robert.

"Really?"

"You couldn't really see yourself in Marrakech. It was horrifying," he reminds me.

"That is not entirely true."

"He was a professional racketeer my dear. We did our own investigation after you left. You were sixth on the list of foreign women he entrapped."

Khadim's life flashes before my eyes. "I think it may have been a cultural barrier."

The concept of the Arabic word "ajnabi," meaning foreigner, had ruled Khadim's professional world for over thirty years of his career. The most profitable industry for men of his working-class background was tourism. The second was to marry a French citizen to acquire dual nationality, which guaranteed social benefits and the ability to travel feely from Morocco.

The guide in Morocco had only one opportunity to better his lot in life and that was at the hands of the tourist in his charge. The djellaba-clad men leading lines of tourists behind them were sewn into a network of kickbacks and commissions earned from taxi drivers, restaurant owners, and shopkeepers. The race was to be outside the most expensive hotels, as their clientele was deemed the wealthiest and the easiest to dupe. Guides routinely bribed the concierges of hotels to ensure that they would be selected for work.

Commissions for guides like Khadim made shopkeepers quote prices where the profit margins soared to 500 percent. Some even paid annual retainers to guides, expecting a trail of tourists brought exclusively to their shops. Khadim had a thirty-year record of standing outside the gates of the Hotel La Mamounia and picking up an unending chain of tourists. He was successful with Cesar and me years ago. Before that, he also married a French woman, fathered a child, divorced, and returned to his country with a French nationality.

I suspect that the boundaries of our relationship had become confused. Khadim thought of me as an "ajnabi" tourist. I, in turn, had raised his status in an egalitarian sense by falling in love with him. Our combined sexual desire for each other was a powerful inducement for the bonding of two cultural polarities. His aegis was much like the history of his country under the French protectorate status. In fact, the objective was colonization. My material advantage had become a bounty that he expected to pillage under various guises. Ultimately, his power of seduction lay in his expert ability to gauge my spontaneity in embracing what was foreign and remote. It was tied into my adventurous and artistic nature.

I place a call to Marrakech and speak to the only colleague and friend he introduced me to in Marrakech.

"My dear, the jewellery he stole from you was pawned in France. This is a police state, and if you sneeze in Marrakech they will hear it in Rabat," Chafiq says.

"So he continues to work as a guide?" I ask.

"Yes, at the same hotel. He is now driving a car which he brought back from France."

I think of the bicycle-riding Khadim who claimed that his choice of transportation reflected his environmental concerns. Marrakech was in danger of heavy pollution. I had swallowed his glib assertion with admiration. It seemed to validate my choice of him as a life partner. He was an evolved Moroccan.

As the pieces of the Marrakech puzzle begin to lock into place, I send a letter to Khadim that I estimate will reach him in three weeks, at the beginning of the month of Ramadan. I simply ask that my journal be mailed back to me.

The Muslim ritual during this month prides itself on eliciting purity.

There is no response.

I finish the first two sections of the book and plan a week's vacation in New York. There is a literary agency I have corresponded with there and I think that I will combine a bit of business with pleasure. I have not been to New York for eight years and lived there from 1973 to 1976. The cleaned up and rather benign city offers its impressive points of interest. I prowl through museums, art galleries and socialize with old friends who are all interested in Morocco.

"Is it the exotic cheap travel destination?" I am asked continually.

I offer a brief sketch without any specific details. However, the break I anticipated from writing is not fully accomplished. The book sits on my shoulder because I am unable to make a critical decision. I stand on the balcony of my host's 34th-storey penthouse apartment at Lex and 56th one evening and finally realize that there is only one way to complete my book. It is also a powerful desire to transform defeat into victory.

The next evening, I am seated at the bar in an Upper East Side restaurant with a friend when a young man sits next to me. He aims a smile at me from a pair of inquiring eyes. His hair is a mass of unruly, ebony curls and his courtesy laced with charm. I am drawn to the warmth and the sense of personal drama that he exudes.

"I am a filmmaker. Call me Heff," he offers after a few minutes of conversation.

"What sort of films?" I ask.

"I made my first feature in Japan two years ago," he says casually.

We talk for an hour and I reveal my creative conundrum to a complete stranger. It is an act of safety, as I imagine we will never meet again.

"This is a hell of a story. I will come down and shoot a documentary short," Heff says.

"It is not a story. This is real," I rise to leave.

"So am I! Have lunch with me tomorrow." He tucks my arm under his elbow as I get ready to cross the street.

We meet the next day at his Wall Street hideout. Stone is one of the oldest streets in the financial district. I walk on the cobblestones and am led to a brick building that houses his office. I am utterly charmed by the environment. He works for a philanthropic foundation and continues with his film work. I see the reviews that the first screening of his film received and am impressed by both his youth and talent.

"This notebook, how badly do you want it back?" he asks.

"It is intellectual property theft, but we are dealing with a culture that is desensitized to all this," I say wryly.

"I am fascinated by this. It's a terrific angle for a film."

"You mean a notebook buried somewhere in the city of Marrakech!"

"Yes, and I want you to get it back. This guy is a bad dude. I hate that."

I FLY HOME TO TORONTO the next morning. He calls me a few days later and I invite him for Thanksgiving. He surprises me over the weekend by flying into Detroit, picking up a rental car, and ending up a block away from me.

"Do you always manage to find your destinations?" I laugh at him.

"I have brought my trumpet, I am going to play for you," he says lifting a small case from the car.

He sleeps in my study and plays the trumpet after dinner. I can picture him somewhere in Paris in a smoky nightclub or at the base of the Eiffel Tower playing siren songs that he is incapable of divining himself. His visit is the most healing gift I have received in months. He also brings a video of his feature film that I do not see in his presence. His work is filled with a raw yet impressive talent and he has the soul of a poet. I send him a laudatory email and he telephones me promptly.

"You are an amazing woman," he says.

"You must continue your career in film."

"Always," he says.

"Never give it up, even if you have to starve," I say.

"I want to interview you," he responds.

"You know the story, let me finish it." I say goodbye.

"Tell me your plans and please stay in touch," he says.

I call my travel agent, book a flight, and arrange for a friend to collect my mail and pay bills for the next month. I make only one phone call to my destination and am assured that I will be picked up at the airport. My computer and two thirds of the completed manuscript travel with me. It is an overnight flight and there is an interesting person seated next to me so we talk the night away until the flight lands in Paris. I transfer from one airport to another and board another flight. The pilot is quite garrulous — he talks about the three countries on the flight path, and although I am seated by the window, I never look out.

When the plane lands, I collect my hand luggage and walk out rapidly. I see familiar surroundings, answer the routine questions posed by the customs official, and wait for baggage. The temperature shifts immediately and my body adjusts to it. I have come prepared. I wheel my luggage cart out of the terminal towards the exit and search groups of faces. There is no one I recognize, and the first dent in my composure surfaces. I push the luggage cart down the ramp on the walkway towards the taxis. My name is called out behind me and I stop.

THREE MONTHS LATER, AFTER THE writing trip, I send the manuscript to my agent. Two weeks later, he telephones me and suggests that we meet.

I am sitting in a pleasant room facing Sam, literary agent. We share a history as he represented my last book, a food memoir.

"What do you think? Do you like the novel?" I ask him.

"Yes I do. I will not represent it as a work of fiction. This is a work of non-fiction."

"It is a novel," my voice has risen and I am wondering if he has gone mad.

"It is the story of your life and that is the power of this story."

"I don't care. I have always written fiction. The last book was different." I feel a tide of panic and nausea.

"This is very simple. You are just converting it from third person to first," he replies blandly.

"I don't need this type of exposure. It works as a novel."

"This is your life. This is real. Think about it. It should do very well. I can sell this book."

I have stood up. "I don't know. I am not certain."

"I am going to work on the proposal immediately. Just a few sample chapters. I am very excited." He rises and leads me to the door.

I am running home. The sky is grey and snowflakes swirl around my face. I am a woman wearing dark glasses who feels as though she has been stripped of her clothes. There have been deaths and burials in my life and the coffin in which I have concealed all this is my manuscript. I have done this artfully somewhere outside myself with my own techniques. I have published five works of fiction and this is my craft. As an author, my conduit to the publishing world is my agent. He is my trusted champion and I feel as though he has betrayed me. Lighting a damp cigarette on the pavement and waiting for the traffic light to change, I am simply praying for an avalanche of snow to descend on me and bury me forever.

I HAVE SPENT TWO DAYS circling my desk and viewing the manuscript folder with fear and a sense of failure. Once again, the sensation of being arrested mid-flight overpowers me. My act of concealment has been shredded. Three months have passed since I have completed the manuscript. A sense of urgency to embrace a new beginning hammers at me daily. I have another day left to speak to my agent as the publishing industry is ruled by seasons. I have also spoken to a few respected peers and they mirror my agent's instincts. I am stunned and feel as though my writing life has been turned upside down. I feel at this point that it is a final act of courage that I am simply not brave enough to manifest. I think of turtles flipped on their backs with their underbellies exposed. This image of their flailing legs and arms depict vulnerability and acts of cruelty perpetrated by tyrants. I see myself as a turtle. I have been flipped over. For the first time, I cannot see the forest for the trees. I am doomed and I am ready to drown in self-pity. Am I going to join the ranks of people who are victims and become detestable?

The next afternoon I am seated by the window in the lounge of the Four Seasons Hotel. This spot is filled with memories of Cesar and a previous life. It is a dodge. I have retreated into a comfort zone where I feel like a delinquent adolescent. It is early afternoon and my computer is before me on the table. I am making an effort I say, wondering if I am clever enough to trick myself. Recklessly, I have also ordered a martini that I have never drunk before in the late morning. Yet the sips of vodka and the first line of Chapter 1 are somehow wedded to each other. All I have to do is insert one letter of the alphabet. It is the word "I." When the index finger of my right hand connects and the word "she" disappears, a silence blankets every sound around me. There is no time to register my astonishment as I become completely oblivious to my surroundings. My fingers are moving on the keyboard and I feel as though I am the captain of a small sailing vessel turning a rudder with precision. All I can sense is that the ocean is calm and I no longer require any navigational chart.

Days later when this exercise is completed, all I feel is that I have finally been introduced to myself. It is a peaceful process and easier than I imagined. Finally, I have reclaimed both my conversations and the people I have had them with. The experience is mine and the life is mine. When I look into the mirror the woman whose face glances at me is not a figment of an overworked imagination. The werewolf does not lurk in this image even though it was suggested humorously by Margaret that perhaps it did. I see Scheherazade, who was a storyteller. Like her, I must tell my stories to save my life, but in a different way. The angles of my face are no longer sharp, and a hint of character spills from my eyes. I see definition and the seasons of living etched on my face, despite the deceptively youthful genes I spring from.

How does one live with a real self? Mostly with humour, gentleness. But also with the surety that compressing a dozen lifetimes into sixteen years is that unchartered act of mystery that can neither be predicted nor controlled. Ultimately, it is not only where we imagine we are headed that counts, but also the true meaning of the mileposts along the way. Will I ever be able to alter the passion with which I invariably engage with life? Chances are I will not, because this is my true essence, and I cannot discard the notion that the perfection of the magical kingdoms where we entwine with others must remain unbroken. Perhaps the single redeeming lesson is that I now accept that caution is not a word synonymous with cowardice, but with knowledge.

It is a full moon tonight! I see it perched above the rooftop garden of the adjoining apartment building. In my mind's eye, it is not the shrouded outlines of the storytellers of the great square Djemaa el Fna in Marrakech that I see, but myself, preparing to reveal secrets from the beginning.

CHAPTER 2

TORONTO, 1991

THE TELEPHONE RINGS IN THE first week of June and I answer it.

"I am having a Gemini party next week and as my favourite Gemini, I expect to see you," says Etti.

"I am not up to it," I reply.

"Don't be a snooty bitch!"

"I am not. I am going through a separation."

"Oh! You will pull through this. You need to get out. It will be good for you."

I stare outside the kitchen window, down the length of the back garden. The roses are blooming in the circular bed and the tall silver Poplar tree stands like an elegant sentinel. After years of growth, the thick cedar hedge separates my home from the one next door. Years of gardening choices and labour have borne fruit and what I feel, as my heart races, is rectangular tranquility. I will never leave you, is the false promise I make to my garden.

Nine weeks ago, I dissolved a marriage after twenty-six years. The troubled, and troubling, husband who hijacked me by romance and brought me to Canada as a twenty-year-old bride does not live here anymore. His departure was not peaceful. It was filled with his custo-mary dark rage and shocking aggression. He had beguiled me into marriage by a dossier of complicated agendas. I had been ensnared by his brooding intensity without realizing that my passion was merely an act of rebellion against the establishment of the country I was raised in, Pakistan. Even when I knew I had made a great mistake, I simply did not have the courage to inform my devastated parents or the conviction to alter the status of my children. However, when I filled four suitcases with his belongings, each empty space and container made my heart lighter. The decision had haunted me for years but when I made it suddenly and irrevocably, it was easier than I had ever imagined it to be.

In these past weeks I have only left the house to visit my lawyer, worked on my second novel, and have not informed anyone in my social circle. I wondered how I would make this announcement, but Etti's invitation opens the door. I will get a divorce within a year and I shall continue to live in my house in a much-desired peace. Perhaps the announcement to my friend will spread the word and ease the path. I have acquired two treasures from this chaotic passage of married life. Two daughters, one who is in her second year at the University of British Columbia and the younger one who will attend McGill in the coming year as well. In many ways, we have all been ready for this eventuality. Yet nothing has prepared me for the encounter to come.

A week later, I wake up on Saturday morning and call Brian.

"Have you been invited to Etti's party?"

"What do you think?" he chuckles. "I am her favourite Gemini."

"It appears that we are all her favourite Geminis. Will you be my escort?"

"Pick me up at six. It is outdoors in Charlie Pachter's patio. We must catch the sun."

My friend Brian is gay, a brilliant artist who lost his companion years ago and has been keeping an eye on me by just appearing at the house and heading to the garden. Here we lie on the grass and chat for hours. He seldom questions me, but displays gentleness and moments of comic relief. It is as though we are playmates, and often he will join my daughter and me for dinner. I know exactly what his mission is and I am grateful for it.

I bake a large sponge cake, hull four boxes of strawberries, and pack a litre of whipping cream. My contribution will be strawberry shortcake. Brian and I land up at the patio on Berkeley Street around six that evening. I am casually dressed in sandals, capris, and a loose smock. There are at least forty people, including two drummers. There is a buzz of merriment in the air and the sky is blue with a sun that is still shining. Etti hugs me fiercely and whispers in my ear.

"You will be fine. Coming out is the best thing you have done."

"Is it?"

"He was never with you anyway," Etti reminds me.

I am seated on the floor sipping a glass of wine with Brian sprawled by my side. It feels wonderful simply to enjoy the sunny evening and observe people. I know most of them and I wave from a safe distance but have no desire to stand up and engage in conversation. I have a newfound reserve and do not wish to discuss any aspect of my separation from my husband. I have moved away faster than I can imagine and am quite relaxed about my new status.

Etti, I say to myself, is right. It is good to get out.

About fifteen feet away from me are four women huddled in a circle and I can see the edges of a pair of trouser-clad legs in the centre. One of the women steps away from the circle and a space opens up. A man dressed in a cream linen suit with an open throated green shirt looks across at me and raises the glass of wine in his hand. I am so startled that I automatically raise mine.

He is now walking towards me. I feel as if he is a unicorn leaping from the pages of a book of myths. Yet the first image is colour. Whether it is the head of pewter-coloured curls or the tanned skin or his vital presence, he belongs in the pages of a glossy fashion magazine. For twenty-six years in Toronto, I have never seen such an exotic man. I find myself standing like a puppet whose strings have been jerked upwards.

"Hello," he says crinkling his greenish-hazel eyes and parting his lips in a stunning smile, revealing beautiful teeth.

"Hello," I mumble like an awkward schoolgirl still reeling from his beauty.

"I am Cesar," he continues smiling; the jaunty silver moustache matches precisely the tint of curls cascading elegantly down his neck.

"I really don't want to be here," I say, as a panic engulfs me.

"Look up at the sky. Just listen to your breath. Don't say a word, just listen to your breath," he commands.

I raise my face to the sky and do precisely that. The panic recedes, as though my entire body has been stilled, slowed down. I cannot be certain.

"Better?"

"Yes," I reply not turning towards him, terrified that like a unicorn he may simply disappear.

"Good. This is a meditation technique for when you want to escape."

I turn to look at him. He is standing next to me, sipping his wine.

"I practise psychiatry. Etti invited me because she said that all her female friends are very interesting women." Again he flashes the smile.

"Well I am not. I am just a writer," I say.

We exchange a few details about ourselves and I move away from him. Women approach us constantly and I notice how animated they become in his presence. I go inside and assemble the strawberry shortcake and return to the patio, where the barbeque is in full production and long buffet tables are covered with food. Accompanied by Brian, I fill up a plate. I am conscious that he is close to us, talking to other people, but keeping me in his periphery. I move away and wander towards the drummers. I dance with Brian and notice that Cesar is also swaying to the beat with his eyes closed, but a body gyrating with sinuous movements that North Americans are incapable of. I am hypnotized by his swaying body, because I sense that rhythm is entwined in his entire being.

Dessert is announced and Etti makes a big production of the strawberry shortcake saying that I made it. I reach for a chocolate dessert and he moves right next to me.

"You have made this with your hands. This is what I want," he cuts a huge wedge, which covers most of his plate.

I am both amused and touched by his gesture and I introduce him to Brian, who seems to know him. I then decide to leave, as a torrent of unusual emotions well inside. It is pure and simple attraction and I am not sophisticated enough to deal with these feelings with ease. Brian says he will stay and I say I am ready to go home. He understands. As I unlatch the patio door, Cesar steps behind me.

"Etti tells me you are separated. May I give you my telephone number? I would love to see you again."

It is a smooth, elegant move but I back away from it.

"Are you in the telephone book?" I say.

"Yes I am."

"Well, you never know I may call you someday."

I run to my car and leave him standing at the patio door. I have not said goodbye to Etti. All I know is that I have been married all my life and have no experience of how to handle myself when a man is expressing interest in me. It is an unknown, unchartered territory and I simply wish to seek the safety of my home. I drive home faster than I normally do.

A week later finds me pacing in my kitchen. I am doing a book review for *The Globe and Mail* and the book editor, Jack Kapica, is a friend of mine. I intend to make money while I work on the second novel, so I have called friends to help. It is my new life plan, despite the support payments that cover most of my living needs. I am reviewing Alice Walker's *The Temple of My Familiar*, which is a barbaric and complex piece of work and I cannot seem to craft the review well. This restlessness is part of the writing life and it is usually handled by tea breaks and much staring into space. However, on this occasion, I pull out the telephone directory and hunt in the professional section under "physicians."

"Hello, Cesar. I did find your number in the book and so I am keeping my word."

I return to my study, convinced I have made a fool of myself. Would he even remember me? Within twenty minutes, the phone rings.

"I am delighted you called. I am delighted that you are so responsive," the rollicking baritone is warm and filled with approval.

"I hope I am not disturbing you."

"I am in-between sessions. Would you like to see a foreign film at the Carlton tomorrow?"

"Wednesday?"

"Yes. We can meet at six."

"Why not?" I reply without a care in the world.

Whether it was the last minute change of plans where we landed at Ouzeri, a Greek restaurant on the Danforth, or the fact that I could not eat the vast array of appetizers that Cesar ordered and sipped on red wine instead, there was a pre-ordained destiny to our talking instead of seeing a film. It was as though a hurricane engulfed us, uprooting past lives, sending us flying into a world of mutual enchantment, life expectations, and a state of love that blossomed and endured where we became inseparable. It was also discovery, made rarer as we had searched for precisely the same response to living. He was exotic and so was I. His ancestry combined Spain and the Dominican Republic, although as the son of a diplomat he was born and raised in New York. After his medical studies, he attended a congress of world psychiatry in Montreal, fell in love with Canada, and moved here. He had a brief sojourn with radical political thought, joined the Trotskyite movement, and then went to Vietnam as a physician to report on war crimes. It was a full palette. He had been married once and was the father of two children. He had courted women and had long-standing affairs but never remarried.

"I have found you," he would say daily, never losing the wonderment in his voice.

He embraced my life experience, my daughters, and charmed all

my friends and he familiarized himself with every wart on my soul and
every idiosyncrasy in my personality. I had been interested in psychology
and found his office library fascinating. He was a voracious reader
and the bookshelves in his office began to fill up with the literary
works I would introduce him to.

He had never cooked in his life and dined at restaurants. I loved
cooking and turned his world around.

"You are saving me a hell of a lot of money," he would smile,
uncorking a bottle of fine wine.

"I will go mad if we go to eat out all the time." I would rifle his
refrigerator stocked with exquisite Chablis and a hunk of ancient
cheese in despair.

Whatever we added to each other's life became a recognized and
savoured delight. My younger daughter, who was six months away
from leaving home for university, and has no memory of her mother
in love, fought the transformed woman and resorted to one last
battle stance.

"He is eleven years older than you Mummy; he is going to die
before you," she curls her beautiful mouth in distaste.

"Leave her alone, her behaviour is appropriate, she is protecting
her turf. I will win her over in three months," my amused lover
responds.

Here was my knight in shining armour, who blanketed me with
a new and dazzling love and championed all my causes. He was so
sure-footed that he effortlessly dismantled every obstacle that stood
in our path. He proposed marriage and designed an engagement ring
for me himself. It was a year-and-three-month long courtship, which
resulted in a new life plan. Daily we revealed our lives to each other
and experimented with each other's suggestions. I learned what it
would be like married to a physician, and he would discuss aspects of
his psychotherapy with me. I discussed books and poetry with him
and we invariably wound up choosing the same films to see.

For a period of six months, we lived out of three homes: his apartment, my home, and his stunning vacation property on Manitoulin

Island. My divorce lawyer cautioned me to make no sudden moves until my divorce was finalized. Cesar pre-empted her suggestions by buying a house for me in Yorkville six months into our relationship.

"I want a new history for both of us. You belong in the city and not in the suburbs. It is our love nest," he grins like a schoolboy.

"Impossible. I have a daughter who is attached to her childhood home. Don't even think of it," I warn him.

The next week, we are speaking on the telephone.

"How was your day?" I ask.

"I had a marvellous lunch today."

"Where?"

"I had two cancellations, so I bought a house," he replies.

"The Yorkville house?" I knew the answer fully well.

"Yes."

"Well then go and live in your house." I slam the phone down.

On a cold December night, we meet at Sotto Sotto on Avenue Road for dinner, and then drive to Yorkville to the Georgian house with a tiny plaque, saying "Endhouse." We bring a bottle of champagne with us. The previous owner left three logs in the fireplace and the first thing Cesar does is to kneel down and light the fire as I walk around the empty house. The flue is shut and within ten minutes, the stunning living room is filled with smoke, which we hastily douse in champagne. Then we make love and leave, knowing that we would break all the rules that had ever been made for us.

A month later, we start furnishing the house. Even my daughter is intrigued by the monumental change in structure. Surprisingly, she voices her willingness to be part of the new experiment. Cesar and I would search the city for furniture to enhance the feel of the house. We both resolved to discard the furnishings of our respective homes and begin a brand new life together. The pale green painted interior reflected the previous owner's tasteful renovation. The marvellous kitchen made Cesar declare passionately and recklessly that he would cook in this house. In turn, the hundred-year-old house accepted with grace all our touches and embellishments.

I use a front hall closet as a study, installing my computer table into it. Rolling the table out and positioning it in front of the front window to write. It is a smaller space, but I manage to fit in perfectly. The back garden contains a large wooden deck and a square of gravel, which I clear, and plant flowers instead. My birthday gift to Cesar is a lilac tree, which took about three hours of digging. Cesar in return clears a much larger section for my roses.

Seven months later, I walk down the stairs to the living room on the main floor. Roses spill out of the fireplace, orchids dangle from the banister and window ledges, the furniture has all been transferred to the basement, and sixty friends and relatives wait for me to marry Cesar in front of the fireplace. When I join him, I offer him the rose that has bloomed this morning. He says "I do" twice when our beloved friend Lynne King, the judge, asks him if he would take me as his wife.

It is bursts of laughter, champagne corks popping, the clarion song of the Mariachi Trumpeters who walk into our wedding dinner, and the kiss that never seems to end. It is a montage from a romantic film. Yet it is not a film because when we look at each other and then gaze at the faces of all our wedding guests, it is just the well-planned and anticipated culmination of a trusted love affair.

The second day after our wedding as we waited to be driven to the airport to fly off to our honeymoon, Cesar holds me in his arms and whispers.

"Do you know why I suggested Morocco for our honeymoon?"

"It will be wonderful," I reply.

"I chose a place which is supposed to be as exotic as my wife."

"You mean the henna on my hands, the rose fragrance, the Kashmiri ancestry, the Pakistani upbringing, the year in Texas, and then singing Leonard Cohen's 'Suzanne' in Toronto?" I rattled off.

"Yes. It is your tapestry, your collective, you have to learn to tap into it." Cesar recedes into his guru mode.

"It is going to a new and foreign country. I can hardly wait."

CHAPTER 3

✿ Honeymoon, Marrakech, 1992

MY BODY QUIVERS WITH EXCITEMENT as the city of Marrakech rises before our eyes. This once imperial city centred in a vast plane, where an ancient grove of palm trees gave refuge to travelling caravans, has defied time. The entire history of the city seems untouched, as the colour red, mixed on a palette with hues of sand and rose is spread on the earth, the structures, and even on the sky.

The sound of hoof-beats, capes swirling, tents being pitched, and camels baying as they sway with heavy loads presses against the ears. My imaginative dreamscape gathered from tourist brochures supplied by the travel agent in Toronto instantly assumes a surrealistic reality.

The architectural wonder appears to be the same for my husband, Cesar, who exhales deeply by my side. The taxi that has transported us from the airport moves though the horseshoe sculpted stone gate carved through the rampart wall and halts at the entrance of La Mamounia Hotel.

The plastered archway leading inside is familiar. I have dreamt about it often enough. The shade of the plaster is terracotta tinged with rose.

"I have arrived," I say to myself. "I have reached the legendary oasis of harmony and beauty."

It is not unlike the sentiments that I harbour for my husband. It is in keeping with our entire union, just like the new wedding bands encircling our fingers. They are two circles of gold with a tri-coloured braid embracing the circle. Our love is like that as well — flowing and concentric. There is no need to ever step out of this circle or come up for air. If one has to perish, then this is the state of preference. It is much like Tommy Dorsey's "Tea for Two" tango, where the refrain tea for two or two for tea is circular and unending. This is the only thing I am sure of as I stand in the pillared doorway of the hotel examining the backless slippers and crimson capes of the white-garbed doormen. The dimensions of the vast foyer stretching beyond our sightline glistens like the interior of a palace, making us both feel that our linen suits are a travesty, and sweeping garments of silk are required to walk through the awaiting gilded interiors.

When we sit together to register, I notice that the impeccably dressed young man radiating a welcoming grace reflects more than consummate hotel management. His heavy lidded eyes shoot out a bemused glint, as though he is saying, "Yes, you are entering the privileged domain of the Hotel La Mamounia, and this will mark you, and it has happened before."

I scribble my three surnames into the forms, unable to drop the previous married name as my passport still carries it. So it becomes a triple-barrelled affair denoting my personal history.

Three men are woven into my identity, shading it with a complexity that even intrigues the manager, whose eyes linger over the signature. Then he inquires whether I am of Moroccan ancestry and I tease him by responding that I have an Eastern background, which could to be similar to the Berbers of Morocco. He beams at me and then ceremoniously hands a key attached to a heavy brass column to Cesar.

The central foyer is drenched in an opulence that resonates off the sculpted ceilings hovering over massive floral arrangements and gleaming marble floors. We are both speechless. The lush Moroccan fantasia unfurling around us surpasses the travel brochures in our luggage. The marriage of Art Deco and Moorish craftsmanship is combined faultlessly by a sorcerer's hands. A pair of European architects, deeply influenced by the Vienna School, has taken the olive grove gifted by an eighteenth-century sultan to his son, Mamoun, and built the most beautiful hotel in the world. Twenty-five acres of land spill around the structure, encompassing the foliage, fragrance of fruit and flower-bearing trees, and a garden bordered by a line of ancient olive trees.

Walking through the foyer, I feel as though the pores of my skin have enlarged and droplets of accumulated toxins are being leeched out. Something older and much sweeter courses through me, as though I have taken draughts of my favourite childhood drink of ground almonds, milk, and honey. This is the drink offered in paradise to all pure souls.

Cesar moves closer, fixing his hazel eyes on me, sensing that a noiseless symphony cascades within me. He seems to be saying, "You are my familiar Canadian wife but there is something foreign and unknown inside you as well." I gaze back at him wondering how long it would take my husband to realize that an old paradise has entered my life. Only this one will be relived in the present and together. Twenty-seven years after my departure from the land I was raised in, the glistening interiors of a foreign hotel that bears no resemblance to anything I can identify with catapults me into my childhood.

The room we are ushered into is appointed in peach and ivory colours, glittering and luxurious beyond belief. Six tall windows display the entire panorama of the ramparts encircling the medina of Marrakech. The colour, vegetation, and buildings leap out of a medieval fairytale. The palm trees are the like the ones a child could draw accurately with crayons. I stand transfixed, and the man I call beloved circles the hollow of my collarbone with delicate strokes. Turning around I move into the heart of Cesar's embrace. The wall-sconces highlighting the waves of Cesar's pewter-coloured hair give him the appearance of a guru, satyr, buccaneer — I can never decide which one.

Nothing changes in our intricate dance of desire.

For more than a year before we got married, our bodies pulsed with sexual fervour that drew indulgent smiles from our friends. The ecstatic nature of our physical coupling makes me feel as though I am reborn continually. Cesar has warm breath and laughs his orgasms out riotously. I have stumbled upon a religion where the only house of worship is the tent of bedclothes covering our bodies.

Standing in the honeymoon suite of Hotel La Mamounia, I allow myself to fly back a year and half ago to Cesar's soft grey bedroom, where I felt like a butterfly with wings drenched in the shadow of unseen tears. I told him that I was not supposed to be with him, synchronizing my breathing with his. He was not deterred, he became a catcher with a gossamer net scooping me neatly, drying my wings, and then releasing me to a larger sky. Now he has brought me to a magical kingdom and reclines on a mound of pillows on the elegant Moroccan bed watching me. Within minutes, I crawl towards him pressing my mouth on the satin of his tanned chest. I want to draw his skin through my mouth into my belly, as though the ambience of this room, which is a confection for the senses, has coated him with the same flavour. He allows me everything, surrendering in turn and taking in turn. Together we enter that miraculous zone where there is neither excess nor restraint in how we share pleasure with each other.

Ironically, I am not unfamiliar with it. I was raised in a Pakistani culture where women, deferential and obedient, spent their adolescence in a protracted dress rehearsal for becoming sexually active and confident. Yet the legions of sumptuously adorned women with hair perfumed with the oil of jasmine and bodies scented with rose fragrance never articulated their sexual lives like their Western sisters. It is as though the brides of Muslim countries are stuck mute the moment they sign their marriage contracts. The only hint of their desire is in their fascination with the yearning delicacy of poetic verse and cryptic comments steeped in metaphoric vagueness.

"Loving you," I tell Cesar, "makes me splendid."

When I say this, it is not the sexual flowering in my late forties to which I refer, but a type of harmony I experienced as a child. This reminds me of my relationship with my father. He was the one who told me to read Dickens and Tolstoy. I was his favoured child, welcomed into his history-obsessed world, where kings and queens cavorted on mountaintop pavilions with peacocks and silken panthers. He regarded his distinguished career as a civil servant with an air of comic gravity and dabbled with compiling historic memoirs of sorts, perfecting his game of bridge and planting rose gardens for my mother. The contemplation of beauty brought tears to his eyes while he taught me not to cry. He recited couplets of Urdu verse and nearly always championed my adolescent rebellions against my mother.

"You have style," he would whisper, "and it becomes you."

Yet the Catholic convent school where he sent me to be educated was dedicated to stamping out my style.

"You must not have these wild notions consuming you," a stern-faced nun would say. "You must restrain this sense of drama. Life is predictable and simple."

The nuns had no way of knowing that it was too late for this because my father had bestowed his personal sanction on me to be both daring and exploratory.

"Life cannot be ordinary," he said, and then he died.

After that, I found it difficult to prove whether his thoughts existed outside the conspiracy we created together. I was too young to realize that everything he imparted prepared me for my life with Cesar, whose level of acceptance rivalled my father's. Cesar's training in psychiatry, his warm Latin temperament and robust *joie de vivre* filled me with confidence. Finally, I could become that sea anemone resting on the bottom of the ocean floor receiving the ripples and collisions of life with equanimity.

It is Cesar, whose chest I use as a pillow, who now imprints my life. It is as though I am not in Marrakech but walking in a field of freshly fallen snow found in my beloved Northern Ontario where the footprints of men of the East do not exist. Finally, I have said farewell to men of the East, fathers, brothers, and husband. I have chosen a second husband who is only interested in watching me flower. Yet the country we have both chosen for our honeymoon is marked by a disturbingly familiar social culture. We are both acutely aware of this in the city of Casablanca, where our honeymoon begins.

The caftan-clad women of Morocco in the markets hold out the same henna-stained palms as mine but their eyes are shadowed by a familiar passivity. Centuries of caution is buried in the folds of their headscarves. Their eyes linger on the hands of my husband who holds me close to him as we walk. They are women shackled to their cultural taboos and they gaze at me as though I belong to another species.

We leave the room and walk down into the garden of the hotel. There are easily a hundred trees spread around. It is not the manicured precision of the trees that enchants us but the symphony of birds who share the same space. The heavens have opened up and the bird songs blanket every other sound. This invisible aviary sends out spiralling crescendos of birdsong while the petals of roses and hibiscus shiver as a thrilled audience. I am convinced that Cesar is a magician and has personally orchestrated this delight for me.

"I want to stay here. In fact, I never want to leave," I say to him.

But Cesar is standing by my side with his eyes closed and head tilted to one side. It is his meditative pose; I am familiar with it. He has escaped into his own private communion with nature. We stand side by side and I wonder what would happen if we had the power to shed our human dimensions and synthesize into the verdant green and the soft feathers of birds overhead. No doubt, Cesar would become the blue heron stalking Manitoulin Island, and I would choose a ruby-tinged cardinal streaking through the skies like a crimson blur. In the lush garden, we experience the first seduction of the grand hotel. No other guest strays into our enclave.

Half an hour later we re-enter the hotel, walk though the lobby, and ask for directions to the Koutoubia Mosque. Cesar is given a little map and he walks to the cashier to convert some money. I wander through the arched doorway and confront a small cluster of men. Instantly, the tallest one moves up to me.

"Madame, I would be happy to be your guide," he says in English.

I am intrigued by his chiselled features and spotless Western clothing. He stands out from the gaggle of tour guides as a peacock does from crows. His entire demeanour is imbued with a courtly air. Then he lifts his wrist and quickly glances at his watch and I think he bears faint resemblance to photographs I have seen of Arab princes riding Arabian horses with falcons on their wrists

I smile at him and reply, "Thank you, but we are just going for a little walk by ourselves."

Turning away, I move towards Cesar who has just stepped outside. Tucking my arm into his elbow, he draws me away.

"The Koutoubia Mosque," he says, "is less than five minutes walk from the hotel."

Outside, a neat pavement stretches ahead and on the other side of the road is a public garden. As we begin to walk, we hear footsteps behind us. We turn and are instantly circled by a group of men who begin offering their services. We keep refusing the offers politely but the men swarm us. This violation of personal space is new and uncomfortable, making it difficult to focus on the mosque rising ahead. The relentless pursuit does not abate. The plans for the leisurely walk are ruined and Cesar's voice gets louder than I have ever heard. The men press closer as would a pack of wolves and one of them moves a hand towards my arm. Cesar's voice explodes and his face turns red with anger.

"Ignore them," I whisper to him.

Cesar halts. The men circle him.

"Darling, we are so close to the mosque, just ignore them and they will go away," I repeat again.

The men study me with an altered expression but continue to shout.

Cesar grabs my shoulders. "We are going back to the hotel." His breath comes out in short explosive spurts.

"Don't get angry darling." I have never seen Cesar like this.

"They are not going to leave us alone," he mutters, savagely propelling me back in the direction of the hotel.

"We are almost at the mosque, to hell with them!" I am shouting.

He leads me back to the hotel entrance, his arm clamped around my shoulders like a steel band. His outrage as the molested tourist darkens his face, making him as sinister as those who pursue us. We enter the lobby breathless and dishevelled.

"Wait here," he commands and marches towards the concierge.

I walk towards the door, lighting a cigarette. At that moment, a forest green two-wheeled horse-drawn carriage stops outside. We had seen them bringing guests to the hotel when we arrived. The regal Marrakech calèche is the preferred and ultimately most charming mode of transportation here. Cesar appears outside accompanied by the tall guide wearing the Western clothing. Before I can react, my husband walks me towards the calèche and steps up on the small step holding his hand out to me. I take it and sit beside him.

"I am Khadim," murmurs the guide who also climbs in and sits opposite us.

"I am Cesar, and this is my wife, Nazneen." Cesar shakes his hand.

When I extend mine, Khadim holds my hand lightly and dips his head in a familiar old world courtesy, which to me is a combination of charm and servility. Cesar beams at me, secure in his protected state. He has hired a guide for a week and has favoured the English-speaking one with the neat appearance. We gaze at the mosque and its tall minaret shaped like a tower from the safety of the carriage as Khadim recites a compendium of historical details. This twelfth-century mosque has a replica in Seville but as a non-Muslim, Cesar cannot enter it. So the calèche draws up beside the great public square across the street from it.

Neither of us is prepared for the Djemaa el Fna square, where people cluster thick as flies. The calèche halts under a canopy of palm trees and Khadim springs out to help us down. Then he uses his tall body to open a small walking path. The spectacle around us makes us halt frequently. Cesar holds my hand firmly. The square is a gigantic open-air theatre and we are hypnotized by it. People clad in long robes with hoods perform juggling acts, parade animals, and dance and sing to music, accompanied by strange instruments surrounded by stalls of food and crafts. Storytellers sit on small wooden stools surrounded by rapt listeners. Trays of medicinal remedies and indigenous cosmetics are spread on the ground and hawkers raise their voices to extol the virtues of the products. Women with veiled faces sit on wooden stools and apply black henna on the palms of tourists. The air hums as though it is hooked to some electrical generator and the energy source comes from hundreds of people brushing and jostling against each other. Camera flashes explode, catching the postures of monkeys and the swaying of hooded cobras.

Khadim leads us through the square with watchful eyes, cautioning me to hold my purse in front of my body instead of letting it dangle from my fingers. We reach a large gathering where people sit on the stone floor surrounding a man. Fascinated, we stand at the edge of the seated crowd. The man in the centre looks at us, stretches out a rigid arm, and points the index finger in my direction. Instantly, I feel as though a beam of energy shoots out from his pointed finger and bounces twenty feet towards me.

"Who is this man?" asks Cesar, noting my expression.

"He is a holy man," replies Khadim.

I cannot tear my gaze away from the man. Suddenly he shouts at Khadim, who excuses himself and moves towards him.

"Local Shaman." Cesar smiles at me.

"He keeps staring at us," I reply, watching Khadim reach his side.

"He recognizes tourists, we may even see a stunt of some sort," Cesar chuckles.

Khadim bends over the seated man, then straightens up and walks back towards us. When he reaches us, we notice that he has a small clear glass in his hand. He holds the green liquid filled glass in front of me.

"He has sent this for you Madam. It is an honour."

"Don't touch it," Cesar's voice rings out sharply.

I peer at the liquid in the glass.

"Why has he sent this, Khadim?" I ask.

"He has sent it for your protection, Madam." Khadim's voice is soft.

"What is it?" Cesar asks Khadim sternly.

"It is what he drinks himself, Monsieur, just some herbs."

I look up at the holy man who watches me fixedly across the distance. I quickly pluck the tiny glass from Khadim's fingers and empty it in one draught.

"Are you crazy?!" Cesar's face contorts with alarm. "There could be foreign bacteria your system is not used to."

My mouth floods with a brackish taste, it is both unpleasant and unusual. Khadim casts an apologetic glance at Cesar but not before I saw a small light of approval when I plucked the glass from his hand. It was as though he willed me to drink. I know my husband's apprehension as a physician is of no consequence to him and his apologetic manner is simply a ruse.

"Let's have some mint tea at a café," I suggest blowing a kiss at Cesar. "Let's get some foreign bacteria inside you as well."

"Tea is fine. The water is boiled," replies Cesar.

Khadim leads us to a little tea stall where glasses of mint tea are being poured with great show. The man holds the teapot at least twenty inches from the glass and pours a stream of tea into a tiny glass, where it settles in a profusion of froth. Khadim hands us the glasses in a ceremonial gesture. The piercingly sweet tea is an infusion of green tea, mint, and hunks of sugar. Under Khadim's watchful eyes, we sip the tea and when we express delight at the national beverage, he smiles approvingly. I have an odd sensation that this deference is extended more towards me than Cesar. I wonder if is because I accepted the holy man's honour and have shown respect for his culture.

I visited a holy man in an orchard in Srinagar, Kashmir, years ago. He was an uncle by marriage and I had grown up hearing tales about his much-celebrated spiritual gifts. I climbed the top floor of his little wooden home on a chilly March morning and when I confronted his reclining form, I experienced the same energy charge that emanated from Khadim's holy man's index finger. However, in Kashmir, I was filled with terror. He simply opened his cataract-filmed blue eyes, shredded a rupee note lying on his chest, and chanted.

"Money will come and money will go!"

Then he shut his eyes and lay motionless in a trance. I was filled with a nameless fear and retreated down the stairs quickly. A wooden splinter lodged itself into my palm with droplets of blood surrounding it. I found it so unsettling that I decided that life could be lived without visits to holy men.

Now I wonder about the potion that I have spontaneously drunk. Why would a holy man in Marrakech think that a bride on her honeymoon requires protection?

CHAPTER 4

🌸 *Honeymoon, Marrakech, 1992*

NEITHER ONE OF US CAN decide whether it is an undershirt that is to be worn under the djellaba, or a regular dress shirt. Cesar dispenses with both. The opening at the throat of the Moroccan hooded robe reveals a triangle of his skin. He slips his feet into the backless local slippers and walks around the room getting used to them. I tie a green silk cord around my forehead and centre the little pendant that dangles from it on my forehead. I have also applied green eyeshadow and brushed it out to the edges of my eyelids. We are acting as though we are off to a costume party and ready to shed our North American identities. Cesar's Hispanic complexion is viewed as a permanent tan in Toronto and my Kashmiri features have a chameleon streak. In the interior of the bedroom, we appear to blend perfectly with the décor. Every item of Western clothing seems to be out of place, but I dislike the Moroccan slippers and wear my evening shoes. We were going to dine at the hotel's restaurant, called Le Marocain. Strolling down the corridor towards the elevator, we constantly glance at mirrored reflections of ourselves like nervous children. Cesar's appearance is almost Middle-Eastern, like mine. The floor-length Moroccan robes add a touch of formality to our gait. When the elevator door swings open and we step out, many eyes turn towards us. The hotel staff are pleased and the guests curious. Cesar tucks my arm closer to him, his possessiveness designed to shield me from the devouring gazes of the largely male staff scattered around us. Le Marocain is located beyond a courtyard that seems to have been lifted from the Al Hamra in Granada. The sculpted stone fountain in the centre is filled with roses. We cross this geometrically perfect courtyard and step into a vestibule that is attended by a stern-faced man flanked by three others in full Moroccan garb. Stiff white shirt collars rise above the triangular neckline of their djellabas. Cesar gives me a despairing look as we instantly realize that he has omitted two essential items of clothing: the shirt and the long white socks worn with the slippers. Observing the tableaux around us and conscious of Cesar's discomfort, I paste the sweetest smile I can muster on my face.

"We decided to wear your clothes to eat your food," I say, relying on tourist naivety.

A smile of condescension ripples across the face of the maître d' and his three subordinates obediently flash broad smiles.

"Please seat my wife, I shall be back in a minute," Cesar tells him.

"You are guests at the hotel?"

"Yes," replies Cesar. "Give me a minute, darling. Order some champagne."

He leaves hurriedly to rectify the error. Although I am happy to wait for Cesar, the man ushers me into the shimmering interior of the restaurant. A forest of marble columns supporting carved arches of plaster surround yet another fountain and a massive chandelier of Venetian glass cascades from the ceiling. The entire restaurant, if it can be called one, floats in an ethereal green with decorative touches of apricot. The softness of colour extracts a lingering concentration. The effect is of such fragile beauty I feel that if I close my eyes for a second, the entire scene could vanish. The traditional Moroccan seating of sumptuously upholstered divans and low circular tables sparkle with formal linens and flowers. I am led to a sumptuous enclave and, as I lower myself on the brocade upholstered divan, I am tempted to kick off my shoes and bury my feet in a mound of cushions, however the four waiters ringed around the table add a formal note, preventing the sybaritic notion racing through me.

Cesar appears in a few minutes at the entrance of the restaurant dressed with the same precision as the maître d'. The starched white collar of a dress shirt fans out above the neckline of the djellaba and his ankles are encased in black dress socks. As he draws closer to our table, I notice with amusement that he has curled the edges of his moustache. He sinks beside me on the couch and orders champagne, waving away the embellished wine list still clutched to the chest of an overbearing server. The portly man has the manners of an executioner rather than a wine steward. In the world of Islamic countries, alcohol still carries a taboo and an exorbitant price. Yet the economic power of the tourists overrides the spiritual will thundering from the loudspeakers of mosques. On this night, the sprinkling of dinner guests in their upholstered pits is obscured by columns on every side. Little do we know that the notion of complete privacy is false, as there are many eyes observing us from the latticework screens across the restaurant.

We watch the champagne being uncorked and poured into glasses. It is tepid with a soapy taste. Cesar sips it, gives a nod of approval, and then buries the bottle deeper into the ice bucket. He winks at me. In the soft glow of candlelight, it appears as though both the irises of his hazel eyes have a fixity I have never seen before. I feel as though his attention is elsewhere. His pupils seem larger than I have ever seen. It is a disquieting moment, as though he is travelling to some interior space that stretches beyond the dimensions of the magnificent restaurant. I am more intrigued than apprehensive, as my husband is an endless source of fascination for me.

A waiter appears, carrying an enormous silver tray that holds out twelve small bowls of appetizers. This is billed in the menu as "salade fine." We taste each one, savouring the marinated vegetables and lentils. The orange salad bloodied by paprika and tossed with slivers of dates and olives wins me over with its originality. Cesar's glass of champagne fills more often than mine; his manner changes abruptly as he becomes boisterous and jovial, engaging the men who serve us with a vivacity that brings them repeatedly to the table. Cesar's French is more fluent than mine. He then dons his spectacles and studies the wine list with the air of a scholar examining some ancient text. He orders entrées from the menu and, like wizards of a bygone era, the waiters keep reappearing in a procession of flowing robes, holding conical serving dishes. Delicate meats flavoured with lemon and figs, morsels of pigeon tucked in sweetened pastry, and the grand finale of the imperial couscous, the national dish of Morocco. It is a circular field of semolina artfully decorated with seven traditional vegetables over a slab of lamb. I look at Cesar in amazement; his appetite is enormous. I have never seen him eat such quantities before. It is as though he simply cannot stop.

CESAR IS ALSO OBSERVING ME. In this new country, we are revealing unknown aspects of ourselves. I eat sparingly and he has accused me of tasting food as though I am conducting a restaurant review. He has no way of knowing that I am also privy to an eating etiquette familiar to my Pakistani roots. I am his trouser-clad wife who had walked with him through the scarlet maple-leaf-clad trees in a park in Toronto two weeks ago but I am also showing him how easy it is for me to submerge myself fully in this extravagant tapestry.

In some ways, we have become anthropological texts written in a familiar script that obliterates the remoteness of the present. Is Cesar conscious that a particular education will mark both of us during our honeymoon? When we dressed for dinner, he said he does not entirely trust the gilded ministrations of the people serving us. Trained in psychiatry, he detects an innate hostility that is skilfully buried. He tells me that it feels as though we are committing some invisible offence levied on the cultural order of this country and we are only protected by our status as affluent tourists. This show of urbanity conceals the watcher within him. I am his cavorting wife with a propensity to disregard the notion that an alien surrounding can be hostile. He has seen me walk through chaos without a trace of fear.

At the beginning of our relationship, this had evoked a spirit of protection in him but within months, he was gratified by the revelation that I am blessed with an unshakeable air of confidence. So he never tells me to be careful, as he knows that I will never be a quarry, and if overwhelmed, I will fight in surprise and yet inform my tormentor that conflict is all too absurd to be really happening. Hazard is drawn to me and Cesar has learned to accept this with ease.

The moment I set my fork down a flurry of movement cuts through the hushed interior of the restaurant. A small group of people appear and music fills the air. A belly dancer and her trio of musicians weave through the columns. Initially all we can see is a blur of tassels, diaphanous veil, and hear the bell-like tones of finger cymbals. Both of us sit on the edge of the divan, leaning forward to catch sight of the spectacle.

"The dancer will dance for you very soon," says the waiter, removing dishes from the table.

I smile at Cesar. "This is the ultimate male fantasy, and it's coming your way, darling."

Cesar lifts my hand and ceremoniously places a kiss on it.

"You," he whispers, "are my only fantasy, but I shall devour the belly dancer."

I chuckle, reminded of the dark glasses incident. A few months ago, we had been seated at a pavement café in Yorkville on a summer afternoon. Cesar wore sunglasses and stared fixedly ahead. I asked him whether he was looking at women and he responded by saying yes, at every woman who passed by. I had laughed and accused him of being a voyeur and his response was that every man anywhere looked at women. This was an essential characteristic, harmless, but present in the normal healthy male.

When the group advances to our table, the alabaster-limbed dancer undulates her stomach and hips twelve inches away from Cesar. The delicate contours of the dancer's face and her smoke-coloured eyes flicker over me but settle on Cesar. She dances for Cesar, tossing her mane of shining hair and using the dance of her jewel embedded navel to beckon to him. The curve of her practised smile makes the invitation both confusing and illusionary. It is a mating call for an unseen partner. From the arch of her poised feet to the spill of her sequin-draped breasts, she is a vision of beauty. My husband sips cognac and keeps his attention on the belly dancer and I wonder as any wife would at how he feels and where his eyes linger.

Cesar, peripherally sensitive, reaches for my hand and holds it in his own. There is a soft smile on his face and he nods his appreciation for the dancer. I feel as though the dancer resembles a young gazelle that has to be encouraged to complete her performance. Her body is younger than mine and yet I am certain that Cesar's fancies have never wandered away. Even when he stands up to tuck a folded currency bill into her sequined brassiere, he is careful not to let his fingers graze her skin.

With her reward jutting out from the cleft of her breasts, she then turns her attention to me. With curving wrists, she beckons to me to dance with her. I shake my head but her eloquent gestures continue and she refuses to move away. This superior will seems to be saying to me, "Show me that we are sisters." I find her charm irresistible and slip off my shoes and rise. Extending my arms and rotating my hips, I sway near her. The beat of the music quickens and we dance faster. I follow the movements as she spins around on her bare feet and I toss a smile at Cesar over one shoulder.

I feel exultant, as though the voices of a legion of women hum through me. It is the dance of women and one of solitude, although it is meant to be the enactment of a promise. The quivering belly, heaving breasts, and curving arms and legs always hint at sexual virtuosity. The sparkling of sequins, faux gems, and semi-clad bodies are in fact an Arab male fantasy, and light years removed from the publicly shrouded forms of their women. The small patter of applause and Cesar's broad smile makes me dip into a gesture of courtesy before the dancer. The dancer's face breaks out into a sweet smile that seeps into her dark eyes. When I sink into the couch, I throw her a fleeting glance of a newfound camaraderie. She stands still for a moment and gazes at me. "Yes," she transmits in silence.

"I have you within me, as I have my mother and grandmother. Their dances were performed fully clothed with ornate ankle bells. This dance is not for men."

"Were you dancing for me?" Cesar hands me a glass of wine.

"Did I make a fool of myself?" I ask.

"Actually I wanted to join you, but you were dancing for each other."

"Did you think so?" I am struck by his perception.

"I remain the tortured voyeur," Cesar clasps his heart theatrically.

His comment startlingly, inserts me into a capsule of memory that travels backwards in time. It was a June evening in a tiny hill station in Pakistan three decades ago. My father, accompanied by a favourite aunt, had taken me to see a film. As a precocious teenager, I had refused to wear a sweater that would have hidden the scalloped neckline of my summer dress. When the car drew up in front of a dilapidated movie theatre, a horde of village men stared at us in dumfounded silence. They were tall men of northern stock. Their reception of the luxury car and its occupants propelled them into celluloid dreams of film glamour. I was equally stunned by their attention. My father moved through them with a stern look hardening the gentle contours of his face. Protective pressure from my aunt propelled me forward. A claustrophobic hysteria gripped me, making me lose my step and stumble. The collision with a man who leapt backwards in terror startled me further. The bulk of his chest brushed against my shoulder. His pungent odour filled me for a moment before I moved away. It took me years to realize that my reaction was sexual. My quivering nostrils and an instant awareness of the weight of my breasts was the response to the force of unwavering male attention.

Cesar's innocuous comment of the tortured voyeur replayed itself with a new accuracy on the streets of Marrakech. I notice that there is no acceptance of spontaneous exchange in the gender segregation rigidly maintained by Moroccan culture. The tourist is referred to as "ajnabi" meaning, stranger, in Arabic. Yet all the implied romanticism of décor and social attitude are permanently arrested. The control came from a repressive social perception. The "Madonnas" of Moroccan society are kept safely at home, while the women of other faiths are stared at, lusted after, and ultimately condemned. I remembered thinking how I had rapidly dismantled the silk-lined patriarchy of my father by crossing over to the other side and living in Canada. Somehow in the face of Khadim I have also detected a hardening attitude as he brushes men away from my path when he guides us through the city. As though his tall frame and his attitude form a fence designed to keep wild dogs away. The unspoken inference being that they are all rabid and I was not to go near any of them.

Later that night, as the gastronomical excesses take a toll on my digestion I drift through a dream. I am in the steam room at my health club in Toronto. I lie on a white towel on the wooden plank seating. The grey fog of steam shrouds the bodies of the other women. Every now and then, someone rises and sluices himself with water. My preference for staying in the steam is based on the idea that only sweat induces a state of relaxation. Eventually when I get up to get a drink of water from the faucet in the corner of the room, a terrifying sight meets my eyes. The three other women stretched out beside me have bodies with missing breasts and genitals. I am wiping the sweat rolling down my face and look at their tranquil faces. A fresh cloud of steam rises from the pipes and spreads into a defined shape. The steam parts, and the belly dancer from the Moroccan restaurant is before me with a straw basket held at her hip. She moves wraithlike, and hands objects from the basket to the women. The women extend their arms and grasp the objects. When a trace of consciousness enters and I recognize the objects I am jerked out of sleep. I open my eyes and sit up. Cesar sleeps peacefully beside me. Then comes the lightning flash of memory and I know that what the dancer handed out were breasts and pubic mounds.

The symbolism of the dream, without the assistance of my psychiatrist husband, filters in with clarity. Women from Eastern societies consider their Western counterparts to be neutered in their essential femininity. They are regarded as being aggressive, masculine, and therefore suspect. The belly dancer had not given anything to me because she knew that we shared a divided sisterhood. I realize that I am being besieged by thoughts that have no place in the happiest season of my life.

I slip out of bed and walk to the windows. Outside, Marrakech is asleep and invisible, as though a vibrant canvas has been covered by cloth. The full moon hovers like a theatrical prop throwing light on the minaret of the Koutoubia mosque. A full sightseeing day lies ahead, and last night's first experience of fine Moroccan cuisine had made us collapse in bed when we had returned. A sense of premonition floods me as though I am being led to some destination neither one of us has planned. How can I share these emotions with my husband on our honeymoon? He is a busy doctor but has taken a month off for the wedding and honeymoon. The last thing I want to do is engage him in my bizarre speculations, which appear without warning at the oddest times.

I glance at the small notebook acquired yesterday. Cesar had asked Khadim where we could buy one and Khadim had disappeared for a few minutes and returned with a small white unlined notepad. He had refused payment for it when Cesar tried to give him money for it. I have written "lunamiel de Cesar et Nazneen" on the cover and kept it in my night table drawer. It is an old habit of maintaining a rough travel journal and then filing it away in folder marked "Travel." Although I never used them in any professional capacity, I am too much of a writer to ever get rid of them.

I enter the baroque bathroom with its carved and painted wooden door and shut it quietly behind me and switch on the light and sit on the edge of the marble bathtub and write. I give a heading to the journal, calling it "Moon over Marrakech," conscious of the moon tilted across the dark sky outside. The moon exerts a powerful grip on my imagination. It appears on the flag of the country I was raised in. My accidental introduction to astrology furthers this curiosity. The sight of the full moon itself always evokes a delighted and wondering sense. The fading henna patterns on the palms of my hands curl around a crescent-shaped design. As a child, my drawings invariably had a moon painted over castles or blue oceans. At the age of forty-seven, I accept the vague and almost shadowy influence of this specific element of nature with ease, without doing any symbolic exploration about it.

There is a knock on the door and it swings open. Cesar fully awake pokes his head through the door.

"Good morning. I hope the food didn't upset your stomach."

"I am fine, I didn't want to disturb you," I reply, hastily closing the notebook.

"The naked writer in cramped quarters," Cesar smiles without stepping in.

"Just some travel notes about this country," I reply, moving towards him.

"I hold Khadim responsible for this, supplying tools for defecting from the honeymoon bed." He pulls the notebook from my hand and places it on a side table.

"What if it is the beginning of a new book?"

"Are you that inspired?" Cesar asks.

"Perhaps," I am deliberately vague, "just some indigestion, and disturbed sleep."

"Giving rise to literature." He has an inquiring look.

I decide not to tell him about my dream and decide it is a perfect time for telling him that we should spend the day without the guide.

"Let's rent a car and pick up a map and have an adventure by ourselves in the Atlas Mountains," I say.

"Sorry, I have already made arrangements with the guide," he replies.

"Cancel them." I resent what I consider the daily intrusion of the guide.

"I do not want to ramble through this country alone and unprotected," he says, his voice softening.

"I can't believe the man who drove through the rainforests of Costa Rica without a map is saying this," I persist.

"Sorry darling, you know the holy man only sent the drink for you, so I remain unprotected in Morocco."

Cesar, who is a superb athlete, dabbling in martial arts, and who has the ability to engage anyone in a comfortable dialogue, is behaving as though we are in some combat zone. This is what I feel as I reluctantly defer to his preference.

CHAPTER 5

🕮 *Honeymoon, Marrakech, 1992*

I AM SPREADING APRICOT JAM on the croissant. It is a new addiction. Decades after Morocco's protectorate status from the French ended, the local chefs continued to preserve their cuisine legacy. France and Spain had carved the kingdom of Morocco in 1912 but the French, under the guise of protectors, had been unable to fully conceal their colonial attitudes. They built residential areas outside the medina, opened schools, and influenced the local cuisine. They also created a social hierarchy based on language. The use of the French language was instrumental in creating a division within the population and threatening the legitimacy of Berber Arabic. This misleading mix of Arabic and French cultures lends a particular mystique and draws visitors like Cesar and myself, who are unable to comprehend either culture fully.

The basket of flaky croissants and apricot jam arrives with coffee to our room each morning. A jam the colour of burned brick is prepared without a trace of preservatives or sugar. The apricot orchards nestled in the areas near the Atlas Mountains send their harvest to the planes below, yet nothing is lost in the flavour that carries the scent of the fresh mountain air and the kiss of the sun. The local breakfast of fried miniature crepes, fried donuts, honey, and strings of dried beef studded in a congealed fat are also assembled on decorative ceramic platters and arranged on breakfast buffets. The largely European and North American clientele of Hotel La Mamounia appear to reject these carbohydrate laden offerings and in a sense so did we.

Cesar opens the door of the bathroom and stands in the arched painted doorway. A bath towel is wrapped around his waist. His hair ends in wet and sleek curls around his face. The East peers out mysteriously from the planes of his bronzed face. Even the ingredients of his aftershave lotion transform into a fragrance where the top-notes of sandalwood rise higher than the others. The sunlight glints off his chest and shoulders and his eyes become a greenish hazel blur. I am bewitched by my husband again, like a child who confronts a unicorn.

Dabbing a smear of apricot jam on my lips, he cups my face with both hands, pressing his lips against mine, transferring apricots, Morocco, and his ardent desire through me. He hovers above like some exotic ceiling mural obliterating everything in sight and making love to me until my body sings and my spirit centres itself.

Khadim, the guide, waits for us in the lobby when we race down an hour later than planned. Cesar has engaged him for the entire trip, slipping him into our circle of two. Part watchdog, part voyeur, he exudes an air that implies that he is extending some privilege for an unnamed sum of money. He has lost the slightly forlorn expression in his eyes we had first noticed, assumes an air of grave responsibility as though two rowdy children have suddenly become his charge. This morning he is dressed in black trousers with a gleaming white shirt. We wear our Moroccan djellabas again. Khadim makes no verbal salutation just a slight dipping motion of his head. Then he extends a hand towards Cesar's leather knapsack. Cesar tightens his grip, gently pushes the hand away saying this is not necessary. Khadim's face breaks into a smile of amusement as he cocks his head to one side. Cesar grins back at him and gives an assertive nod. I watched the little tableaux, and sense that Khadim's amused smile is a bit shaky. In fact, it conceals an elusive injury dealt to his notion of tourist behaviour. This is something Cesar is incapable of understanding from his occidental vantage.

Khadim then turns his gaze to me and I keep my expression neutral.

"You are wearing Moroccan dress."

"How do we look?" I ask, expecting some reaction. It is slow in coming.

"It looks very good, Madame," he replies gravely. "You look like our women."

"Wonderful!" says Cesar heartily. "And me?"

"But of course," replies Khadim, not convincing either one of us.

Outside the hotel entrance, a tan Mercedes of unknown vintage and a local chauffer wait for us.

"The car is good and so is the driver," murmurs Khadim, opening the door for me.

Cesar raises his camera and instantly takes a photograph of Khadim holding the car door open. Khadim flashes a broad smile. None of us knows at that moment that the significance of this photograph will take fourteen years to reveal itself.

We sit together in the back holding hands. It takes less than ten minutes to leave the city of Marrakech behind. A straight road heads towards the Ourika valley sprawling in front of the range of Atlas Mountains. The pastoral vista is gentle. On either side of the road, there are cultivated orchards, a shallow river, and small homes made of ochre coloured plaster. This is a postcard scene. We stop the car along the way and stand in the brisk mountain air to take photographs.

"How about a small house right there?" Cesar points to a meadow. "And one goat for you, darling?"

"You would like that?"

Khadim of the watchful eyes is right behind us.

"Yes," replies Cesar.

"And Madame?"

"I will milk the goat and make chèvre." I flash Khadim a mischievous smile.

"I cannot see that." Khadim shakes his head.

Cesar grins, pulls me away, and whispers, "He is staking a claim on my wife. He has superior knowledge of you."

We get back into the car stifling our laughter, and brace ourselves for the next volume of tourist information as the car heads for our next destination. I lose interest but Cesar listens to it all intently. It is a therapist's trick meant to assemble some sort of profile on a patient. I am certain that Cesar sniffs something beneath the overly courteous exterior. He finds Khadim a challenge. Yet Khadim exercises a control where all points of reference are impersonal. This particular smokescreen requires a particular intelligence. Cesar has told me that Khadim's refusal to wear the long Moroccan robe that other tour guides do and his neat grooming are elements of a narcissistic quality that is also nuanced by a political complexity. Nevertheless, Cesar has confidence in him and wants to extend camaraderie rather than formality.

The sharply winding mountain road curves unexpectedly and stops by a small stone hut. Standing outside the hut is a young man wearing a blue robe and a loosely wound turban around his head. We are unaware that his appearance is designed to make tourists believe that he could well belong to the tribe of the fabled blue men of the Moroccan Sahara who appear in guidebooks. Khadim gets out of the car and speaks to him in Arabic and the man gestures to us to come inside the hut. We follow Khadim into the dimly lit interior of the hut.

Inside, the man with the trailing indigo robe and turban assumes a different aura. We stand surrounded by vessels of hammered metal and colourful ceramic dishes. The floor is littered with straw baskets filled with necklaces, rings, and bracelets of beads. His appearance is almost medieval. Khadim informs us that he is a Berber selling authentic crafts. The Berbers are nomadic mountain tribes of Morocco and its original inhabitants carry a multitude of bloodlines that go back to the invasions of Carthage and Rome. They are a sedentary, agricultural tribe of people, who had resisted the colonial domination under the French protectorate status and even managed to retain their customary law tribunals. They enjoy an exotic and somewhat elevated status of indigenous people among the urban communities of Morocco.

In the cocoon-like interior of the shop filled with shimmering objects, we both visualize the Berber in a remote desert seated on a camel. The organic dye extracted from the indigo plant seeps into the faces of these men through the turbans with which they conceal their heads and half their faces. The man standing before us transforms into one of the "blue men" riding camels in the desert, inspiring legions of artists who have split the monochromatic vista of Morocco with splashes of blue. From a distance, the men appear to be blue obelisks moving through golden sands.

We look at the objects in the hut and examine crafts that have a crude primitive charm but do not appeal to either one of us. I sift through the jewellery. The knowledge that both the turquoise and the amber are fake resin will come months later when I return home. Khadim engages the man in a conversation and tells us that he is confused as we are dressed in Moroccan clothing. Cesar humorously tells Khadim to tell the man that confusion is a good thing. Then he tells me to browse and he steps outside.

"My husband is not a shopper," I say to Khadim.

"I will stay with you, Madame, to make sure he will make a good price for you," Khadim stiffens his shoulders.

I am acutely aware that he expects me to buy something so I pick up a small metal box studded with amber and a pair of turquoise earrings and hand them to Khadim. The Berber looks at Khadim's palm and shakes his head. He draws the blue robe aside to reveal a leather pouch fastened on a cord wrapped around his waist. He opens the pouch and draws out a small lump of paper. Twisting open the paper he lifts a strange looking bracelet and hands it to me. It is a silver cuff attached to four chains that end in rings. It resembles the bridal hand jewellery worn in India and Pakistan.

"This is very old, only Berber women wear this, and they will like it in Canada," says Khadim using the guide's bluff with great ease.

He has taken the bracelet from the man and now holds it up against the lamp as though he is checking its authenticity. Then he extends it to me. It is ornately decorated. The central motif on the bracelet is a butterfly with the body fashioned out of turquoise and carnelian. The chains that settle on the back of the hand have an identical pattern in a smaller size and so do the rings. The curling tendrils shooting out of the bracelet duplicate an Art Deco motif. I know this is not a piece of antique jewellery and am uncomfortable with both men who anxiously wait for me to try the bracelet on. I wish Cesar would reappear so I could muster the strength to walk away. Although it is an attractive bracelet, I resent the pressure exerted to make a purchase.

"You know how to wear it?" Khadim's eyes bore into mine.

"Yes," I reply brusquely, taking the bracelet from his fingers.

I slip the rings on first and then fold my hand to slip the cuff of the bracelet on my wrist. Cesar walks in.

"It's stunning, and made for you." He lifts my hand and kissed my knuckles.

"I am not sure, I have so much jewellery that I don't wear."

"Don't take it off, it goes with your clothes." He pulls out his wallet.

The Berber aims a broad smile at Cesar realizing that the sale had been made. But Khadim's eyes have changed; there is both a hardening in his expression and disinterested coolness in his body language. It catches me off guard and I realize that his presence is intrusive. A series of unvoiced signals have become part of the communication between us. Is my husband aware of this?

"What do you think Khadim, wasn't this just made for my wife?"

"Masha'Allah!" Khadim murmurs correctly.

"Ah yes! By the grace of God," Cesar's hearty baritone rings out, winning a smile from Khadim.

The next destination a few miles away is a stone mill that Khadim insists we visit. The car halts besides two small plaster huts where men in blue-hooded robes lounge against the walls. Khadim leads us towards the mill located in one of the small rooms. There is grain inside the circular stone mill. Cesar insists on photographing me and asks me to move closer to the mill in the centre of the room.

"Put your hood up," he says. "Perfect!"

We are almost on top of each other in the small space. The floor is carpeted with sand and wheat chaff. The roof is so low that Khadim hunches over while Cesar kneels with his camera on the floor. My sandaled feet sink in the ground as I lift the hood of the robe over my hair.

"You look as though you've stepped right out of the Bible," Cesar chuckles.

The flash on the camera explodes and I feel an excruciating pain lance through my stomach. I scream and another needle seems to have pierced my right hip and I double over in pain. I am terrified by the pain.

Cesar lunges towards me.

"What is it?" his face contorts as he struggles to straighten me up. Khadim retreats and steps outside.

"Something, like a needle went through me, three of them," I pant.

"Let me." Cesar grabs a bunch of fabric around my legs, and shakes it.

"I've been bitten, I felt it," I moan in fear and pain.

"We have to go outside. You have to take this off, I need light to examine you." Cesar pulls me towards the door.

"No," I push him, "there is no privacy outside; I am not wearing anything under this."

"I will tell Khadim. Stay with me." He pulls me outside the doorway into the sunlight.

He returns within seconds and raises my robe up to my stomach. There are four swelling mounds of flesh on my stomach and hips. Each has a miniscule dot in the centre. They look like insect bites and Khadim has informed him that this is not a scorpion region. The pain subsides and the swollen mounds of skin grow larger. I am more shocked than hurt, but my husband has never heard me cry out like that. I stand with my elbows rigidly to my side, waiting.

"Let's just get out of this place. Some insect bites and if you were allergic you would have reacted by now, I was scared that it may have been a snake." He is no longer my husband but the doctor.

Gathered outside the hut is the cluster of men who gaze at us with curiosity. Khadim waits near the car. Cesar and I walk to it in silence.

"My wife has been bitten by an insect of some sort."

"Ah," murmurs Khadim, not looking at me.

"You are not feeling dizzy or any numbness anywhere?" Cesar looks at me anxiously.

"No, I am fine, I can just feel the swelling now."

"Would you like to go back to the hotel? It is almost afternoon," Cesar asks me.

"We will have lunch at a relaxing place, Monsieur. It has been arranged. You will both relax," Khadim says to him coolly.

"No, I am fine. Let's get something to drink, but I don't know about my appetite." Khadim's lack of concern annoys me.

The car travels on the winding mountain road for another fifteen minutes until it reaches a restaurant perched on a hill. The location is stunning. The stone terrace commands a view of the entire valley beneath it. A man with a broad smile on his face waits for us at the entrance. He embraces Khadim and leads us up a flight of stairs. A table has been set up for us, but no other guests are present. We are enchanted by the azure sky and terraced valley wrapped around the restaurant. Khadim sits with us and orders bottles of mineral water. Cesar lights my cigarette and I reassure him that I am fine.

"Do you think this can be called the honeymoon sting?" I laugh, feeling myself recover.

"That's it, probably a mosquito or a sand fly."

"It was a wasp. I saw one sitting on your hair, but I thought it had flown away," says Khadim.

Cesar's head jerks in surprise. He looks at Khadim for a moment.

"So when you put your hood up darling, it got trapped and tried to escape wiggling down and biting you along the way. You are not allergic are you?" My husband peers at me.

Cesar's explanation and Khadim's shocking comment stun me. Had he seen a wasp sitting in my hair and not said anything?

"In my hair?" I ask him indignantly.

"Yes, I thought it would fly away, so I did not tell you," Khadim repeats woodenly.

You are lying, Khadim, I think to myself. You wanted me to be bitten by the wasp.

"I suppose none of us noticed it in the mill," Cesar shrugs, sensing my anger.

"You are no longer in pain, Madame?" Khadim glances at me.

I lift the glass of water and drink it without replying and then get up and walk to the stone balcony and lean over it. Instinctively, I feel that Khadim's customary gravity cannot hide a particular light in his eyes. It is like a cautioning light, one that implies that I have deserved this little punishment. It is all too bizarre for words. I need to explain this to Cesar, who has accepted Khadim's notion that the wasp would fly out of my hair. The emotions swirling inside prevent me from returning to the table. I feel as though a shadowy cultural collective is pressing upon me.

The right to inflict pain on women who merely appear to be transgressing slips into my world. I am no longer on my honeymoon in Morocco wearing a Berber bracelet on my wrist and about to have lunch in the most exquisite spot I have ever seen, but hostage to a storm of conflicting thoughts.

Cesar waves to me and so I return to the table.

"The view is breathtaking."

"Are you with me? You seem so far away," he says, intuitively.

"I took a little voyage."

"I hope I was with you."

"It would have driven you mad." I gaze at my husband.

"An adventure?" he persists, intrigued.

"If you must really know," I face him squarely, "think of *Heart of Darkness.*"

"Joseph Conrad breathing over us as we wait for roast lamb." He points towards Khadim and the waiter, who are carrying an enormous platter towards us.

We head towards the table as Khadim places the platter in the centre of the table and the other man arranges plates and cutlery on the table. We look at the food dumfounded. There is enough meat for at least ten people.

"Khadim, please join us," says Cesar, amused at the quantity of meat.

"He has prepared this especially for you, Monsieur." Khadim cuts a large chunk of meat and places it on Cesar's plate.

"How could he roast this in fifteen minutes? Amazing country!" says Cesar.

"When did you arrange this, Khadim?" I am beyond trusting him entirely.

Khadim silently and meticulously slices wedges of the lamb and places them in my plate. He wields the bone-handled knife with practised ease. Then, ignoring the cutlery, he rolls pieces of meat into the flatbread and eats with great relish. The crisp skin conceals the buttery soft meat and is delicious. I try again.

"It's almost half a lamb." I still cannot get over the quantity of meat in front of us.

"It has been cooked especially for you, Madame," Khadim beams at me.

"I don't think so Khadim. Perhaps it's been cooked for you."

The words shoot out of my mouth before I can control myself. Cesar is incredulous. Khadim drops the piece of bread in his fingers on the plate, rises from the chair, and swiftly walks away.

Cesar looks at me and then at Khadim. I know he is thinking that the shock of the insect sting still lingers, and has resulted in my hostile comment. I feel as though Cesar is almost feeling sorry for Khadim.

"Being a little harsh, don't you think?"

"Was I?"

"It doesn't matter darling. I am happy to pay for this even if we only have a few bites. I am sure he made arrangements in advance. After all, this is how they make their living. I am going to bring him back." Cesar gets up from his chair.

"Must you?"

"Yes. He is a very polite fellow and won't understand. What prompted that anyway?"

"Well, I can tell him I didn't really mean it," I give in.

"No, I will tell him. This is a man's country."

It takes a few minutes for Cesar to return to the terrace with Khadim, who once again starts slicing meat and putting it on our plates.

"Please don't. I cannot eat anymore," I try to stop him.

"What you cannot finish, we will give to the children," he responds.

There are no children visible. In fact, there is no one around; only the bright afternoon sun and the sweet-smelling air. Have I really been unjust or do I continue to feel a sense of personal intrusion from the guide? Cesar is also my closest friend and yet the things I want to tell him remain frozen inside. Khadim has the ability to hurl me into a cultural zone resembling that of my childhood. Have I, in fact, never fully escaped the legions of Eastern men whose repressive attitudes I have been educated to abhor?

The drive home is also eventful. A Berber market has assembled along a great meadow across the river. Khadim asks the driver to drive beside the meadow. The teeming humanity makes us stay in the car and simply watch the scene. People look at the car in curiosity and some even move closer. We are fascinated by the donkeys laden with goods and people with makeshift wooden stalls outside. An old man, bent double under a pyramid of clay vessels strapped to his back, sways besides the car. His face turns to my side of the window. I smile at him naively, and watch in disbelief as he purses his mouth and aims a gob of spit at the window. I draw back, startled by the insult.

"Amazing man," says Cesar who has only seen the great load the man carries. "What's that on the window?"

"He spat at me," I reply.

Khadim's head jerks back towards me from the front seat. He mutters something to the driver and the car halts. Before either one of us can respond, he leaps out of the door and crosses to my side and blocks the path of the swaying man.

"Stop him darling! He is just an old man," I cry.

Cesar tries to open his side of the car door but a crowd of people have suddenly appeared by the car.

"Darling, you really have to stop creating provocations." He looks at me in exasperation.

"I haven't done anything. He is an old fool. Let Khadim handle this."

"I will not. I don't want a riot in the middle of my honeymoon. Stay in the car." He pushes the car door open against the melee of bodies, slides out, and firmly locks the door behind him. Curious faces peer into the car and I put on my dark glasses. The driver sits unconcerned. Then I roll down the spit festooned window a little and the odour of unwashed bodies and animals roll in. I rewind the glass upwards. I can see the top of Khadim's head followed by Cesar's. After a minute or so, they elbow the crowd aside and get into the car. The driver leans on the horn, the crowd parts to let the car roll onwards. The drive to the hotel is a silent one.

In the elevator, Cesar looks at me.

"It was quite dramatic. He removed one of the clay pots and held it in front of the old man. Then he smashed it under his nose."

"With what?"

"His bare hands. He held the pot in one hand and used the other to strike it. Like a karate chop."

I am in the bathroom watching my reflection bouncing off the mirrored walls. The steam lifts from the hot water filling the bathtub. I am examining the small reddish mounds on my stomach and hips. The mirrors begin to cloud and I can hear Cesar ordering coffee from room service. I remove my clothes, slip one leg over the ledge of the tub, and feel as though a hand brushes my shoulder. I turn my neck and wonder if I have really felt fingertips slide off my shoulder. The fingers belong on a large hand that is not my husband's, however, in the empty space around me, there is no one.

CHAPTER 6

✿ *Honeymoon, Marrakech, 1992*

CESAR IS SWIMMING IN THE pool. I am lying on the padded chaise holding a book across my chest, and watching my husband. I am not the only one, as other eyes are also watching him. To say that he swims is an understatement. It is more as if he dances in the water. The stroke is a crawl, but his arms and shoulders ripple with movements of a Balinese dancer. The elbow rising to etch a scroll in the air before it disappears and his long-fingered palms cup the water backwards. He does not slice the water or part it vigorously. Instead, he becomes liquid himself. The water, ultimately receptive to the sinuous rolling torso, breaks and restores its surface rhythmically, as though a portion of the reptilian brain has plucked memory from its collective and willed the body to simulate it. The sleek head with its helmet of platinum curls identify him as Cesar, and not some sea-creature who has strayed into the pool of the Hotel La Mamounia.

As the midday sun changes the colour of the pool water into glittering turquoise, the contemplation of my husband becomes an act of languid meditation that slows my pulse and stills my thoughts completely. Even the sound of voices near the pool does not disturb the weight of my silence. With this silence also comes the pleasure of baking gently in the sun, sipping cool drinks, and reading pages of the "Alexandria Quartet," which I personally equate with bliss. Added to this is the delightful chorus of birdsong in the gardens surrounding the swimming pool. Finally, a day without Khadim.

Cesar floats on his back for quite a while. I wonder if he is opening his eyes wide and allowing the burning sun to penetrate his retina. It is something he does even at home in Toronto.

"The sun has lithium and this is needed in the blood to ward off depression," he has explained to me.

Of course, I have relegated this comment to his mysterious world of psychiatry. Maybe he is storing it up for when we return to a grey Toronto winter. He then swims to the edge of the pool near me and hangs on the ledge.

"Come on, I will take you into the deep end."

I get up and kneel down by him.

"Sorry darling, I am not ready yet," I reply.

"I would never let anything happen to you. I will swim beside you. You can do it."

I shake my head and retreat to the lounge. My love for him is boundless but my fear of deep water makes me head to the shallow parts of pools and shorelines of oceans. He has accepted this for months as he heads off for deeper water, but he has not given up trying.

When he climbs out of the pool, a pair of attendants greets him with towels. They appear on cue and he savours their ministrations. I watch him, amused at the way he enjoys draping the towels around his shoulders. The faces of two young Moroccan men are full of an effeminate grace. Both are dark-complexioned, with curly hair and long-lashed dark eyes and smiles on their faces that never waver. This attention paid to personal service outranks any other hotel we have ever stayed in. In many ways, they remind me of Khadim. At this point, I do not know that Khadim has left a message at the hotel for Cesar. Cesar has made some plan with him without consulting me.

"How would you like to dine in an authentic Moroccan home tonight?" he asks.

"I would love that. So we can see the real life."

"And they are cooking especially for us. Don't ask me who — it is a surprise," he warns me.

I smile at him because he knows that I love surprises. This is a perfect day. A break from sightseeing with the opportunity to actually write the postcards I have gathered. Who is Cesar's local contact, I wonder, but know that he makes friends easily and has always been a resourceful traveller. I have decided to allow him to surprise me. An hour later, while Cesar dozes off on the chaise longue, two figures clad in white towelling robes appear at the far end of the pool. The distinction between sanatorium and hotel merge for an instant. As though the chaotic resonance of the rose-coloured city of Marrakech invariably overwhelms the central nervous system and the only place for healing rests within the vaulted confines of this luxurious hotel.

The man is in his late sixties and of an indeterminate Middle-Eastern appearance. His companion is younger and bulkier. She also wears dark glasses and her hair is concealed by a white towel wound in turban style. The wrist clutching the expensive designer handbag is laden with gold bracelets. The pool attendants lurking in the shrubbery pop out on cue, fussing with the cushions of the chaise longues. The air is charged with activity, dispelling the silence. The woman's voice pierces the air, shrill with the sound of complaint. She speaks in Arabic. Before she sinks into the chair, she kicks off her open-toed heeled shoes and one flies away. As an attendant kneels down to retrieve the shoe, her companion addresses her in a sharp tone.

"Do you suppose Madame is a handful?" Cesar whispers by my side, now awake.

The man looks at us apprehensively, as he is aware that his noisy companion has drawn our unwanted attention. She adds fuel to the fire, opening her robe and sliding it off her shoulders. Her large-bosom stuffed into a garish bathing suit, commonplace on European beaches, causes a harsh response from the man. The result is a heated exchange. When the man's voice becomes almost menacing and the woman's lowered, she draws her bathrobe back over her upper torso. We continue to watch under the protection of our dark glasses.

"It's because you are here," I say. "She is not supposed to be on view for another male."

"Here! By the pool?" Cesar's voice rises. "Are they Moroccan?"

"I don't know, but they are Arab-speaking, and it doesn't matter. She could be in Cannes, and it would be the same."

"She is not exactly a cover girl."

"It doesn't matter. She is his wife, or mistress, or even a daughter, and the men will make them feel as if they are whores."

Cesar gazes at me pensively.

"It is a male response that plagues men in many cultures."

"It has nothing to do with being male. It is a political statement," I reply sardonically.

Cesar laughs. "You have to observe peacocks. The females do not have the glorious tail."

"No darling. This is tribal and cultural."

"Well I don't particularly want other men to examine your bikini and this sarong," he playfully pulls at it.

"No. You are nothing like these men."

"You mean the dark, predatory, possessive rage?" He is laughing at me.

"Precisely."

"You are wrong my darling, given the right set of circumstances I could easily be all of the above."

Lunch is served at the other end of the pool. It is a sumptuous buffet, dotted with at least ten servers. We sit at a table and find ourselves directly opposite the couple who had attracted our attention. The woman removes her sunglasses and the towel twisted around her head. She faces us squarely while her companion has his back to us. She has a swarthy, attractive face, coarsened by dark hair, which has garish strands of blond shot through it. She examines us boldly with a touch of coolness to her expression. I smile faintly. The woman holds up the large menu in front of her. Cesar, seated next to me, turns his head and just at that moment, the woman lowers the menu and beams a smile at him. Amused by her transformation, I kick Cesar under the table.

"I think you have made a conquest."

"The lady is quite a tiger," Cesar says softly. "She will eat us both up."

"Until she is punished."

"A touch of paranoia about the local male. He looks quite harmless?"

Cesar's comment has barely escaped his lips when the woman's companion heads towards the buffet. He looks at us briefly and nods, and the expression on his face sobers us both. His dark eyes are ringed by weariness, as though the responsibility of his companion weighs him down and, in some incongruous fashion, he expects us to understand. A chill invades my body, recognizing his expression. It is an old sensation called the Dance of Marionettes. The women of Eastern countries, whether shrouded or visible, are like skilful acrobats clad in seductive clothing. They never rotate within their skins with spontaneity or relaxation in public, only sag to collapse in privacy. Just the way puppets do after being consigned to a box when the show ends.

The grilled fish is expertly filleted at the table for Cesar. I chose to pick through the delicate web of bones myself because I feel more connected to what I eat in this fashion. The couple sitting at the table eat in silence, as do Cesar and I. There is no desire from either table to bridge the cultural divide. Cesar consumes the entire bottle of Moroccan wine over lunch. The Grès wine is similar to a California blush and lighter than a rosé. His appetite and his vitality seem more robust than ever before, as though his entire metabolism is powered by a furious engine. I decide that it must be the relaxation and being away from his work. When the crème brulé arrives for dessert he polishes it off, smiling and saying, "Pacing myself for the feast tonight."

Khadim waits for us in the lobby later that evening. He intends to play host to us in his own home. Filled with curiosity, I climb into the taxi with Cesar. The taxi moves away from the grand hotel to unfamiliar streets. Khadim no longer displays the attitude of the serious tour guide, now acting as though he is bringing old friends home for dinner. He has mentioned that, like us, he is also newly married, and I wonder if his wife speaks English. The barren neighbourhood where the taxi stops displays no evidence of Moroccan architecture. The two-storeyed boxlike home in front of us is devoid of any embellishment.

He pays the taxi driver with a great flourish and ushers us in through the metal gate. Cesar holds the large box of Swiss chocolates we have purchased from the hotel gift shop for Khadim's wife.

The overgrown shrubbery in the front ends at a small porch. Beside the open front door, a young woman sits on a crude wooden bench. Her head is bent over a white kitten sitting on her lap. Intent on stroking her pet, she gives no indication that she has noticed us. Khadim reaches her first and speaks to her in Arabic and she looks up. The childish contours of her face explode with a beauty that leaps off the pages of a Renaissance art book. A shy smile dimples her fair-skinned face and her eyes swim in a bluish-green haze pin-pointed by jet pupils. Her hair, swept back in a crumpled satin ribbon, is a mass of auburn tendrils. It is a Berber face, touched by many ancestries. She presses the animal closer to her and looks not a day older than sixteen.

"My wife, she is called Sharbat," says Khadim.

The girl gazes at us sideways and does not get up. Although we are charmed by her beauty, we are shocked that she is the wife. There could easily be twenty years between them. Cesar slowly extends the box of chocolates and his entire body is held with a stillness, as though confronted by a rare butterfly that might suddenly dart away. The young woman presses deeper into the animal. The white aureole of the kitten's fur fans around her cheeks and both pairs of eyes are eerily similar. The kitten's pink tongue flickers out, duplicating for one unearthly second the exact shade of the girl's lips. Cesar moves the box of chocolates closer and a set of plump fingers closes around it. Khadim ignores her and ushers us inside the door, his wife oblivious to our departure.

Looking back, I see that the young woman with the perfect name has disappeared. Sharbat is the juice of fruits and pressed flowers in the Persian culture. However, even drinks made with sweetened dairy products and scented with rosewater are called sharbat. Street vendors in Middle Eastern and South Asian countries rent the streets with exhortations to drink it. One sip, they chant out, will catapult one into some magical realm, and the refusal to do so only hints at lack of judgment. I am acutely aware that although the new bride outside is a visual feast, it is only Khadim who will control her destiny.

We enter a room that has the appearance of a living room. Stiffly upholstered couches flank three walls and the fourth sports an enormous television set.

"Please," says Khadim. "You must sit."

We sit down, taking in the tasteless formality of the empty room with the plastic-covered circular table complete with a vase of artificial flowers. The room is dimly lit by two wall fixtures, which hold naked bulbs. Even the large maroon carpet beneath our feet has a dullness that shows no relation to the geometric wonder of the Berber carpets in the markets.

"How long have you been married?" I ask Khadim.

"Like you, Madame, just recently. The first time I married young, this time my wife is young."

Cesar casts an amused look at Khadim. I know exactly what he is thinking. Our sombre guide has also succumbed to the lure of youth and beauty. Youth in itself is a powerful intoxicant and when it comes graced with beauty then it is considered a rejuvenating force.

"Will Sharbat," Cesar pronounces it like sherbet, "join us?"

"She will go to her mother, they will bring us tea," replies Khadim, looking every inch the lord of the manor.

"Has she finished her education?" I ask, immediately hating my absurd judgmental question.

"Yes," Khadim looks at me squarely.

Sharbat's mother, who is middle-aged and dressed in the long caftan and headscarf, arrives with the tray carrying mint tea. She eyes me discreetly, never quite meeting my gaze. When I hold out both hands to receive the glass, a sudden transformation occurs. She swoops down and holds one of my hands, turning up the palm where the henna designs have begun to fade. She beams at me and then talks in Arabic to Khadim who responds to her and nods his head repeatedly.

"She wishes to know if you would like the henna to be redone so it does not fade away." Khadim cuts though the torrent of words pouring out of his mother-in-law.

"Now?"

"Yes, she will do it for you," Khadim smiles at both of us.

"We don't want to trouble her," Cesar looks at me.

"It is no trouble. It has already been arranged. She is very happy to do this for you."

I sense that the woman will be disappointed if I refuse, and perhaps Khadim is displaying Moroccan hospitality in all its colours, or simply making amends for the wasp incident. However, the recipient of this small pleasure will be Sharbat's mother, released just for a moment from her appointed station. So when the small tray carrying a bowl of henna arrives, I offer one hand. The woman applies a clear liquid to the palm of my hand and then creates a fresh design over it. She asks Khadim to tell me that the clear liquid will ensure that the henna will be strong and intense. She works quickly, and when the smell of garlic rises somewhere close by, I mistakenly think it comes from her, completely unaware that the clear liquid is pure garlic juice. Then the herbal tang of henna masks it, sealing it into place while the henna dries and hardens.

The appearance of Sharbat without the kitten creates a charming diversion. Sharbat sits next to her mother and smiles at me but ignores Cesar. They speak in Arabic.

"I would like to show you the video of my wedding. It is traditional Moroccan," says Khadim to Cesar.

"Yes, of course. We would love to see it," Cesar replies enthusiastically, thoroughly intrigued by the informality.

Why had we not fortified ourselves with a drink before leaving the hotel? The small glasses of mint tea that are pressed upon us make us feel waterlogged. It is also difficult to resist looking at Khadim's wife, even though she ignores us. Instead of the kitten, she now presses into her mother's bulky form. When Khadim inserts the video into the player, both women leave the room.

"They will prepare the dinner now," he announces.

I rest my hennaed palms on my thighs as the video begins.

A staccato rhythm fills the room and Khadim, seated on horseback, bobs along the screen. It is the groom's procession to the bride's home. The camera pans the faces of the people surrounding him and for a split second lingers on his face. His aquiline features and dark eyes are caught in a hawkish predatory light and do not resemble any of the laughing faces of those walking beside him. There is endless filming of an archway and the rooftop of a home strung with lights. Khadim tells us that his wife's father is a man of some economic stature. All this while the henna dries on my palms and the garlic juice seeps through the pores of my skin to an unimagined depth. Sharbat bobs into view, veiled behind a fluttering cloth and a tasselled cap. A clutch of women around her, guiding her as one would a blind person. Her appearance resembles a miniature walking tent, her face protected and shrouded behind a headdress. Within seconds, she disappears, replaced by the banal sweep of a camera showing a meal being consumed. Crates of soft drinks lined up against the walls of a large eating hall and communal platters of Moroccan food being picked at. The only sound accompanying the video is the drone of Arabic music. No actual part of the ceremony is shown on the video.

I raise my voice above the clamour and ask Khadim where I can wash my hands. He leans forwards and stops the video, which freezes on men dancing. I scrub my hands in the wash basin of a bathroom with rough and primitive fixtures. Flowers and geometric patterns in a vivid orange leap off my palms, but they are accompanied by the stench of raw garlic, which makes me nauseous. I soap my hands repeatedly but cannot get rid of the smell. There is knocking on the door as I have spent a long time. I turn to meet the inquiring gaze of Sharbat and her mother. Embarrassed, I hold out my palms without making an issue of the smell of garlic. I am led to a smaller room where Cesar and Khadim are seated around a circular table. Sharbat sits next to Khadim as I sit on his other side close to Cesar. The mother staggers in with a gigantic platter of couscous. A box of Kleenex and glasses of water are placed near us. Neither plates nor cutlery appear. Khadim simply lift strands of meat and places them on the section of the platter facing me. He then unceremoniously tosses a chunk of meat near Sharbat as well. Cesar, realizing that communal eating from the same platter is the custom, lifts a scoop of the grain and vegetables and puts it in his mouth.

"This is delicious," he says, giving me an encouraging nod.

I instantly dislike the forced intimacy of fingers being dipped in the same dish. Also, the smell of garlic from my hands makes it difficult for me to swallow the food. A rage directed at my predicament coils inside. The subservient attitude of the two women also makes me uncomfortable. Why have Cesar and I permitted this folly to take place? Socializing with a guide who has now trapped us within the primitive banality of his domestic life is a mistake, threatening to upset the charmed circle of our honeymoon. I am offended at the way Khadim puts small scoops of food near Sharbat.

"Do you always select her food for her?"

Khadim glances at his wife, who is sucking on a chunk of chicken cartilage.

"If I do not put it in front of her, she will not eat."

Sharbat throws him a merry smile and responds in Arabic. Cesar watches Sharbat indulgently. At that moment I stifle the annoyance I feel at Cesar, who examines this eating ritual as though rare fossils were placed in front of him. Then it is over, as Sharbat rises and awkwardly lunges out of the room. Khadim, unperturbed, simply comments that she is going to feed her kitten. Within minutes we also get up, declining the offer of mint tea and ask Khadim to find us a taxi. His offer to escort us back to the hotel is firmly declined by Cesar.

"You have shown us great Moroccan hospitality, and honoured my wife," says Cesar adopting the local etiquette.

"It is nothing." Khadim looks at me gravely and places his right hand over his heart.

"Please thank them," I stumble on the words, "for the henna."

"They are pleased to do this for you. You are one of them, so you will always have our heart, and our protection."

Cesar feels that Khadim's declaration of spiritual kinship to me is respectful even though it subtly excludes him. Within the seductive tentacles of Moroccan society, Judeo-Christian societies are relegated to the horizon. The pull of this invisible fraternity is so powerful that I can see how impressed Cesar is. I know that he had mentioned earlier to me how charmed he felt by some of Khadim's graces, which make him utter lyrical sentiments as though he is discussing the weather. Cesar, in the throes of these emotions, moves forward and embraces him.

I HAVE TUCKED BOTH MY hands between my thighs and cannot fall asleep. I feel that the garlic has permeated my entire body. One recurring thought is that garlic, apart from culinary use, is also considered protective. In homeopathy, it is regarded as a purifying and cleansing agent. The women in Khadim's home have chosen garlic, but what is the protection for? And who has decided that I am in need of it?

Cesar moans in his sleep. I touch his face and his eyes open.

"I have had a bizarre dream," he says and I switch on the bedside lamp.

"What was it?" I watch him sit up in bed and then get up. "Was I in it?"

"No." He gets up from the bed and walks to the window. "Actually, it was Khadim."

"I need to wash my hands, I can't get rid of this smell." I sit up in bed.

"Don't," he says. "I cannot smell it, besides it will be gone in a few hours."

Cesar pours some cognac into a glass.

"I am clearing my head," he winks at me.

"Can I hear about it?" I ask him.

"Ah, dreams and symbolism." He sits in the armchair.

"Do I get to interpret it like you do with mine?"

"Yes, Doctor," he says blandly, then takes another sip of cognac.

I sit on the edge of the bed near him and we are now both fully awake.

"I am in a desert terrain that has large rocks. I am riding a horse. Khadim, who is wearing his black trousers and white shirt, is also riding beside me. But I am wearing the hotel's bathrobe. My knees are pressed against the horse and in the pocket of this bathrobe is your Berber bracelet. Then the image shifts and I am standing within a circle of men. We are all wearing Moroccan robes and there is dagger on a cord attached to our waists. I am chanting. We have come for her. We have come for the bride. Then Khadim says they want the gift. I shout that I am the gift and I push my way out of the circle and Khadim, who is with me, smiles. He shouts, "This is my brother." The next series of images are these. Khadim is holding a white cat. Sharbat's head is attached to the cat. Then Khadim kneels down to stroke the cat and she plays with an object on the floor. I look down at the cat and see what she is holding between her paws. It is Sharbat's severed hand with your Berber bracelet clasped on the wrist. The cat then pads towards a bowl. It is filled with apricot jam. I shout at Khadim that Sharbat is eating your breakfast, but Khadim just chants words in Arabic that I cannot understand. That is when I woke up."

I place my hands on my husband's eyes, blanking the screen in his head.

"Well?" He removes my hands and looks up at me.

"No dream analysis on our honeymoon." I lean down and kiss him.

CHAPTER 7

❀ Honeymoon, Marrakech, 1992

I AM NOT CERTAIN IF this is an afternoon to wander through a necropolis, even if it houses the remains of sixty-six members of a ruling Saadian dynasty. Even the cachet of a mausoleum built in the late fifteenth century and discovered in Marrakech in 1917 fails to excite me. I walk behind Cesar and Khadim, trying to block out the drone of Khadim's guide repertoire. I would have preferred to browse through the pottery lane in the souks, loose my heart to some frivolous object and carry it back in triumph. This is the afternoon to let the rose-tinted city play its final siren song for us before we leave for Fez the next morning. It is not an afternoon for antiquity and death. But Cesar has cajoled me out of my resistance, marched me down to the lobby, and apologized to Khadim, who had waited patiently for two hours.

The sombre chamber has the air of a room lifted from the Alhambra in Grenada, Spain. The lacy marble frescos fanning out from pillars topped by arches, the dull sheen of yellowing marble draped over coffins, and the violation of a sixteenth-century royal decree by invaders does not engage me. Khadim lifts his face, cups his hands, and silently offers a prayer at the exquisite "mihrab," a prayer niche. This prayer, he informs Cesar, is for departed souls, and the glance he lances me with is almost accusatory. He is aware of my lack of spiritual interest. Cesar remains still, inhaling the dank and oily flavour of the death chamber, examining ceiling and walls with a pensive look. I feel myself detaching from one reality to another, reclaiming a childhood memory.

IT IS THURSDAY NIGHT AT the Mazar, which is the tomb of a Sufi mystic in Karachi, Pakistan. A narrow lane forks off from the playgrounds of the Clifton Beach with its roadside stalls and vendors. Towering above the end of the lane, fifty steps made of stone end at the rounded cupola and pavilions of the shrine. The lane is choked with stalls of flower sellers. Red- and fuchsia-coloured roses are heaped in conical mounds and surrounded by garlands of jasmine. I am walking behind my mother, whose arms are laden with flowers. The scent of roses is so overpowering that I feel as though an enthralling mutation has occurred. My breath, hair, and face have entered the heart of the flower. Then through the heady fragrance rises the scent of jasmine with a sharper and more piercing note of sweetness, heralding its own presence. I feel airborne floating on clouds of entwining fragrances. Not even the flower sellers, who are a crude and cynical lot, aiming gobs of betelnut-stained spit on the street, can disturb my anesthetized state. I climb the steps to the tomb, carrying the flowers that my mother has shifted to my arms. I am the custodian of fragrance, I think, reaching the threshold of the shrine lined with rows of shoes.

"Cover your head," says my mother arranging her chiffon scarf and slipping out of her shoes.

The spectacle rising before us is startling because of the number of people packed into the large chamber. They are seated around a mound of roses covering a marble encased coffin. A narrow path is left clear for people to walk up and place the flowers.

"Do you want to put the flowers on the coffin?" asks my mother. "He was full of love, his spirit enters the heart, and all wishes are granted."

Within the packed melee of the chamber, my mother transforms. Her topaz-coloured eyes glow and a smile of pure abstraction plays across her lips. I feel as though I am losing my mother to some force hovering in the air around us. I am scared that if I turn, some other change might become visible. At that moment my mother instinctively leans forward and cups my face with both palms and whispers, "Go. You are taking my place today."

I look at her and then turn towards the path carrying the flowers. When the cascade of roses and jasmine slide from my hands to settle on the huge mound of flowers, I hurriedly rejoin her.

"I have brought you with me to hear the 'Qawali' and we will go upstairs to hear it." The "Qawali" is a musical recitation comprising of Sufi verses sung by classically trained singers and musicians. Both my parents are fond of listening to them. As an adolescent I was familiar with the music and rhythmic clapping, but the lyrics sounded like passionate exhortations accompanied by ferocious facial gestures.

I sit with my mother on the second floor, face pressed against a circular balcony with an ornately carved marble railing. We are hovering above the vast chamber below. The soft lights glowing in the wall sconces beneath us turn the mound of red flowers into a pool of crimson. The throng of people part and seven men wearing long white shirts settle on the floor in a row. Their musical instruments are placed in front of them. When the musicians remove the covers and start warming up, the sounds of the "tabla" and the harmonium spiral upwards. A vocal hum accompanies the music and I feel my mother's hand circling my own. It is an unexpected intimacy. I feel as though the hand clasping mine transmits energy, planting the first seed of an unimagined sisterhood with my mother.

The husky voices of the two lead singers begin chanting one word. It is the word love and sung in changing cadences and expressions. Each cadence becomes a snare falling on the ears but wrapping itself around the heart. The melodic refrain never alters, simply turned the singing into notes of exultation. The entire assembly of people sways as I do, hypnotized by the clapping and music. I feel all tension leave my body. The ecstatic faces of the musicians turned upwards, the scent of flowers pressing on all sides produces the same delight as seeing a thousand balloons floating in the air.

Standing in the burial chamber of the Saadian Sultan, three decades later, I realize that this childhood incident was my first spiritual experience, where the devotional songs of Sufis had transformed a shrine into a field of flowers and I had entered an altered state. As the Saadian tomb lay hidden from sight for two centuries, in a smaller span of time so did the validity of my lapsed faith. What astounds me is that nothing in my parents' meticulous religious instructions had resulted in that sense of surrender. I can read the Quran in Arabic and recite prayers learned by rote but it has always been a forbidding exercise. Divine love no longer hid in the pages of text. Instead, it finally emerged as a sensorial assault. A burial tomb designed as a place of devotional prayer shifted its perspective and a group of magicians wearing garlands of flowers and dressed in white shirts were responsible for my claiming an affiliation with a particular faith.

I walk away from the second chamber when Khadim launches into yet another lengthy narrative of Moroccan history. Cesar frowns at me but I head towards the exit. I choose a different path, walking along a narrow corridor that ends at a wooden door. The door opens into a sun-baked courtyard where a straggly garden is planted in a few raised beds. Beyond the courtyard, the city dwellings press together. The silence of the courtyard, the flashback of memory, and the slightly depressing environment of the tombs makes me feel tired. I decide to find Cesar, and as I turn towards the door, I see Khadim. He stands with his hands at his hips and we face each other across the length of the courtyard without moving. I wonder why he is not with Cesar.

"Monsieur Cesar is waiting," he says finally.

I walk towards him, pushing my sunglasses on top of my head. When I reach the doorway, he does not step aside.

"You do not like the tombs?"

I watch a tiny muscle quiver along his right jaw. I wonder what his current torment is and realize that once again he has become invasive. I blame Cesar for this because he has created this bizarre dependency on Khadim.

"No," I reply coolly, "I find them depressing."

"As a Muslim you do not give your prayers for the dead," he retaliates.

"I am only interested in the living," I reply.

I am furious with his arrogance, furious at the anger he provokes in me. I want to slap his face and dismiss him on the spot. Instantly, a smile appears on his face as though he has gauged my feelings and witnessed my anger. Then his entire manner changes as he surveys me from his height as one would a wayward child. With the lightest of fingers, he slides the dark glasses from my head down to the bridge of my nose.

"Now, you will not see," he says theatrically, quickly moving aside so I can walk through the door.

"Where is my husband?" my voice is rising.

My equilibrium is shattered by his sardonic gesture, and I am disturbed by his boldness. I whip the glasses from my face, yanking a strand of hair painfully and hurl them at him. Then I race down the corridor, not remembering which entrance to turn into. There is a sound behind me. I re-enter one of the smaller chambers that is empty, and leave it, heading towards the central chamber. I hear footsteps behind me but refuse to look back, certain that Khadim is following. When I sense that he is almost behind me, I turn around to confront a smiling Cesar.

"The blind leading the blind." He kisses me lightly.

"I thought you were waiting outside."

"I wouldn't leave you in a tomb darling, not yet anyway." He puts his arm around my shoulder.

"I am ready to leave this place," I tell him.

"I wonder where the trusty guide is?"

It is the perfect cue and I tell Cesar that it is time to end his services. Cesar says that he has already made arrangements with him to accompany us to Fez, because he is the best tour guide in Marrakech.

"He really gets on my nerves."

"But how absurd darling, he is so respectful of you," Cesar protests.

Khadim reappears then and walks up to us. My dark glasses stick out of his breast pocket and the solicitous tour guide expression is pasted across his face.

"Ah, Khadim, you see I found my wife," Cesar chuckles.

Khadim stifles a soft laugh and then rolls his eyes in a droll gesture at Cesar.

I can see the camaraderie and am stunned at how it has developed in a space of five days. It is like watching the ocean and seeing the crest of a wave turn silver in the sunlight for just a moment. One minute it is there and the next it disappears. However, its weight presses upon me and isolates me further. Khadim is like a spider that has the ability to encase us both in a silken web that holds the duality of comfort and entrapment. I cannot blame Cesar entirely. It has also been easy for me on occasions to slide backwards into my culture of birth, which was filled with solicitous family retainers. When Khadim parts crowds of people with his tall angular frame and carries the parcels of our various shopping exploits and I walk through easily, I adopt a familiar behaviour pattern and simply appreciate Cesar for providing this service. Yet now all this exposure to a guide assumes the complexity of some abstract painting where colours pitted against others swirl and merge within an imprisoned space. Our honeymoon in this exotic and history-laden region has also become an undecipherable ménage à trois. Cesar acts as though he is in the company of an old friend and his reservations of being in a foreign environment are forgotten.

Walking to the car, I struggle with emotions. The tilt and joust of my childhood world dislodges the present, gives birth to a pensive vulnerability. I feel currents of apprehension ripple through me and wonder if Cesar, whose fingers are latticed though my own, will receive the transmission.

"These are yours, Madame."

Khadim extends my dark glasses through the car window towards me. I notice that the thumb and forefinger pinching the glasses have perfectly square nail beds. The large hands that crush clay pots are also capable of holding objects with delicacy. Retrieving them, I turn towards Cesar, who has not commented about why Khadim has my sunglasses. Khadim waves to us, and as the car heads back to the hotel, I lean against Cesar, my face turned, wishing that his shoulder would transform into a hard oyster shell, where I, like a pearl, could lie embedded without any risk. Khadim's presence, much like the edge of a serrated knife, has created a frenzy within me, from which Cesar and I have to escape.

When we return to the hotel, we head for a final swim at the pool. On the way to the pool, I bump into a fellow author from Toronto. Catherine squeals with delight and hugs me. She asks what I am doing in Marrakech.

"I am on my honeymoon and we leave for Fez and Rabat tomorrow."

Within moments, the parameters of a familiar world restore my humour. We plan to meet later that evening, introduce our husbands to each other, and have a drink.

I arrange casino chips in three neat columns and glance at my watch. I have spent fifteen minutes playing blackjack, losing and recouping, concentrating on the rhythm dictated by the turn of the croupier's wrist. The casino, with its Belle Époque décor, has a languid hush to it, drawing a sprinkling of observers and fewer players. Cesar has stopped at the concierge's desk in the front lobby to finalize arrangements for Fez. He is deferring to my wishes and is not extending Khadim's services for the trip to Fez and Rabat. I know that all requests at the Hotel La Mamounia are treated with great elegance. One journeys as opposed to travelling in Morocco, and all this can be achieved with a delicacy similar to the process of inserting inlaid brass in a ceramic vase. Each city has a unique mood and colour. If Marrakech is the red city then Fez is a city bathed in a creamy gold hue at sunrise. The hotel Palais Jamai in Fez will arrange for a guide if we need one.

"Insurance, insurance," lisps the croupier as he flips over his Jack of Spades.

I toss him a smile, refusing to be intimidated. I have my own system of allowing the house to exact its dues fearlessly. The two South American men seated at my table smile at me mischievously. A woman gambling alone in the city's most exclusive casino arouses their interest. One of them offers me a glass of champagne, which I refuse. Behind me, I distinctly hear the Arabic word "Haram" float in the air. Curious, I turn around only to see a waiter fussing with a silver tray. He does not raise his head. I know that the exclusive casino is also forbidden to the local population so the staff are used to seeing foreigners who consume alcohol. Therefore, the injunction, or what is forbidden in Islam, could have been directed to me because of my appearance, which is often mistaken as Moroccan.

I gather my chips and rise from the leather stool. Moving towards the cashier's booth, I am intercepted by one of the dark-suited hotel employees. He hands me an envelope. It bears my name in Cesar's handwriting. The note informs me that he is going to be delayed in joining my friends and me for a drink. I am both amused and curious. The upside-down heart drawn next to his signature fills me with tenderness for his customary sentimentality. If I close my eyes, I can see this exercise of penmanship in the careful withdrawal of the fountain pen from the breast pocket, the slight squint of concentration to his eyes, and the flourish of his sprawling signature. There rests within Cesar a ritualized sense of order that rules even mundane activities. This order marks him with a predictability that heightens my knowledge of him. If the note had been written in pencil, it would not have been from Cesar who can be found with a fountain pen in his breast pocket even in the middle of a hurricane. One edge of the heart is always more bulbous than the other. This knowledge of Cesar is imprinted in the circuitry of my brain.

I walk out of the Casino to the hotel and along the lush corridors pausing before the doorway that leads outside to the pool and gardens. Stepping out, I walk on the path to the left, avoiding the pool area, and head towards the pathway lined by rows of olive trees. This is Cesar's favourite spot in the gardens and he often chooses a bench to sit on, smokes a cigar, and examines the olive trees. Evening breezes lift and rustle the leaves of the trees. It is a whispering sound but strolling through it, I feel an unseasonal chill seep in through my silk camisole and trousers. I look down the pathway and wonder if I am alone. White roses in the beds close to the trees glint in the night. Cesar's image rises in my mind and I halt. A premonition rising in my thoughts makes me turn back.

I head for the small bar named after Winston Churchill. Catherine and her husband are the only people in the bar. They wave to me and I join them. I apologize for Cesar and say that he will join us shortly. Despite the exotic environment, both of them express an inability to assimilate culturally. They also voice their mistrust for the guides they had spent time with.

"You know Scott Symons lives in Essaouira," says Catherine.

"I know."

"We should go and hunt him down." Catherine's eyes sparkle with mischief.

"I am on my honeymoon, and we are leaving for Fez," I tell her, somewhat tempted by the adventurous notion of meeting a Canadian writer who has settled in Morocco. Yet we know that they are ready to return home. Cesar fails to make an appearance even after an hour, so I say goodbye to them, walk to the front lobby, and casually inquire if there is a message for me. The manager behind the counter makes an elaborate play of rifling through a book, and then informs me there is none.

The room has been freshened up for the night. I slip off my shoes and lie on Cesar's side of the bed. The message button on the telephone placed on my night table glows, but is unseen by me. It is only when I hear the sound of the door opening that I realize I have fallen asleep.

Cesar lurches into the room, stumbling against an armchair and then sinks into the one beside it. His clumsy movements tumble the vase of apricot roses on the table next to the chair onto the floor. I move towards him and sense another movement. Khadim stands in the opened doorway.

"He needs to sleep, Madame." He steps backwards and quickly shuts the door behind him.

"Are you all right? Where were you?"

"I wanted to say goodbye and pay him. We went for a drink. I think I may have caught something." He tilts his head back and closes his eyes.

"What?" I am startled. "Should I call a doctor?"

Cesar opens his eyes, raises his head, and gives me a weak grin. "I am the doctor. It's all right. I will be fine — I just need a bit of sleep."

His hand reaches for mine, moving along the length of my arm, fumbling and finally grasping my hand. I cover it with both of mine, gripping tightly as my mind races. I am also outraged at Khadim for depositing my husband in this condition and disappearing without an explanation. His presence at the threshold of our honeymoon suite is also a violation of our privacy.

"I need to change." Cesar rises. "Just an experiment with an herb in the house of a local shaman."

The next morning when we check out of the hotel and walk out to see the car that will drive us to Fez, we are both alarmed. The red Mercedes has seen better days. The original paint is now reduced to a mottled brick colour and the dark leather upholstery is cracked in places. Still an air of shabby elegance hovers over it, and the driver, leaning against the fender, puffs on a cigar. We both feel as though we have stepped into an Egyptian film set and a young and beefy Omar Sharif will stroll by. Cigar clenched in his mouth, the driver supervises the loading of our luggage into the trunk as though he were the custodian of a great treasure. Doormen from the hotel gather around to say farewell and discreetly tuck Cesar's folded dollar bills into their sleeves. The manager presses a cellophane cone filled with roses into my hands. Cesar, completely recovered from the previous night, bristles with excitement. The journey ahead to Fez moves between us as a new adventure.

Then Khadim arrives. A small bag slung over his shoulder and a bunch of white narcissus in his hands. He walks up to Cesar, dips his head, and clasps Cesar's hands in a double-handed grip.

"Madame, for you," he then turns to me, "so the journey will be a fragrant one."

I give him a wry look.

"Thank you Khadim," I accept the flowers, "but they will die in the car."

"Nothing dies on the way to Fez, Madame."

"Is that a historical fact?"

Khadim smiles at me, taking the sting out of my condescension, and refusing to pick up the gauntlet. The arc of his smile tilting my reservations about him and dislodging them as easily as one would a sandcastle. His smile broadens further, making my hostility vanish as though it had never existed in the first place. I shift the flowers from one hand to another and turn to Cesar, who has once again pulled out his camera.

"One for the road," he says, focusing on Khadim in the viewfinder.

The driver comes towards us. The cigar has disappeared. He is a chunky man stuffed into a maroon wool jacket that, like his car, has seen better days as half the buttons are missing.

"Salam-aleikum, I am Rasul," he announces. Then he switches to a rough English. "No problem, Fez. Road good."

Sitting in the car, I whisper to Cesar that we are being driven to Fez by a prophet. That is the meaning of the driver's name. I place the flowers on the ledge behind the back seat and they gently perfume the interior of the car. We hold hands and wave to the staff as the car sails out of the circular driveway of the hotel. The city of ramparts, the tower of the Koutoubia Mosque, and ancient masonry disappear rapidly behind us.

"Do you think we will ever return?" I ask Cesar.

"There really isn't any need to because we are taking it with us." he taps my forehead, lips, and finally my chest. "Here always."

I gaze out of the window, recording the landscape, and wonder if it is possible to go beyond the camera's eye to a third and mystical eye. Marrakech has tugged at the edges of my spiritual ambivalence and captured my imagination. The encounter with Khadim has become a bizarre conduit to this spiritual fragmentation. I am also certain in my sense of fatalism that nothing really happens without a reason. I can hear the pages of a book rustle somewhere in my imagination. In fact, what is dying on the road to Fez is the unexamined part of our lives. I tried last night to find out why Cesar went to a local shaman and what substance he ingested, but I have failed. Cesar said it was a disappointing experience and I did not press him further. I know someday he will give me more details himself. Will we even remember this incident? We are still on our honey-moon and headed towards another city filled with legends.

CHAPTER 8

TORONTO, MAY 1999

I AM WALKING TOWARDS THE front hall to greet him. My pulse still quickens at the sight of Cesar. Although we have been married for eight years, I am confident that this tiny miracle will always remain intact. We have never been away from each other for more than two weeks. Usually, a type of collision embrace takes place, as I race from some part of the house, dodging obstacles along the way. There is no clear path to the front hall. The house exercises its own restraint, as it is Victorian. Perhaps it gives him the extra seconds needed to place his briefcase carefully on the chair. The he kisses me purposefully, and what his lips and breath convey is the undiluted force of his presence. I am conscious of who he is when I return the kiss and seal the exchange. In eight years, the greeting has not changed.

On this May evening when the door opens, I hear a rasp of breath: it is a jagged intake of air, which cannot be expelled, feels as though an iron band circles my throat. I take a step backward, stumbling against the sofa. Cesar stands motionless, examining me with the face of a stranger.

As I straighten up, images flash across my mind. I see Buddhist monks swathed in kerosene robes on the path of self-immolation. My nostrils quiver, like an animal catching the scent of blood. My eyes settle on his midriff and I am counting the dots on the lower half of his tie. No force can make me raise my eyes to his face. We stand apart from each other, mute. Cesar is waiting for my response, and I consider this an act of savagery. Every strand of hair on his head is missing and so is his glorious moustache.

Somewhere in the course of his appointment-filled day, he has headed to a barbershop and all the wealth of hair ended up being swept off a floor. He has returned to me with a naked bulbous head and a clean-shaven face, robbed of grace. The flowing moustache concealed the contours of his upper lip and now I know why. The contour of flesh above the lip swells out and reveals a sinister curve beneath it. It's as though I have never seen this face before.

I turn away because I cannot comprehend the act. It is not only the change to his physical appearance that I find oppressive, but the energy around him. I am terrified by the intensity of my shock. It is as though the front hall covered by our beloved salmon-coloured rug from Marrakesh has become a minefield, and Cesar is responsible for this. It contradicts every notion of expansiveness that flows between us. It is simply not only his amazing hair, coils of pewter-coloured waves that are gone, but with it the intimacy of my knowledge of him.

In my eyes, he has become a grotesque stranger.

I turn away, retreating to the top floor of the house where Janet, my guest from England, is playing with her three-year-old son.

"Are you all right?" She looks up at me.

I shake my head very slowly. She turns away and goes halfway down the stairs. Within moments, she is back. Janet lifts her son and gathers his toys, and tells me she is taking him out for the evening. I wait until they are ready and walk down with them.

I can hear ice cubes tinkle in the glass of scotch Cesar is pouring for himself in the kitchen. He does not greet Janet and remains unseen. I walk rigidly to the front door and open it to step outside on the porch. Cesar's car is parked behind mine, but I do not want to return to the house so I drive his. Janet remains silent and I am grateful for that. There is no way to tell one of my dearest friends that my husband has shaved his head and I am so disturbed by it that I cannot make a sound.

I drop them off at another mutual friend's home. Janet silently strokes my face in a farewell gesture, choosing not to break the silence.

I drive the car aimlessly circling the neighbourhood and then park in front of a restaurant.

"Where's Doc?" asks Tony, the owner.

"I don't know," I reply, sinking in a chair.

"What would you like?" he asks carefully as he has never seen me here without Cesar.

"I would like a glass of Shiraz."

"Yes, your favourite."

I take a sip and feel as though my throat is scorched by acid.

"What is the matter?" Tony is watching me intently.

"It tastes like boiled blood."

"I can change it."

I take a sip and then, another. "There is nothing wrong with the wine, it's me."

Tony rolls his eyes sympathetically and moves away with studied nonchalance.

I do not leave for a while. I hope the wine will dull the agitation inside me.

When I return home, I can see that the lights are dimmed on the first floor. I climb up the stairs and halt before the closed bedroom door. It is not quite 9 p.m. and no light spills out from under the door. I open the door quietly and see Cesar's sleeping form. The bald head is pressed into the pillows. I change in the bathroom and slip into my side of the large bed and place a pillow as a barricade near me. This act shocks me. The gesture makes me feel ten years old. If I do not see him then he cannot see me and read the terror in my eyes. I exhaust myself by examining my inability to talk to Cesar, and finally fall asleep.

When I wake up in the morning, he is not there.

I race downstairs and notice his small gym bag lying on the kitchen counter. I look outside and see that his car is missing. I make coffee and open the Saturday papers as I hear the car pull into the driveway.

Cesar walks into the kitchen wearing a small wool cap on his head and hands me a bag of fresh croissants from Patachou. It is a Saturday ritual that he never misses. We do not kiss. He picks up the gym bag and says, "I am leaving now, I want an early start." He moves towards the doorway and I still cannot move.

"See you," I whisper to his retreating back, still rooted to the kitchen stool.

The front door slams shut and then I race to the front window, his grey Volvo rolls out of the driveway but his profile under the peaked cap is unrecognizable. He does not look at the window and I turn away.

He is going to our Manitoulin Island vacation home for the long weekend, and I am staying in town with my visiting friend. Janet and her son return by noon and I finally explain my silence.

Janet chuckles, "Cheer up, some of it may grow back over the weekend. I know he has the most beautiful head of hair in this town, but it might be some male thing."

It is Saturday evening and I miss Cesar already. I cannot believe that we parted without kissing. I refuse to think of the missing hair and know I will apologize when he calls.

On the island, Cesar usually drives to town to telephone me when he arrives. The drive from our glorious home tucked in the forest is about ten minutes. He has not called me, so I pick up the phone and call the caretaker, Jim, who takes care of our property and greets us whenever we return.

"No, he hasn't spoken to me," says Jim.

"Well, he got in yesterday. Can you drive by and ask him to call me please?"

"There is no one at the house. I was there yesterday to check on the water pump. No tire tracks either. I would know."

"That is not possible."

"Perhaps he stopped somewhere else on the way."

"Please go in the morning and ask him to call me," I say.

It is late Sunday night and I call Jim again. He assures me that he has been to the house twice and there is no sign of Cesar. I think he will arrive home by tomorrow night for his Tuesday morning patients. I call Jim twice on Monday and get the same answer. Is this our first official fight? Is Cesar annoyed at my reaction to his shaved head?

It is the last day of May and I think of the extravagant plans he has made for my birthday in three weeks. Everything is fine, is the mantra I keep repeating, but I already know this is a lie because one small act has disrupted the order of our life.

I am wearing Cesar's green bathrobe, seeing the sunlight fade outside and grappling with an unimagined predicament. I cannot seem to get rid of the pinpricks of fear that stab me. Janet and her son have taken the flight home to London.

I make seafood paella for dinner and arrange roses on the dining table. This will be my peace offering to my husband whom I now miss as though we have been separated for a month instead of a weekend. I go upstairs, switch on the television, and settle on the couch. It turns out to be the longest wait and somewhere around 3 a.m. I fall asleep, exhausted.

When I wake up it is 10:15 on Tuesday morning. There is no sign in the house that Cesar has returned. I dress quickly and drive to his neighbourhood office. My heart pounds as I race to the corridor of his office and bump into a patient who says she has been waiting since 9:30 for her appointment. The office door is shut. Instinctively, I lie for him and tell the woman there must be some delay — he is travelling — she should go home and will hear from him later. I do not have the keys to his office. There are only two sets of keys. Cesar has one, and his bookkeeper, who does his monthly bills, has the other. I drive home and call his office number. His answering machine comes on, and I leave a message for him. I telephone Jim on the island, who says that no one has seen his car in town and he has checked with the neighbours as well. The house phone rings and another patient calls and says that she has an appointment but his office door is shut.

I am a doctor's wife and know about damage control. I give the same excuse. Then I return to his office and paste a notice on the door citing a family emergency and delay in returning to the city. His colleagues across the hall are annoyed, as patients have been going there and asking about him.

I have the sensation of being Alice falling down the rabbit hole. I field his telephone calls for three days, racing back and forth to the office with the locked door. I have told no one that my husband is missing and I have not heard from him and neither have his patients. On the fourth day I break down and call my best friend Malka, and Gordon, a Catholic priest whom I have known since he was sixteen, and Paul, a respected friend who is also a writer. They insist that I call the police immediately, then they come to my home. Three police cruisers sit outside the house, but only one police officer comes inside.

I AM SITTING WITH DETECTIVE White at the dining table. He is middle-aged with a stamp of weariness on his face as he informs me that Cesar is now a missing person. He tells me that he will inform the police on the island to search for him and his car. I need to search his office in case he left a note. His next comment, that he could have driven his car into the lake, shocks me into a terrified silence.

"You have no idea who you are talking about," my voice breaks.

"Was he depressed, suicidal?" he asks, flashing me a sardonic look.

I can't answer his preposterous suggestion but simply pick up Cesar's photograph from the mantelpiece and slide it across the glass table towards him.

I can sense that Detective White is suppressing the irritation that marks some of his questioning. I know he is wondering, "Who are they?" Malka with her enormous green eyes seated upright on a chair. Her luxurious black Jaguar blocking the driveway outside resembles the jaguar lurking within her. She is my protector. Gordon is always standing close to me. His spectacular physique, down to the muscular forearms, gives him the appearance of a male model instead of a Catholic priest. Then there is Paul, my writer friend, with his scruffy beard, bulging stomach, bloodshot eyes and brandy-laced breath asking precise questions in his Oxonian accent. I quell the irritation about his cheap brandy, as though a more expensive brand would have made any difference. I am invading Detective White's head and wondering if he can feel that everything is wrong here. I have put a glamorous photograph of Cesar and myself in front of him so that he realizes who he is dealing with. Cesar is wearing a white suit with a lavender shirt and tie and his sweeping mane of hair and rakish moustache make him look more like a movie star than a doctor. We are not some runaway cheap statistic is what I want this detective to understand.

Yet the power of the three other people in my home has made him feel as though he is being supervised and the expectation is that he alone can end the devastation saturating me seems to annoy him as well.

"I need some more details please, so I can go back to the station and work on a profile of the doctor," he says, not looking up from his notepad.

"How long will all this take?" I don't want him to leave without giving me some hope.

"We have cases like this every few years. There are no surprise endings. Some men are born bastards; others kill themselves or are just ducking for cover."

"Excuse me," Gordon steps a little closer to me.

"You mean he had a short haircut?" Detective White asks me ignoring Gordon's reaction.

"No! It was all gone."

"Was he completely bald?"

"Yes."

"Has he ever done this before?"

"No. I couldn't recognize him. He doesn't even have any clothes with him." Tears are rolling down my face.

"You don't think he was depressed or that he thought about suicide?" Detective White makes his parting comment, snaps the notepad shut, and takes his leave.

I pace the empty house, moving from room to room, as though I may turn a corner and find Cesar standing before me. Finally, the exercise leads me to the front window and I watch the street. The front-hall closet door reminds me of the laundry at the cleaners. I cannot remember if I have collected it or not. I open the closet and gaze at Cesar's heavy winter parka hanging right in the middle. I do something that I always did in the winter when he wore it. If I forgot gloves, he would put one of my hands in his pocket and warm it with his own.

I put my hand in the pocket nearest to me. I imagine that that I will find his warm hand with graceful long fingers in this pocket and the horror of his absence will simply fly away. Instead, there is something hard and I pull out his wristwatch with his wedding band looped through it. A shaft of pain travels from my palm to my heart. This is what Cesar did every night before going to bed. The watch always lay on his night table. Cesar had misplaced his wedding band once and had been desolate until it had been found and, after that, he would always loop it through the watch for safety. How did the watch reach the pocket? Had he meant to take it with him and simply forgot? Yet the heavy winter jacket is not required for a late May weekend on the island.

I race to the telephone and tell Detective White about what I have found. He sounds irritated, as though this revelation has negated his theories, and I have inconvenienced him. I slip off my band and then wear Cesar's, keeping it in place by wearing mine in front of it. I am keeping us safe. No part of our life will ever slip away. If Cesar is missing then he expects me to be the custodian of our life until he returns.

The next day I discover that Cesar has not kept me safe. Both his bank accounts are frozen when the banks discover he is missing. Four days ago, he would have made a deposit into our joint account, which I use for household expenses. There is also a strange message from a financial trustee saying that his first payment is late, and all Cesar's personal assets will be in jeopardy if he is not contacted immediately. I recoil from this message on our home answering machine in shock. What circles the edges of my existence is more bizarre than terrifying.

Has Cesar just stepped out of character and decided to take a trip without informing me? Then he will return any minute. I keep repeating this to myself.

I have parked my car and decided to walk into our bank. The ATM in my neighbourhood has rejected my three attempts to withdraw cash. When I reach the teller, I am informed that the balance in the account is forty-seven dollars. I hold the receipt in my hand and fight the waves of nausea rising within.

Cesar is known both in his personal and professional life as being generous to a fault. He is a physician with a comfortable income and our life is always stable. It is inconceivable even to imagine that he is responsible for this. Yet I realize I need some help and return home to call Harry, a lawyer. I find Harry's number in an old telephone book and dial it. The voice at the other end informs me that Harry is no longer a lawyer and has accepted a bench appointment as a judge, and offers the number to me. Harry cautiously informs me that I must immediately call the old firm and speak to Sharon. I have seen Sharon once in the offices of the law firm that handled my divorce. I remember being quite mesmerized by the beauty of the petite fine-boned woman with striking eyes.

The next day I am seated before Sharon, who listens to everything.

"Do you understand your predicament?" Sharon's eyes are silvery grey searchlights.

"No. It's a mistake. It's been nine days and he will be back." I am sobbing again.

"We have to go to court to protect you. That's why I am here." Sharon slides the box of Kleenex towards me.

"I don't know what to think. I can't trust my emotions, my life has been stolen." I am quoting my friend Paul's response to parenthood.

"You are not going to collapse and I am here to make sure this does not happen."

I am exhausted. "What about his car? Someone would notice it. It can't just disappear."

"Do you know how many missing cars we have in this country?" Sharon's tone is sharp.

"Have they stopped looking?"

"Was he depressed?"

"No. I never looked at him. I never saw his face. I couldn't bear what he did to his hair. He treats depressed and suicidal patients," I am whispering to Sharon.

I AM IN THE KITCHEN marking off the last day of the second week. I do this with a black marker and realize that the marks I have made look like tombstones.

My loss has no geography but the damage is precise, measured by sleepless nights and a lack of appetite. Every thought of Cesar is like a hand grenade where, although the pin is released, the explosions are time-released. So it is a fragrance, the sight of his clothes in the closet, or even a photograph that becomes the trigger for these explosions in the heart.

Even though I feel that I am concealing this great pain, I can now see it reflected in the eyes of my friends. Paul has almost settled in the kitchen and drinks coffee laced with shots of brandy for hours. He is putting together clues just the way he does in the books he writes, but remains mystified. Malka sends platters of food prepared by her housekeeper that lie untouched. I have now become a statistic and the joy of my married life is stripped and harshly transformed by the words of the daunting legal argument Sharon has prepared. Cesar and I have a new history and yet I am convinced it is not ours.

Sharon has summoned me to her office again. She tells me that she is immediately going to court armed with a desertion and abandonment plea to ensure that all Cesar's assets are transferred to me and the frozen bank accounts opened. I have been working on a new book that will take months to complete.

I hate Sharon at that moment and tell her that everyone is mistaken and Cesar has not deserted me. I say that my belief in our love is unshakeable and that this faith is better than any legal argument.

Sharon draws a sharp breath. "He has great financial liabilities that you were not informed about. He was trying to settle them. If he does not return, this will cripple you and you will be destitute in that stunning home of yours, which the bank will foreclose on. I don't think a book-in-progress will generate any income for you."

This is the cannon she fires. The next comment is equally searing. "Can you raise some money immediately? I have a plan."

I AM WALKING THROUGH THE pale green interior of my home, which is called Endhouse. Cesar and I have a lot of art decorating the walls. I am staring at the primitive intricacy of the Berber design sprinkled though the apricot-coloured Moroccan carpet, and wonder if my days of walking over it are coming to a close.

Sharon has succeeded in frightening me. I call Detective White again, who tells me he has no news and his tone suggests that I have joined the list of women with missing husbands in some data bank.

I telephone Cesar's best friend, a physician in Michigan. He was Cesar's witness at our wedding and he is very fond of both of us. He first asks whether I need any money. His thoughtfulness savages my dignity, but I pull up the drawbridge and automatically refuse. Then I instantly erase the conversation from my mind and all the images flitting through my brain.

I open Cesar's closet and bury my face in the forest of trousers and jackets. This is the most tangible proof of his presence. My eyes are closed and I hope that somehow the clothes will smother me. Finally I withdraw and walk to the clothes hamper lying under the dressing table and pull out the turquoise blue shirt lying on top. It is hardly soiled and carries traces of his cologne.

I remove my blouse and wear my husband's shirt. Standing in front of the mirror and carefully buttoning the shirt, I notice that my cheekbones rise sharply from my face. I have difficulty recognizing myself but my survival instincts are sharp as I move towards the telephone.

JOHN IS MY FRIEND CATHERINE's ex-husband. Cesar and I had kept our friendship with him. It was easier to be fond of John than Catherine, who demanded that Cesar and I choose sides. We had refused, so we lost Catherine and wound up with John. John arrives in ten minutes. When he bends down to embrace me at the front door, I am aware that I have dampened Cesar's shirt with my tears. I have lost my ability to control this. Silently, I take him upstairs to see the painting. We stand in front of it. It is a haunting work of art, spelling the history of an entire nation. It is a large work and invariably attracts a great deal of attention from anyone who visits our home.

"I thought it should be donated to a Native cultural centre some day," I say.

John turns to me and I see his eyes glow with wonder. "Don't be ridiculous. You need money and I am going to buy it."

I tell him what it was purchased for. I have never sold anything in my life but am aware of the value of the works of art in our home. John draws out his chequebook from his pocket. He has come prepared. He writes the cheque and places it on the ledge of the bookshelf. It is a delicate gesture, as though the sale of valuable art in the middle of the night is a clandestine act, which will besmirch our combined dignities.

We remove the painting from the wall and carry it down together. I help him carry it to the car. He wedges it in the back seat, but it sticks out from one end so he holds the door with a rubber cord and secures it on the roof. My heart turns over as the car pulls away, but I now feel as though my tears have dried up permanently. I go inside and make another call. My voice is cold and brusque. It is the voice of a woman who has sold a dream for an absurd sum of money.

Leo arrives the next day with a pained expression on his face. He looks at the work over the mantel of the green marble fireplace in the living room. He expresses his delight at the reframing that I selected before it was hung.

"I know it well. I am sorry I can only offer you what the gallery paid Joso for it."

"It's all right," I reply evenly, concealing my shock.

I lift the painting while he places the cheque written in advance, on the dining table. Before the door is shut, I go upstairs and bring down another painting to cover the bare spot. Although it shifts the ambience of the room, I am beyond caring.

I have now experienced another dimension of loss, but I have also raised a significant amount of money without leaving my home. I slide a CD of Chopin nocturnes into the stereo with steady fingers, and step out into the back garden. The music filters in softly and I do not cry. Instead, my thoughts unexpectedly turn to my father and a childhood injunction I seem to have been violating in the past two weeks.

I am re-examining a childhood incident, and this is what I remember.

I have slipped right over the horse's head and landed unhurt on soft ground. The terror of my feet slipping out of the stirrups and my face pressed sideways on grass is heightened by the clamour of voices around. I am lifted by my father who whispers in my ear, "Brave girls don't cry." He walks back rapidly towards the black horse, as I struggle in his arms and lean backward. I am convinced that the docile horse I ride weekly is no longer my friend. It is my first fall and it rocks my eleven-year-old universe. I hear the word "Shaitan," meaning devil, being repeated by the groom who accompanies us.

"I don't want to ride," I wail to my father. "He is going to do it again."

But my father reaches the horse and lifts me back on the saddle. Despite my fear, he slips my feet through the stirrups.

"You are riding Lucky-Dip and you must let him know that."

My father firmly places one of my hands on the horse's neck and makes me stroke him. Lucky-Dip's skin is warm and silky and some part of my fear recedes. Then he places the reins in my hands and says that horses are sensitive animals and have moods just like people. Even the gentlest horses can act up for reasons that are not visible. If we can enter their world, he continues, we can find the reason.

I know that my overpowering love for my father will prevent me from letting him down, and I begin to relax. My father also adds that I am old enough to know that the rider must take care of the horse as well, because if a horse falls and breaks its leg, it would have to be destroyed. Noting my fearful expression, he quickly adds that it is an act of kindness, a way to end suffering. He smiles at me and reassures me that I will not fall down again.

I am aware that this childhood incident had danced away years ago and become a shadow memory, until this moment. I cannot recall how the day ended or was ever conscious that the notion of embracing duality had been so powerfully imprinted in me by my father. I loved and trusted him implicitly but was unaware that the first seeds of a character ethic had also been deftly inserted into my carefree childhood. I was too young to understand fully the concept of annihilating beauty if it turned on itself or others. I never fell off a horse again, or ever saw one that had to be shot.

CHAPTER 9

TORONTO, 1999

SUNLIGHT POKES THROUGH THE CLOSED shutters of the bedroom windows and I can sense a trickle of light seeping through the sheet covering my head. I am playing a shoddy game of pretending to be in a cave with no desire to let anything in. Even the eagerly awaited summer has become a mockery because although I water the garden haphazardly, I no longer look at the flowers but quickly retreat indoors. Can I only know pleasure in Cesar's presence? Are other married couples fused in this way? Have I come to view the universe through his eyes, and as he is not here, have I lost my sight?

This does not convince my family doctor, who insists on seeing me because some friends have made a call to her. I have no intention of revealing my weight loss and lack of appetite and am confident that I will breeze in and out of the doctor's office without being detected. I have never a cooked a meal for myself nor eaten it alone. How can I tell my conscientious doctor that I can brush my hair, apply cosmetics, and choose appropriate clothing — but it was always the intensity of Cesar's gaze that made me aware that I had a body, hair, and a smile. Is this a trick, or have I simply obliterated all my history before I met him?

It pleased me to begin my life with him and so I cling to this distorted notion secretly. It is the best game of all and one that helps me observe that another day has passed.

I am also mastering the art of compressing grief into a sliver of steel. It is a family tradition. The female half of my ancestral clan floating continents away is split by triumph and despair. Two-thirds of the women are plumped with sleek lives and the remaining few are disaster-prone heroines. The sleek ones insert the steel into the spines of those who need it. The exercise is in reality a family conspiracy. Yet I remember the lesson; even though the conspirators are missing my imagination is still rooted in this practical mythology. However, unlike then I still expect a knight in shining armour to fulfill his destiny.

In my case, it is Detective White, in Missing Persons. I call him from the kitchen each morning and evening as though Cesar is a button that I have misplaced. The kitchen is my command post for dealing with disaster. I no longer prepare food but am sifting grief and watching doom simmer. Instead of food, I ingest Detective White's comments about drawing blanks. This daily ritual makes me dodge passivity and punctuates my life. The calendar on the wall displays the names of the people I have to meet, whose job it is to inform me of the terrifying details of the chaos Cesar has left behind.

The details fill me with a particular shame. Cesar has not only abandoned me but also eighty psychiatric patients who must seek treatment elsewhere. His patients flood our home at Christmas with an army of cards and paper bags filled with homemade gifts.

The telephone suddenly rings on my night table. It is Federico, a recent acquaintance and a prominent psychiatrist. He and Cesar had worked together in their earlier years at the Queen Street Mental Health facility. Yet my friendship with him began over a dinner party at Margaret's home. I was seated next to him and enthralled by his reputation in the field of treatment of victims of torture as well as his romantic and courtly demeanour. He combined psychiatry with life, art, and cuisine. Federico was Spanish and I had been learning Flamenco dance in Toronto. We were delighted to discover each other. I also trusted him instinctively. Federico suggests that the time has come for me to search Cesar's office and the vacation home on Manitoulin Island personally. There could be some clues I am better equipped to notice than the police. Although he makes it sound as though I will be playing detective in some novel, I am aware that he is engaged in some mysterious exercise that he does not share. The duplicate set of keys are with Cesar's bookkeeper and I finally ask her to courier them down to me.

Two hours later, when the doorbell rings I leave my bedroom and receive the padded envelope. When I pull out the keys, I grip them so hard that the loose end of a small metal ring punctures my finger. A scarlet dot of blood blossoms on the finger and I immediately suck on the finger, tasting both the blood and metal. "This is who you are," I say to myself, "don't buckle." I place the keys on the mantel-piece next to a framed photograph of Cesar and myself. He embraces me and my head is thrown back in laughter. It is a wedding photo-graph taken spontaneously. Gaiety and safety leap from the photograph. I feel as though my real self is imprisoned in the photograph and the woman standing in front of the photograph is an imposter.

Malka arrives to accompany me to Cesar's office. She looks elegant in cream-coloured linen. Instead of attending a board meeting for the various philanthropic ventures she and her husband are dedicated to, she will play sleuth with me. Her enormous eyes are tinged with heroism and her slender frame is rigid. Before she reverses her car out of the driveway, both of us put on our dark glasses as though we are criminals who are about to commit some heinous act.

When we reach the office door and I turn the key, I can feel her breath behind my neck. I know she is terrified and distressed by my pain, but is aware that I cannot do this alone. I push the door open and automatically stoop to collect the stack of mail resting behind the door. The reception room is empty. Malka shuts the main door behind her and both of us gaze at the door leading to the consultation room. Neither one of us want to open it. This is my life, so I walk up to the door first. She is right behind me.

I turn the key in the lock and slowly open the door. The room is empty and familiar. It feels as though Cesar has slipped out for lunch and I am flooded with relief. The coffee mug, my photograph in a silver frame, and a cushion almost sliding off the black leather couch tell me that Cesar is alive. I reach for the blue wool cardigan he wears in the office and bury my face in it. Malka plucks it out of my fingers, and tells me we have to start searching. I glance at the desk calendar on the small table and see my birthday passed, encircled in red.

The telephone rings, the answering machine clicks on, and Cesar's rich baritone voice floods the room. It's as if nothing has really happened in three weeks. Then another voice pierces the room. It is an irate patient demanding a response to her calls. My delusional joy is shattered instantly and I move towards the large double closet housing his filing cabinets. I am violating the ethic of his profession by going through each drawer and perusing medical records from beginning to end. No letter or personal correspondence gives a clue to his disappearance. When I finish, I notice the tall fig plant by the window and wonder how it has survived. He will return to this, I tell myself. He was attached to the plant and took pride in the fact that he kept it alive for years.

I sit on his armchair and telephone Federico.

"There are no clues," I say.

"Is anything missing?"

"Nothing that I can notice."

"Is his appointment book there?"

"Yes, it is here by the phone."

"Look at the last day, before he left for the weekend," Federico commands.

I look at the page. All the afternoon appointments have a line through them. The paper is depressed as if the pressure applied to drawing the line was close enough to tear it. A thick black line slashes down to the bottom of the page. It is an angry line.

"He only cancelled the afternoon's appointments," I say.

"So it was a sudden decision."

I know that Federico is processing this information in a different way. Then I notice that Cesar's briefcase is missing. Cesar always left it at the office on the weekend. I know it is not in the house and all I can remember is a small gym bag in his hands the morning he left. Was it in his car? It meant that he stopped at the office on the way to the cottage and picked it up. I am familiar with its contents: prescription pads, chequebooks, vials of pills, and medical journals. Cesar was a physician, not a businessman.

"Someone will have to take care of all this, and store it. I am taking you to your doctor's appointment," says Malka.

"Nothing moves, he is coming back," I tell her flatly.

I AM SITTING ACROSS THE table facing my doctor. When I tell her that I am fine and not hungry, she pulls opens the drawer to her desk and pulls out a package of biscuits. When I refuse, she nods and then scribbles on her medical pad and calmly hands me the slip of paper, saying that I have an appointment with another doctor half a block away.

I am angry. "Why do I need to see a psychiatrist?"

She gives me a warm smile. "You are going through a hideous trauma and he is trained to deal with this. Trust me, you will like him."

"There is nothing wrong with me, I miss him every second, I can't stop thinking," I blurt out. Tears are flooding my eyes.

Half an hour later, I am seated in a brown chair next to a water cooler. A tall man wearing a creased white shirt calls my name and ushers me in. The small vestibule we pass through is plastered with medical certificates. The inner office is a small room and I sit in an armchair. The psychiatrist sits across from me and puts a writing pad on his knee. Then he looks at me and his gaze is both piercing and contemplative. I wonder what he will say, as I have never been to see a psychiatrist. I know that he has the advantage of information given to him by my doctor. Can he sense the twilight zone I am functioning in? It is as though we are sitting in a bar waiting for drinks to arrive.

My face is expressionless but there is a twinge of discomfort. His blue-grey eyes are like twin lasers burrowing into the coils of my brain. "Warning! Circuitry being examined is the unspoken inference." You are Merlin, I think silently, just hand me the magic spell.

All I want to do is go home and call Detective White again. However, the fixity of his gaze becomes a superior force. He has used silence as a move to bend my will. I want to say something trivial to mislead him but when I open my mouth, like an undetected geyser, a torrent of words and tears gush out. I am stunned, both at myself and the speed with which his pen moves across the writing pad. There is no trick, wise suggestion, or prophecy that he offers but within forty minutes, he slips into the guardian niche.

"We can't let the system shut down, and that is my job," he says briskly.

I walk out of his office without any prescription for sleeping pills or tranquilizers, troubled by the thought that I have given a false promise to return next week at the same time. When I return home, I do not call Detective White. Instead, I open the door to the refrigerator and pull out a tub of yogurt. Merlin, I decide, has cast his spell, and I actually feel a pang of hunger.

Paul comes by that evening. He sits in the straight-back armchair in the living room and gazes into the brandy snifter he holds. The police seem to have given up and the car has simply disappeared.

"I know he is alive," he says. "But we need to find him, so let us go over everything again."

I can see his logic. We are both writers who are given to stretching the imagination. I think of the Caribbean island where Cesar took me for a vacation and introduced me to relatives he had not seen for twenty-five years. Cesar's father was a diplomat from the Dominican Republic posted to New York where Cesar was born and raised until he was a teenager. I still have some of their names and telephone numbers.

Cesar was completely estranged from both the culture and the relatives on the island, but Paul and I now consider this a possible clue. We spend the evening dialling telephone numbers and investigating in Spanish, which we cannot fully comprehend. It is a fool's errand and when Paul finally leaves, he makes sure that the back door to the house is locked. He embraces me and I cling to him for a moment. I am clinging to hope and see the shadow of pain ripple over his features.

"Lock up, it will be all right," he says gruffly and disappears into the night.

Late at night, I sit in bed and make a list of things to do tomorrow. Every now and then, my eyes wander towards Cesar's silver hairbrush sitting on top of his dresser. Eventually I get out of bed and pick up the brush. There are three strands of silver hair lodged in the bristles. I pull one out and it coils backwards on my fingertip. The spontaneity of the curl tells me that my husband is alive. I have this memento of his living presence and, through it, I can trace the waterfall of waves and curls on his head, which makes me giddy with pleasure. So I make it a talisman of sorts, as faith cannot be an abstract emotion for me. I will use anything to give it tangible presence. Despite the collective shock of those who know me and their judgment, I sense an unknown force like some retrograde planet at work. I will continue to believe that Cesar will return until I am knocked senseless.

Morning brings a call from Sharon the lawyer stating that I must be in her office at noon.

"The trustee who was handling your husband's financial affairs has hired a lawyer who is a specialist in this," she informs me without any ceremony.

"Why?" I ask, still not understanding the complexities of Cesar's financial liabilities.

"They are nervous. If we do not buy out the proposal, they will go to court and overturn the decree I have won for you. Also, the island property is only in his name. I have to consult an expert, who charges $1000 for the consultation."

"It is not a problem."

"He needs a certified cheque."

I am shocked. "That is an insult."

"Do it," Sharon commands. "These are not the battles you have to focus on."

Where have these battles come from? The hurricane of fear makes my heart race again. If Cesar knew what was happening to me he would come back. This is the mantra echoing in my soul as I return home. My writing desk, a gift from Cesar, is now littered with papers and bills. The book I was working on is completely abandoned. I have been derailed. If this were not happening to me, I would make it a story and write a book, is another thought that also pricks my soul. Prominent Ontario physician disappears into thin air! Novelist wife hounded by creditors! But my computer remains shut. Instead, the fax machine spits out legal documents every day. I finally understand the true meaning of the word *chaos*. It is like an octopus, each weaving tentacle followed by another. Cesar has left and placed me in front of a firing squad.

This is not the man I know.

The house is silent. I mute the sound on the telephone and turn off the volume on the answering machine, but I cannot escape. Each room is filled with his presence. His reading glasses sit on the side table of the study and I have not removed them. Each day I am mesmerized by the intimacy that hovers over them. I go to the bathroom and open a bottle of his cologne and inhale. Citrus and a hint of sandalwood enter my nostrils, moving upwards to the brain. Electrical impulses create pictures in my mind. I see his fingers gathering a handkerchief and tucking it in the breast pocket. I feel as though he is standing in front of me but I only see my reflection in the mirror.

Again I race to the closet and bury my face in his clothes and feel my equilibrium return. Then I walk to the Chinese lacquered cabinet where each drawer holds personal items belonging to him. I open the first drawer and see it is empty. Both Cesar's Canadian and American passports are missing. My finger, on which both wedding bands are jammed together, flails and jerks as I open each drawer, hoping to find the passports. My thoughts are tinged by the first notion of betrayal, as I alone know all the underpinnings of his exercises stamped with order and precision. Cesar opened and then closed cereal boxes with elastic bands. He emptied his pockets each night with the order of a military drill. The small turquoise comb folded into a white handkerchief, the wedding band looped into the wristwatch. The leather wallet folded on the crease with the miniature Swiss army knife placed by its side. The passports could only have been removed by Cesar, and now it's as though all the elastic bands have snapped.

Detective White is non-committal when I give him this information. It is a long shot, he tells me, in a soft voice he adds that he will add this information to the file, but I must get on with my life.

"Where are you?" my heart screams to Cesar. How can love and betrayal rest side by side? When you come home you will see that I am bent out of shape and rapidly becoming unrecognizable.

I race downstairs and notice the winking light of the kitchen telephone. I press the button and listen to Cesar's friend in Michigan saying he is travelling and should be home in three days but wishes to talk to me. I play the message again, focusing on the cadence of his voice, hoping to pick up a signal of sorts. Is there anything tucked into the sonorous and accented tone? But I remain uncertain.

All of a sudden, seventy-two hours are an eternity. Overcome by this and feeling as though I am entering some realm of lunacy, I step outside the house to the back garden.

In seven weeks, my neglected garden is shocking. Peonies drag on the ground and unclipped roses send out leaves covered with dark spots. The lilac planted for Cesar has bloomed and dried without being celebrated, but the waterfall of white Spirea blooms is blinding. I thought that nature would pick up its cue from the lifeless home inside, but it confronts me with a tangled abundance.

The beauty of the flowers I planted years ago become a punishing force and then I remember the psychiatrist's comment. An external world that blazes with colour and life can turn murky when the interior mood is weighted by loss. My garden has escaped total ruination, and like my life, I am determined to salvage everything I can. I pick up gardening shears and rescue the plants, flooding the beds with water. The afternoon turns into evening and the emerging order of the garden restores my sanity. I will still cling to the notion that my love for Cesar is eternal. When I walk on the streets of my city and see couples together, I want to dash up to them and say I am this too.

A large white envelope arrives in the mail next day. I have cashed out some investments I have had for years. The safe money I was instructed never to touch has been converted into a cheque. I inform my lawyer that I can satisfy the trustee and clear Cesar's debt. Sharon cautiously suggests that I sell the house and plan a life based on the equity I will receive. I know that she is a salvage expert. She treads into the war-zone of dissolving partnerships and transforms catastrophe into practicality. I cannot tell her as yet that I refuse to be a statistic and my pride will not let me accept any judgment on Cesar's disappearance. The house is our shrine and all that has flowed through marks the radiance of our life together.

We were married in front of the green marble fireplace in the living room. In a rapidly shifting life, my home is my best friend. The night before he shaved his head, Cesar was my loving husband. What if he has had an accident in his car and become an amnesiac like a character in film? He could be living the life of a stranger without an element of choice. His frozen bank accounts, opened by court order, reveal that he has not made a single withdrawal.

Federico's suggestion of going to the Manitoulin Island home is next on my list. The five-hour journey by road and ferry terrifies me. Safety has now become the house with Cesar's photographs leaping out of frames. It is almost sacrilegious to invade the nine acres of deep forest lining the shores of a lake, considered by Cesar to be his personal sanatorium. He only cleared enough land to build a pine Canadian log house with strategic vistas to the water. A quarter-mile long driveway leading to the house is lined by a border of wild daisies.

There are driftwood sculptures outdoors and works of Native art inside. There is no telephone or electricity — just a propane line for the stove and refrigerator. There is also a solar panel on the roof, which generates electricity for the house. When Cesar first brought me here and I walked through the stunning home he had created, he said, "I have harnessed the sun," referring to the solar energy.

I had thought he was the sun himself as he warmed every aspect of my life. Over the years, I had only added books and colourful dishes. In our absence, the home is maintained by Jim, who lives permanently on the island. We only vacation there on long weekends and during the summer. Guests are never invited, except once when I went alone with Katherine and Rosemary, my two writer pals. We called it a Brontë weekend.

Cesar felt that the energy he used in therapy with his patients was replenished on the island. It assimilated his rhythm. We wandered in the forest, swam, and lay on the large rocks by the water. It is a perfect hideout for both of us. It is a place where transformations take place.

Often, Cesar would sink into long silences and move slowly. Or he would chop wood furiously, tramp through the woods, and swim halfway across the lake. He always planned to be on the island for the full moon.

On such an occasion, I woke up in the loft-style bedroom we slept in. Moonlight flooded the loft. Through the large glass windows, the water of the lake had turned to silver. Cesar was not in bed. Instead, he was sitting on the kitchen table staring out. The moonlight spilling in through the glass windows bathed him in an opaque haze. He turned his head and I remember being frightened, almost disorientated, by his expression. For a split second, I felt as though he was lost in some reverie that could not be invaded.

"Watch," he smiled. "It is a full moon and I am turning into a werewolf."

A few minutes later, he draped me in a blanket and took me outside to see the moon disappear behind the first blush of sunrise.

CHAPTER 10

TORONTO, 1999

"HE HAS BEEN SEEN IN Santo Domingo."

My entire body folds over. I hear a moan trailing through my breath as relief floods over. The receiver of the telephone slides from my ear to my chest and I am sitting on the floor. My world has shifted and I think it has become normal again. My husband is alive and only a three-hour flight away. There is not a trace of judgment in my thoughts, just euphoria. I am certain that I have regained my lost identity and am no longer the victim of some monstrous hoax. The friend from Michigan continues to talk on the telephone, but I have difficulty concentrating on his words.

"The person who saw him was confused by his appearance, apparently he has no money, and nobody knows where he is staying."

"I will fly out today!" I am shouting on the telephone.

"No, wait until we have more news. Something is wrong here. Just wait, I will make calls and get back to you."

I call my travel agent and inquire about flights to the Dominican Republic. Then I race to the basement where our luggage is stored. I pull out a small suitcase for myself and another to pack clothes for Cesar. The suitcases are wedged behind a large tubular light. When we moved into the house together, it came with Cesar's belongings. He told me it was a lamp he stared at to absorb light during the winter months. He was dismissive, as though it was something he no longer required. So my curiosity was also fleeting.

Now I call Paul and he comes over. Together, we sit in the kitchen, get the names of hotels in Santo Domingo, and call each one. Cesar is not registered in any of them. Paul repeats Manuel's instructions and says I cannot fly off to a place where I have both a language and cultural barrier. Also, I need to give Cesar time to contact me. He is puzzled about the location. Cesar had dispensed with his Caribbean ancestry thirty years ago. Both his parents were dead and he had no siblings. He planned a trip to Santo Domingo five years ago to satisfy my curiosity and had contacted two male cousins, who received us warmly. Cesar's father had belonged to a prominent family of the country. His maternal relatives had all settled in New York, but he had no ties with any of them. Unlike myself, I never detected any traces of nostalgia in Cesar for the land of his parents. He regarded himself as an American who had chosen to settle in Canada. It was only his appearance and fluency in Spanish that revealed his Spanish and Caribbean ancestry.

I call Detective White.

"Do you know there is a warrant out for his arrest?"

"I beg your pardon?" I am wondering if he is mad.

"He failed to appear in court, so a warrant is issued automatically. Of course, it can be dealt with if he returns. But he could still get arrested at the airport," says Detective White.

"I am going down to find him." I want to end this call immediately.

"I would not do that. We can ask Interpol to look into it."

"He has done nothing wrong, Detective White. I don't know why I called you." I hang up.

I am outraged at Cesar's new status and decide not to call Detective White again. I can't escape the feeling that it is me, and not my missing husband who is engaged in some illegal activity.

For three days, there is no further news, and Paul convinces me to wait. Manuel from Michigan telephones again to say that Cesar seems to have disappeared. Perhaps he was there for just a short while and on his way home. If he hears of anything, he will let me know. I am to wait at home.

A week passes and I brush against the two suitcases lying on the kitchen floor every day. I call the numbers of his two relatives repeatedly and they have no knowledge of his being in the country, know very little about his life in Canada, except that he was a successful physician. I am too embarrassed to tell them about the devastation he has left behind. They assure me that if he were in Santo Domingo they would know about it.

The second week also passes and I find myself seated in the psychiatrist's office again.

"Was your husband taking any medications?" he casually inquires.

One night in the earlier days of our marriage, I saw Cesar open a small vial of pills.

"What are these?"

"Oh they help me get a rested sleep before the week starts." He swallowed two of them.

"Are they sleeping pills?"

"No. More of a relaxant. Most doctors overmedicate themselves," he drops the pills in his briefcase with a rueful smile.

"I had no idea you have trouble falling asleep."

"I am the doctor, remember?" He walks me out of the room.

At that moment, I felt intimidated as most people do by physicians. I did not have the knowledge that my husband had of medications. I did not have the confidence to talk further about a matter in which he obviously had a superior and thoroughly professional judgment.

The psychiatrist also asks me to describe Cesar's personality, and smiles at my passionate descriptions. I have no way of knowing that he absorbs each descriptive word as though he examines it under a microscope.

"I want to go and find him," I say finally.

"Isn't he capable of finding his way home?"

"Something is wrong. I feel he has had an accident of some sort."

"A rescue operation?"

"I want the truth," I reply. "His entire life is here."

"I support you, because you will go there wearing two hats; you may lose one but will come back wearing the other."

"What do you mean?"

"The wife and the writer," he suggests.

Leaving his office, I realize that his quixotic loyalty to my mission strengthens me. He simply nodded at me, as though the dossier of horrors resting in the folder on his knees did not exist. As though I had just announced that I was going to the hairdresser.

Yet the days that follow turn bleak and lifeless again as I cannot seem to find the courage to go to another country to look for him. Someone from Santo Domingo offers the telephone number of a house where Cesar could have stayed, but whoever answers states he is not there. I keep a journal of my daily activities, and wait for the telephone to ring. My journal is written as though it is a novel. At some instinctual level, I know that contact between Cesar and myself is imminent.

I am also forced to store the contents of Cesar's office in the basement of the house, as the office rent is now overdrawn by three months. The College of Physicians asks about Cesar's whereabouts, as some of his patients have complained about his abrupt absence. I lie and tell them he is away on a leave of absence.

This is the point at which the house starts to become unbearable, and the stress of my predicament brings a new emotion to the surface. I am looking for an escape from my life. It becomes the uppermost thought in my mind. Our beloved home, the Endhouse, has become a crypt. Each room is now a museum of grief. Even the tall weeping willow positioned over the house is no longer charming but melancholic. My predicament is eroding my spirit day by day. Once again, a stranger begins to inhabit my soul. I thought that the telephone was my lifeline but this notion has also proved to be false. So I step out of character and lift a page from Cesar's script, deciding to create movement. I plan to simply walk out of a life that has become unbearable. I can no longer count hours and days without action of some sort.

I AM SEATED ON A plane, stunned by the speed with which I have planned the trip and the callousness with which I have abandoned my home. Cesar has the keys to the house and, if he returns, he will find my explanatory note and contact number. My destination is Newport Beach in California, the home of an American friend from my schooldays. He greets me warmly at the Los Angeles airport and drives me to a charming home complete with a large garden and a view of the ocean. It is a stunning environment and my bedroom is exquisitely appointed. Resting on the night table is a bowl filled with water on which a single gardenia floats. The scent of the gardenia catapults me into my honeymoon with Cesar, where in Marrakech the gardens of Hotel La Mamounia perfumed the air and Cesar plucked a rose each night to wear in his lapel. I take the gardenia and crush it into a tight little ball in the palm of one hand. One small flower will not have the power to hurl me back into the maelstrom I have taken some respite from.

Within the sympathetic confines of a home where I am reassured that my visit can be as long as I please, I pretend that I am a convalescing by taking long walks on the beach, exploring the small town and allowing myself to be entertained. However, each morning I work on my journal in the garden. I miss writing the book I have abandoned and am terrified that I will lose the ability to write again. And yet the shape of this journal is like that of a detective novel.

There is a Cuban gardener who appears daily. He is responsible for cutting the gardenias left in my room. I often chat with him companionably, as I am an avid gardener myself. Then one day he disarms me.

"Signora, you are a beautiful lady but your eyes are always sad."

"I have lost my husband," I reply.

His face clouds with sorrow but I quickly tell him that Cesar is not dead. Disarmed by his pure empathy, I spontaneously reveal my personal catastrophe to a complete stranger.

"But we can find him," he rises from the grass and stands tall.

"I have often telephoned the house where it was thought he may be staying a few weeks ago, but my Spanish is not good. It could be a wrong number."

"You have this number?"

"Yes," I reply.

We go inside the house and I hand him a small piece of paper. He dials the number, speaks rapidly in Spanish, and hangs up.

"It was the maid. I told her that there was a parcel for the Canadian doctor, and she said he was not there. I told her I will call again. She thinks I am calling from Santo Domingo. He lives in this house."

I stare at him in disbelief. This is the number Paul and I had called from Toronto numerous times to be informed that no one knew of Cesar's whereabouts.

"Thank you," my voice trembles as I turn to go to my room.

"Wait. He is there, but not close to the telephone. I have been told to call again in five minutes." He has a resolute expression in his eyes.

I am rooted to the spot. When he dials the number again, he speaks in Spanish and brusquely asks for Cesar, referring to him as the doctor. The clock winks on the oven and within thirty seconds I hear him repeat Cesar's name twice. Then he nods and hands me the receiver.

"Darling," I say softly.

"Yes," replies Cesar, slowly.

"What happened?"

I AM STANDING VERY STILL, feeling that if I move I may lose my step. The gardener has left and I am replaying every word of my conversation with Cesar in my head. It is terrifying, because it appears that Cesar is completely disassociated from the reality of our life, but he has given me his address. I have simply listened to the few things

Cesar has said and whispered goodbye to him. It is impossible to either berate him or demand explanations. The Cesar on the telephone is a complete stranger with a soft and halting voice. My questions have been chased right out of my mouth by a paralyzing shock. The contact I have yearned for is incomprehensible. I return to my room, pack quickly, and make arrangements to fly home that night.

THE FLIGHT TO SANTO DOMINGO leaves on time. I am sitting in the window seat and gazing at the clouds outside. The pilot makes an announcement. Something is wrong with the plane. I remove our wedding bands from my purse and slip them both on my middle finger. Mine slips on easily and Cesar's ring covers half of it. It is how we used to sleep, half his body sprawled over mine.

"It's to make sure you don't escape," he would tease me.

I wonder what it is that I love most about my husband. Was it the weight of lavish desire or merely his ability to make me carefree? Even when he kissed me, it felt as if he filled my lungs with air. Like his own brand of helium, designed to make me float upwards to the heavens and never descend. When he stirred sugar in my cup of coffee, the spoon always rotated a few extra rounds, even though we both knew the sugar had long dissolved. His stewardship of our love was meticulous and still this vision blossoms in my mind.

The plane is not turning back, announces the pilot. There is no hazard, just a computer error solved by technical wizards on the ground. I slip the bands back into my purse again. Had the plane crashed and my body been found, the bands would affirm my history. The finger released from the clump of metal has become free and weightless. Cesar's name followed by "Amor Eterno" is the inscription inside the ring pressed against my skin. This sentiment is now unpredictable and I want him to place this band on my finger again. Yet like the pilot, I am not turning back either, simply racing towards a destiny I have no preparation for.

When the food tray is snapped back, I place the spiral ring notebook in front of me. It is an act of discipline. I now feel that it is simply not enough for me to be perched on the edgy of an abyss, I must record it as well. It is a perilous act as I am both subject and archivist. And I wonder if my eight-year knowledge of my beloved husband is largely imagined. Cesar is a subject as well. Even if I have joined us at the hip, it will be my language that will flesh him out. At this moment, I would have preferred to use music rather than words. A symphonic exercise ruled by the bowstring of the cello and air valves of the flute. The power of language is finite. Within my shifting life, the recordkeeping itself is subject to change over and over again.

The notebook sits in my lap unused until the plane begins its descent. When it lands, I rush down the stairs into the full blast of Caribbean heat. The blinding sunshine, Hispanic faces, coconut trees lining the small airport, and throaty decibels of Spanish all quicken my pace. A porter wheels out my luggage. I follow him to the exit. He tells me in accented English that the Apollo Taxi will take me to the hotel where I have a reservation. I inquire about this taxi and he beams at me and says it is the only company that is reliable, always comes. He presses a small card in my hand.

There is a crowd of people pressed against a barrier and I sense as though a hundred pairs of eyes observe me and smell my fear. The taxi draws beside me and I give him the name of the hotel. Meringue plays on the radio and the air conditioning is fitful. The taxi speeds along a highway and winds through the city to deposit me in front of a picturesque hotel with a large wooden door. When I register, my pen falters at my married name. The room is large and appointed with Spanish colonial furnishings and a ceiling fan overhead. The bathroom has an enormous marble bathtub. On the bed, I lift the telephone and ask reception to dial Cesar's number.

"Buenos dias," says Cesar.

"I am here," I say.

"I am coming."

THE TROPICAL RAINSTORM UNLEASHES ITS fury. Sheets of rain flatten the foliage of trees and unpaved roads become rivers of shifting mud.

I see this scene from the window of my hotel room. This is no longer the situation in a fictional tale. I am about to confront truth. Had it been a work of fiction, I could say that Cesar waits outside a house under the front terrace for an Apollo taxi to arrive. He could wonder if he had enough money for the taxi. I would also place myself in an Apollo taxi racing to meet him. The taxis would glide by, missing one another. It would become a tale of star-crossed lovers!

At this moment I have no way of knowing that Esperanza, a cousin whom he has not seen for forty years, has given him refuge in her home, or that she delicately places money on the edge of his bed every week. He buys a bottle of Dominican rum and a pack of American cigarettes that last him all week. He walks everywhere and has lost the weight he should have years ago. He has no income, as he has landed in the country without his professional certificates and cannot even apply for a work permit. He has survived by detaching himself from the life and the woman he loved and in his mind exists as a warrior in an alien world.

If this were fiction then I would create favourable solutions and convert Esperanza and her husband into heroic souls. They would shower him with affection and see to all his needs. The missing car scenario would be resolved in this fashion. Cesar has sold his expensive car in Miami for fifteen hundred dollars. He purchased a one-way ticket to Santo Domingo and then bought three pairs of black jeans and packs of black T-shirts and shaving razors and boarded the flight using his American passport. He has avoided the two cousins that I met, one of whom has just been appointed a state minister.

As he is coming to meet me, he has taken care with his appearance by polishing his only pair of shoes, trimming his moustache, and dabbing on the cologne that Esperanza put on his dresser one day. He will most certainly feel as though he is off to a romantic assignation. There are no thoughts of anything else in his mind as he watches the rain and waits for the taxi that will find its way even through a hurricane. He will find his way to me and it will be a happy ending after all.

I UNPACK AND ORDER COFFEE. Then I place my toiletries in the bath-room and take out my arsenal of vitamins. Cesar had put me on them years ago. I shower and change, drink coffee, and wait for Cesar. It is over an hour before the knock comes on the door. I turn the heavy handle twice.

He stands in front of me dressed in worn black jeans and a black T-shirt, lean and muscular with a head of short, silver curls. The face is heavily tanned, turning his hazel eyes to shades of green, and the smile curving beneath the moustache is familiar and beloved. The mahogany doorframe gives the moment a surrealistic touch, as though he is a painting that has come to life.

"Sorry, I was waiting for Apollo." He steps in with one stride, pulls me into his arms.

The blades of the ceiling fan overhead revolve slowly, lifting the edges of the white bedsheet covering our bodies. The rainstorm has ended and the afternoon has turned to evening. I open my eyes, savouring the exquisite languor infusing my body. My face is pressed into Cesar's collarbone and, even in sleep, he is holding me. I slide from his embrace and he wakes up and holds me tightly against his chest. This is how the world is kept at bay by both of us for a while.

In silence, we walk to the bathroom to shower together. Cesar glances at my array of cosmetics, bath soap, and vitamin bottles and says he has missed everything terribly. I gaze at him in silence, my fragile equilibrium pierced. It is the first admission of pain from him about his predicament, overwhelming both of us simultaneously. Nothing else is said as we wash each other's body under the stream of cascading water with well-remembered touches.

Now we sit on two armchairs wrapped in towels and devour the food I ordered through room service. Our movements are like a pair of matched horses but the cues emanate subtly from Cesar. He still retains the ability to pace our activities and as always, I follow with ease. Cesar has no way of knowing that although a part of my brain is utterly soothed by the ecstasy of our reunion, the newly acquired wariness quivers with the alertness of a hunter. I will not reveal this to Cesar, not yet.

"A breakdown," I repeat the word he has just used.

"Yes. I fled from everything and landed up here."

"Is this a medical condition?" I am trembling.

"Yes."

"Is there a cure for it?"

"Yes, but not here. I have to go home."

"Home!" I am screaming at him, losing the deceptive calm I have been displaying. Then like the rainstorm, I hammer and tear at Cesar, telling him all the details of the horrifying chaos of our life in Toronto.

"The house?" Cesar asks slowly.

"It is safe and your office is sitting in the basement."

Cesar's expression is grave and he is watching me. He can see the signs of the damage and I know he will rely on his skills as a therapist and not a husband to restore me. I am his dancing, laughing wife whom he will continue to shield from the truth because I am the most precious part of his life. This is what he tells me, as he admits to being dazzled by my heroism and humbled by my love. But he is filled with confidence.

"We are going home tomorrow. I can fix everything." He gets up and puts on his clothes.

"You can't. They are going to arrest you."

"Rubbish! I am going to call my lawyer. He was working on this case."

I look at Cesar in amazement. He has become brisk and authoritative again — the man I am familiar with — not the one who has talked about a nervous breakdown. Cesar opens his empty wallet and pulls out a card and places a call to Toronto and talks for a while and then hangs up.

"It will take him a week to go to the same judge and make an explanation, so I have to wait here. Did you bring any money with you?"

I show him the folder of American currency Malka has given me. He looks relieved and then makes another telephone call, speaking rapidly in Spanish. He has called Esperanza and she and her husband are coming to the hotel to take us home for dinner.

"No. I don't want to go anywhere. I need to be here in a space that is mine. Do they speak English?"

"They are highly educated and refined people. You will like them," Cesar responds softly but his face clouds with apprehension.

We are seated in a patio of the hotel surrounded by lush tropical foliage. I am wearing a white summer dress with a long strand of grey pearls around my neck that Cesar gave me as an anniversary gift. They were left in a toilet case from our last trip and I just discovered them. Nothing matters except that miraculously, Cesar has managed to make me feel as though we are on a vacation in a romantic hide-away in the Caribbean. We are no longer partners in a *danse macabre*, but sun-kissed lovers in a paradise. The power exuded by Cesar is dazzling, as he sweeps away the debris of his flight and my ensuing trauma and the assurance with which he speaks about restoring our life immediately.

My thoughts about the woman whom I will meet are mixed. I have feelings of great hostility for her. When they arrive, the tall imposing older woman with dark hair piled up formally, ignores my handshake and simply embraces me for a long time. Her body language conveys a silent empathy for the well of tears that has gathered inside me for five harrowing months. Her husband is a barrel-chested man with a kind face. He is a lawyer and she is a well-known television person-ality on the island. They do nothing but express delight at meeting me. They tell me that Cesar was troubled, but the way he talked about me and our love for each other, they felt sure I would come to take him home. When I asked them why they didn't contact me, they say these were Cesar's instructions.

Esperanza rises and asks me to accompany her to the other patio where there is a collection of beautiful orchids. The men stay behind. As we stand beneath a canopy of rare orchids dangling through a ceiling trellis, Espernaza tells me that she owes a great debt to her cousin.

"He is an angel sent to me from God," she explains.

"My son," she continues, "had a serious drug addiction and Cesar has played therapist and assisted in his rehabilitation. In three months, my son is cured. For this, I would give my world to this cousin I have not seen for forty years. Now my prayers are answered, and his world has come for him.

"He refuses everything except food at the house. He wears the same clothes and the maid washes them every day. He came to us not well himself, but he heals my son. It will be an honour to have you both in our home."

I lift the rope of pearls from my neck, drape them over Esperanza's head, and hush her protest; I am garlanding a queen. In the cool night air we are simply two women who have rescued the same man. I have no concept at this point what a breakdown means, although it appears that I have endured one myself and, in a protective gesture, I exist in the moment, without a thought for tomorrow.

Although I know that I am being offered carefully selected information by my husband, I am relieved by our reunion, and an overpowering feeling of love for him. This is a choice I make with full consciousness. If Cesar had suffered a heart attack or some other ailment, I would have reacted the same way. The cure he hints at lightheartedly also restores my confidence. In a ludicrous fashion, which I cannot recognize at this moment, it is as though I have been to the doctor for a visit and been reassured that a simple course of treatment will banish a mysterious ailment forever.

DOMINICAN REPUBLIC/ TORONTO, 1999

CESAR AND I WALK DOWN a short flight of steps to his room. It is a storage room in Esperanza's home that has been converted into a bedroom. The bed is narrow and the concrete walls are unpainted. A small wooden table with a lamp sits near one side of the bed. The lamp has a red shade, which adds a garish touch to the room. On this table sits a small wooden picture frame with a seven-year-old photograph of me. This is the photograph Cesar always carried in his wallet. Adjoining the room is a cement shower stall with a toilet and washbasin. A small stack of washed and neatly pressed laundry sits at the foot of the bed. The room has the appearance of a monastic cell and I find it painful to view this evidence of Cesar's home in exile.

Cesar is aware of my distress and rapidly collects his clothes in a small bag and his toiletries from the bathroom. We walk back upstairs silently where Esperanza is waiting to drive us back to the hotel.

When we say goodbye to her, she lifts Cesar's hand and places it in mine.

"You are each other's home," she says.

Then she looks at me and says, "Mucho Amor."

It is almost a handing-over ceremony — Cesar's passage from one woman to another. Both of us are unaware of the emotions that keep Cesar silent as he kisses his cousin on her cheeks.

We return to the hotel room and put Cesar's clothes away. We will spend the second night together and I will fly out first in the morning. Cesar will follow in two days, on the advice of his lawyer. I am also given strict instructions that when I pick him up at Toronto airport, he is not to leave the house until his appearance at court.

Throughout the day I think, "How will he feel knowing that two-thirds of his material life is missing?" I have also cashed out my investment account to settle legal bills and all his liabilities. But I have saved our home, and the contents of his professional life sit in the basement. We are together and he will put our lives back together. I have implicit faith in his ability to do this.

He takes me out that night on a short walk from the hotel to an empty outdoor restaurant. It is in the colonial section of the city and has an ambience of being lifted from a film set. There is a garden with a few tables sprinkled on the grass. On one side is a tiny hill with a concrete dance floor and two musicians. The music is romantic and Spanish. A waiter appears and places menus in front of us, and without missing a beat Cesar orders a bottle of Spanish champagne.

"What is a nervous breakdown?" I ask him again.

His face becomes very still. The he starts speaking. It is bizarre story, which I hear right to the end. The sips of champagne and snatches of music add a misleading touch of lightness.

He felt an overwhelming pressure the day he shaved his head, he tells me. This feeling accompanied him on the drive to the island, so halfway through he changed directions and headed for the U.S. border. The passports were in the briefcase because the American one had to be renewed in six months so he kept them together to remind himself to do it. They were in his briefcase for weeks. He forgot to put the briefcase in the front hall closet when he came home from work. The briefcase lay in the trunk of his car for safety. He put the watch and the wedding band in the first garment he saw in the closet, also for safety.

A real estate investment in the United States acquired before our marriage and that offered him a tax shelter had instead created a financial loss, so he was behind in his taxes for a year. He was settling the matter with the help of a financial trustee, but when he felt the pressure, he buckled, and simply walked out of his life. He was crippled by the feelings that I would never forgive him and neither would his patients.

I am hypnotized by these details. His storytelling skills are brilliant. His manner is forthright and his contrition evident. I tell him that his beloved island home was used to settle part of his debts.

"Ah!" he says, and sits quietly for a while.

"I will have the office set up in a week. We will replace it, darling. Forget about it." He rises and holds up his arms.

To the chords of "Bésame Mucho," our favourite Spanish love song, he leads me to the little concrete square in front of the musicians.

We are dancing alone, clinging to each other. He is a superb dancer and the stranger within me is receding. My cheek pressed to Cesar's feels as it has always done. I know exactly when he will twirl me around. When he does, I will fall into his arms without stumbling.

When we return to the table and the salads arrive, he winks at me and fishes out all the avocado slices and piles them on my plate as he has done for years. I watch, eternally fascinated by the way he debones his fish. He wears his glasses and looks as though he is performing surgery with great delicacy, while telling me about the danger of a fishbone getting lodged in the trachea. I have heard it a thousand times before and smile as I have always done. This is how the balance of my universe is set right. It is the undiluted force of our intimacy that chases away the strangers living inside us. Added to this, is that despite the knowledge of a personal and professional life that is in shambles, Cesar exudes an unshakeable spirit of a survivor.

"AMOR ETERNO," HE WHISPERS IN my ear before kissing me at the security barrier at the airport the next morning.

I walk away, carrying the imprint of his embrace and a song of hope in my heart. When I turn around for the last look, he is still watching me. I fall asleep in the plane. It is my first untroubled sleep in months. When I arrive at the Toronto airport, I want to do cart-wheels on the gleaming floors. The taxi cannot travel fast enough to get me home. The front porch light is on and I unlock the front door and go through the house, turning on all the lights.

That night I sleep on Cesar's side of the bed.

During the day, I restock the refrigerator with all his favourite food. At the flower shop, I stagger out with an armload of roses and collect newspapers and magazines and a bottle of his favourite Scotch and race home to freshen up the house.

I telephone my best friend Malka first, and her voice quivers with relief.

Paul shocks me by not being fully convinced. "I want details of this breakdown. He is a bloody doctor himself. Is he aware of what you have gone through?"

"He is going to thank you himself," I plead with him.

I spend time placating him on the telephone, casting his judgment away, telling him that the horror has ended and he must stay a true friend and support my happiness.

It is about four in the afternoon and I am waiting for Cesar at the airport. Just when I have almost given up, he strides through the glass doors. His bronzed face gleams and his eyes widen with delight. He then drops his bag and embraces me. An avalanche of kisses descends on my face, mingling with tears. He tells me he used the American passport and has managed to get through. Outside, when we reach the car in the parking lot, I hand him the keys. He slides into the driver's seat and adjusts it, then pulls the car out and drives us home.

He enters the house first and walks through all the rooms. His gaze halts at the changed painting over the mantelpiece but he says nothing. Then he goes down to the basement, now filled with his office furniture and filing cabinets. He surveys the scene without commenting. He returns with his black leather appointment book. I am in the kitchen and do not see it in his hand.

Cesar recreates his professional life with speed. He spends hours on the telephone calling his patients and talking to them. Fifty percent wish to return to him. But he has lost half the practice to other doctors. He finds an office close by and arranges for his furniture to be delivered there.

His attendance in court is dramatic; he is arrested and released within ten minutes. The judge is sympathetic to a doctor who has suffered from a breakdown. I am in the courtroom with Federico. Cesar is standing with his lawyer. He is wearing a navy wool pinstriped suit and looks well-groomed and dignified. I find it almost absurd. Five well-dressed people in a courtroom attending to what is regarded as an error. As though a magic wand has been waved and five harrowing months have simply disappeared.

"It will take him some time to recover. You have to be patient my dear," Federico whispers.

You are wrong, I say silently, gazing at my husband in awe.

Cesar has also gone to see a therapist who is an old colleague of his.

"What did he say?" I ask.

"The physician will heal himself," responds Cesar, smiling at me.

"I went to see one myself," I tell him.

Cesar looks surprised. "It's all over darling, everything will be fine. You don't need to see anyone."

The dynamics of our domestic life shift. One car is missing and I drop Cesar at his new office each morning and he walks home in the evening. Cesar calls all his colleagues seeking referrals. His income will stabilize within the coming months and I am not to worry about anything, is what he tells me daily. I am to relax and work on my book.

I cannot tell Cesar that I am not writing these days but researching psychiatric texts. This is my secret. But each evening at 6 p.m., I write a poem. I call this new creative venture the six o'clock poems. Sometimes I read them to Cesar in the evening. We play chess regularly and I notice that my game becomes more aggressive. I often lead with the Queen, an exercise fuelled by misguided confidence. Cesar always takes the game but assists me along the way. The geography of love widens. It now includes a new state whose borders are yet to be mapped out. An element of watchfulness develops in me, yet Cesar is the husband I continue to love passionately. His behaviour is predictable, familiar, and gentler than usual.

Cesar returns from his office each day looking happy and calm. He does not tell me that he is not interested in taking the medication that his therapist has recommended. He does not tell me about his great resistance to drugs of this sort. All he exhibits is a vitality that is more seductive than ever and an enormous zeal for restoring our life. Each day, he tells me that I will never go through this experience again. We are back to where we were and exchange ideas about our life.

"What are you writing?" he asks.

"I am struggling."

"I thought you had the novel all worked out," he smiles at me.

"No, I am confused," I reply.

"About what?"

"Fiction based on non-fiction."

"Sounds fascinating. You will work it out," he holds me very close to him.

I AM HAVING A DINNER party. I have invited Paul, Malka, and Federico. This is a way to thank them for their support. The house is filled with flowers and the dining table is set with the silver Berber dinner plates we brought back from our honeymoon in Morocco. I use this arrangement for special occasions and then sprinkle rose petals on the tablecloth. It is a Moroccan touch I have kept alive for all these years.

Cesar is wearing an elegant jacket and I am wearing a silk caftan. It is a full show of colours intended to tell our friends that order is fully restored in our lives. Or like a magician's trick, the disappearance and chaos was simply a mirage.

Paul is pleasant but remains guarded, Malka is emotional, and Federico spreads a sense of ease around the dining table. Cesar is questioned about the Dominican Republic as though he has just returned from a vacation. I am in my element because I love cooking and am delighted by the response of my guests. Cesar is never far from a bottle of wine. He is a jovial and attentive host. After dinner, he takes Paul out to the garden to smoke a cigar. When they return Paul has lost his guarded attitude. They walk into the house together like comrades.

"He has gone through hell, when he drove to Miami he had no money, only a gas card. He slept in the car," Paul tells me.

"I know. All his chequebooks were at home, and the accounts were frozen."

"He is a doctor. He will make it back again," says Paul.

"I am not worried. My love has returned."

"Are you writing?" he skewers me.

"Not yet, we are in the middle of the second honeymoon." I smile gaily at Paul.

A few days later, Cesar stands in front of the refrigerator and talks non-stop while I slice vegetables for dinner. He tells me about a business plan he's thinking about. He vibrates with excitement and there is a peculiar grandiosity to his speech. I am noticing it for the first time.

Then he changes the subject and says, "I have been asked to participate as a guest lecturer at a community college. I have checked out five books from the library to do some research. I intend to make some notes tonight."

I am aware that his part-time bookkeeper also handles his occasional correspondence. I say, "I can type up your lecture on the computer when you are ready."

He brushes my offer aside and continues to talk through dinner. An inspired Cesar is not out of character, but when he talks, his eyes have a fixed look to them. It is almost as though he is not aware that I am seated with him.

Although I am drawn to his ideas, on this occasion it appears as though a mass of them seem to be jammed together. Suddenly, I feel cold. I check the temperature on the thermostat. It is perfectly comfortable. Cesar continues to talk as we clear the dining table together and load the dishwasher. Then he dashes upstairs and changes. He walks into the guest room with the stack of books and a writing tablet.

"See you later," he says.

I am asleep when I feel Cesar drawing me closer to him in bed. My body offers its habitual responsiveness. When I wake up in the morning, I feel as though we made love all through the night. It is 5 a.m. and Cesar is not in bed. I am still sleepy so I do not get up. The next time my eyes open, it is 6:15 a.m. I rise and know instinctively that Cesar is not at home. Walking into the kitchen, I notice that coffee has been made. The health club we both belong to opens at 6 a.m. Cesar swims there most mornings before going to the office.

I call the health club and ask if he has checked in. They say he headed to the swimming pool. I drink a cup of coffee, change, and go outside to pick up the newspaper from the porch. My car is still there and I wonder why he took a taxi to the club.

I decide to surprise him, have breakfast at the club with him, and drive home together. Then he will change and I will drive him to the office. This is what I tell myself but there is a shadow tucked into this innocuous thought. This shadow makes me drive the car faster than I should. It stays in place until I park the car in the parking lot of the health club.

I climb the front steps to building and catch Cesar dashing through the exit turnstile. The colour in his face is high, as though he has gone through physical exertion.

"Darling, have you finished?" I ask, moving to him.

Cesar steps through the security gate hurriedly and roughly turns me around back to the exit, speaking rapidly.

"I have done thirty laps. I have full appointments all day and I have to see the accountant at lunch."

Outside, he races to the car. He pulls out his own keys and gets behind the wheel. I step into the passenger side, amazed by his rush. My brain swirls, something is wrong with my husband. He is behaving differently. When did he go to the club, and how fast did he swim the laps to be showered and ready to leave now? He is driving as though he is being pursued. The car reaches the driveway and he dashes out first and goes upstairs to change. I try to stop him, saying I will make breakfast. He says he has no time; he needs to work on the lecture at the office. He will catch a taxi on the street.

Then he comes down fully dressed for the office and crams vitamin pills into his mouth with a glass of water. Now I am aware that Cesar is in a state I have never seen before and I spring into action with a speed that astounds me. I race him to the front door and get into the driver's seat. Cesar follows immediately and sits besides me. He talks rapidly about his schedule and he makes flying hand gestures, but does not look at me.

I drive in silence, feeling as though I am in the presence of a wild and dangerous animal. I do not say a word but have made up my mind that when we get to the office I will ask him what is wrong with him.

I reach the office. He gets out before the car fully stops, walks towards the two-storey building, and opens the outer door. He always kisses me goodbye and today he does not even look back.

I park the car and race after him. As I get through the main door, Cesar is already opening the inner glass door that leads to the offices. He steps through as I run to it. As I step forward, Cesar shouts and pushes me violently, slams the door and locks it from inside. His face is contorted, his expression completely unrecognizable. I bang on the door with my fist. I cry out in terror and ask him to open the door, but he disappears towards his office.

I am stunned by his repelling gesture but this does not paralyze me. Instead, it galvanizes me into action. I race to the public phone outside the office. I telephone Federico and tell him precisely what has happened. Then I call Cesar's office number and leave a message saying I want to see him. After ten minutes, I go home. There is a message from Federico saying that he has contacted the doctor Cesar sees, but he is on vacation in Europe and cannot be reached. I am to stay at home and wait for him. He knows exactly what the problem is.

I AM SITTING ON THE sofa in the living room. The doorbell rings and Federico is standing there, his hair ruffled by the wind and a grave look on his face. He leads me to the living room sofa and sits with me.

"He is hypomanic, my dear."

"What?" I have never heard this word before.

"He is in the middle of severe mood disorder. He is a manic-depressive. He cannot see patients in this condition. He is not responding to my call. He has to be hospitalized immediately and properly diagnosed. He is a danger to himself and to his patients."

"That is not possible," I whisper to him.

"I have suspected this for a while." Federico brings the full weight of his profession to his tone of voice.

"I knocked on his office door, but he would not open it. His entire disappearance is almost a textbook case. But he is highly intelligent and he has been hiding this for years."

"His doctor is not here. What do we do?"

"You are his wife and you have to commit him immediately."

"I can't do this to my husband. He is a doctor. He is not insane."

"You are the closest person to him. It has to be done."

"When?"

"Now! We have to go to city hall and see a Justice of Peace who will issue the order to the police to take him to the psychiatric wing of the hospital."

"I cannot do this!" I sob. "I cannot commit my husband, who is a psychiatrist, to a mental ward."

"There are medications that will stabilize him, he will be under observation, and a diagnosis will be made. You will be helping him. Nobody has done this before. He needs help. He cannot see patients in this condition. It will destroy his career."

"This nervous breakdown is a disease."

"He cannot help it. But he must be treated. It will be handled appropriately; the admitting doctor will interview you at length, and then make a decision. They will keep him for seventy-two hours for observation. But he will be angry and not forgive you for this."

I see my stunningly conceived house of cards fold in front of my eyes. As Federico explains the symptoms of manic depression, parts of a giant puzzle lock into place. The boundless energy and vitality Cesar was blessed with is in fact a type of mania. The long silences and the meditative withdrawals, brilliantly concealed from me, are the product of depression. The pendulum has swung from one extreme to the other for my beloved husband most of his adult life. In between there are stable periods.

When I first met Cesar and fell in love, it was June when he was seasonally manic. He masked it as a summer awakening. He displayed a staggering sexual prowess, was the last person on a dance floor, and shopped with an extravagance that left me breathless. The verbal grandiosity that I noticed yesterday was also a symptom. According to Federico, the act of leaving his office and having his head shaved bald was the result of a depressive episode.

This is my biggest test as a wife. Am I a woman who fell in love with a disease? The behaviour dictated by mania is the one that had swept me off my feet. Cesar's vivacity and dynamic presence affected most people who were exposed to him. It is not his exotic Hispanic ancestry that accounts for his temperament, as Cesar has coached me for years, it is in fact the inferno created by the polarities of mood shifts that mark his true personality. Has this happened to other people as well?

Federico is prominent in his field and now sits in our home and writes a report to give to the Justice of Peace. I tell him I need five minutes to change my clothes. I go upstairs and do something I have not done for years. I am utterly lost and seek some act of consolation.

I pull out a dark green book from the top shelf of the bookcase. My father had given me this version of the Quran, which has both the Arabic text and the English translation side by side, when I left his home and settled in Canada. Although I was tutored as a child to read the Arabic script, knowing that it could pose a language barrier, he ensured that I could understand the text fully in the language I had the greatest comfort with.

I resort to a ritual of divination I have heard about, but never experimented with. I sit on the edge of the couch in the den and close my eyes and take Cesar's name silently in my mind. I close my eyes and open the text randomly. I then read the opening stanza of the page. Whatever is written is to be taken as a message. It is an act of absolute and blind faith, and at the moment of my greatest trial, I seek consolation from the faith that I was raised in.

I open the 42nd chapter of the Quran entitled "Al-Shura" meaning the counsel. It is a chapter that encourages Muslims to make it a rule to take counsel in all affairs of importance. When I walk down to join Federico, I am ready to take the step. Now the boundaries of my married life will be defined in ways I could have never anticipated. I regard the act of concealment on Cesar's part to be an act of love and of protection, and am unaware that this is also a symptom of the ailment. I rejoin Federico and sign the clinical declaration he has written for me based on the narration of the events I have given him.

When I return from city hall and the police department where the order is delivered, I then wait for the call from the admitting doctor. Everything has been explained to me in detail. The police will go to Cesar's office and knock on his door. If he is in session, he will have to conclude it immediately. The police will then escort the doctor to the hospital and, in all probability, the patient will see all this happening. I have been instrumental in savaging his professional dignity.

The telephone call comes around noon. The only thought in my mind is that he is safe. What I do not know at that moment is that my love for him will grow larger as it now has compassion folded into it. I am ready to face Cesar, not across a chessboard, but at the threshold of his secret, and I have no way of knowing what the outcome will be.

CHAPTER 12

TORONTO, 2000

I AM WALKING SLOWLY DOWN the corridor towards the psychiatric wing. It is an oppressive environment with many heavy doors and small portholes of glass. Behind these doors I imagine that a crazed world exists where an angry Cesar is being held against his will. I would give anything not to be here. The white-coated figure waiting at the end of the corridor is the doctor who wishes to interview me. When I reach him, I am jolted by his youthful demeanour. He greets me, leads me to an office, and makes me feel comfortable. The penetrating gaze and clinical manner add a weight to his young, unlined face. He tells me that the most important diagnostic information comes from the spouse or family members of the bipolar patient. Within an hour and half, he gathers information on all aspects of Cesar's moods from season to season. He also tells me that Cesar is older than him, a colleague, and highly intelligent, so his task is fraught with skill and delicacy. It is also typical for a bipolar person to deny the condition completely. Doctors also address manic depression as a bipolar disorder. Cesar, he shocks me by adding, has completely denied all aspects of his behaviour in the past twenty-fours hours and has suggested that I am lying. He has also concealed his disappearance for five months from the doctor.

"In such a case I would have to release him in forty-eight hours, but I am not convinced. I know the history and I have great respect for Federico. I am keeping him for seventy-two hours. I want you to go home and rest."

"Why wouldn't he want to be diagnosed and treated?" I am completely bewildered.

"The medication controls the manic highs. That is the only time a manic depressive feels alive," responds the doctor.

"Can I see him please?" I suddenly want everything to stop.

"I am afraid not. Please don't worry. We will call you when we are ready to discharge him." He takes me to the door.

"I really want to see my husband, I want to tell him why I did this," I am close to tears.

"Please go home. You can call in the evening and check at the nursing station. You will not be able to speak to him, but they will tell you how he is."

Walking back, I think that if I knew where he was, I would sit outside the door and just wait. I am reminded of war wives with faces pressed against barbed wire searching for imprisoned husbands. Instead, I am walking with the doctor towards the exit door and he has no intention of letting me stay behind.

I AM AT HOME READING a book. In fact, I am devouring the book. It is called *An Unquiet Mind*, written by an American female professor of psychiatry at the prestigious John Hopkins School of Medicine who is herself a manic-depressive. I cannot put the book down. Not only does it describe everything exquisitely, it also reveals how the doctor managed to conceal her ailment from professional colleagues, patients, and family members for years. It spells out the trail of self-destructive patterns that create financial, conjugal, health, and professional hazards. It expresses in lyrical prose the matchless sensations experienced during mania. The propensity for alcohol and drugs used excessively to control the mania, which in turn heighten the depression, is aptly described. It reveals with spellbinding courage the perspective of the disease from both the eye of the healer and of the afflicted. It makes me open the first drawer of the chest in the guestroom and read the labels on all the vials that Cesar has prescribed for himself.

A singular pain enters me as I feel a sorrowing and maternal love for Cesar. This is not a flaw in his personality but a disease marked by blood chemistry, possibly genetics. Its symptoms are difficult to trace and its diagnosis and treatment difficult. It redefines my role of being a wife and will make me into a caretaker of sorts. I piece together every incident in our lives and retrieve the annual calendars I am used to saving. They show bursts of high energy, spiralling enthusiasm, and bouts of reckless spending followed by periods of long silences.

In fact, I have adjusted to his rhythm perfectly, tailoring my behaviour to be a harmonious and matched companion. I have, without being aware, solidified his denial of the ailment. I have always believed that I was sensitive to his professional life and eternally fascinated with his unique temperament. It was how I loved him perfectly. Not only has he loved me passionately but, in fact, what he has done both subtly and powerfully is to teach me to follow the mood swings of his ailment without suspecting that he has a mental disease. It has been a consummate act of deception carried out in the hallowed space of love. Cesar is also eleven years older than me and is acutely aware of the cultural reverence I extend to him. It is the product of my upbringing, where seniority is equated with wisdom and, like most people, I regard a physician as being highly knowledgeable.

Despite the new and overwhelming information I have gathered from the book, naively I place my faith in the young resident in psychiatry, who has assured me that the seventy-two-hour observation period will be maintained and a diagnosis confirmed. So the next evening I call the hospital nursing station to inquire about Cesar, I am informed that he was discharged three hours ago. With a sinking feeling, I call Federico.

"I am not surprised, my dear. He telephoned me and was very aggressive. He must have even called his patients to support him. The weekend staff changed and the new resident was no match for him."

"But he has not called me?"

"He is not ready to confront you and will hold you responsible for this." Federico's warning falls on my deaf ears.

Once again, my expectations enter a fictional realm. My star protagonist is Cesar who I believe has stepped out of character. He has discarded both hope and promise and used his formidable skills to subvert his treatment. But I am viewing his entire mission as a consummate game played by a brilliant mind. I have to marvel at the speed with which he has played this game.

He has also spoken to Federico because he suspects that I have been guided by someone professional. Or is he simply averting any jeopardy to his professional career? Do I use this as new journal entries or will Cesar redeem himself by ensnaring me with an altered perspective? In my agitation, I wonder if I am truly capable of separating the imagined from the actual. Is my ultimate hero Cesar, taking risks with his power to sustain our love? In that case, he will use every ounce of superior knowledge about my nature to preserve his oasis. He often calls me his "oasis."

When the call comes to sever my life in half, I am numb with shock. Cesar's voice on the other end informs me that he is separating for a while and will be arriving to collect some of his clothes.

I do not believe him, but when a taxi halts in front of the house and Cesar walks into the front hall without greeting me, I am filled with apprehension. He collects a suitcase from the basement and goes up to our bedroom as I wait downstairs. My silence is the defence mechanism I choose. I am convinced that when he returns downstairs he will talk to me. I am wrong.

"Please don't worry about anything. I shall make deposits into the chequing account for everything," is the perfunctory statement he delivers without looking at me as he walks towards the door.

"We can handle this together," I cry out.

The word "together" bounces from the ceiling and walls like a primeval dirge. It emanates from the depth of my wounded heart. It has no effect on Cesar whose unhalting steps lead him outside to the waiting taxi.

My life has once again become unimaginable. All communication between Cesar and me has halted. I do not know the location of the furnished accommodations he has taken. In fact, I re-enter the realm of a separated woman without any warning. I often dial his office, listen to his voice on the answering machine, and then disconnect, knowing fully well that his phone will display the house number. I continue to keep a journal and do not tell anyone that Cesar is not living at home. His behaviour is meticulous as he continues supporting all the household expenses by depositing money in our joint account. There is no accidental encounter. I refuse to wait outside his office and confront him. He will have to open the door himself. There is also an optimistic side to my thinking, where I feel that he may be taking some treatment and will return when he is stabilized.

I have devised a plan to survive without Cesar. Often I will go to the neighbourhood cinema and watch a late show. There is another bedtime ritual I perform that continues to surprise me. The green Quran sits on Cesar's night table and I meditate and then open a page with closed eyes. I take whatever is expressed on the page as a guide. The historical occurrences have no interest for me, as I am only drawn to exhortations of belief and protection. It is crisis that leads me to the text and the consoling element of this activity puts me to sleep easily. The activities of my daily life do not alter. I go to the health club and exercise, write in the afternoons, and devise ways of making the long evenings go by. I will not accept that either my marriage or my love has ended, until the accountant who jointly files our taxes calls at home wanting my receipts. This is when I panic and call Sharon, my lawyer.

"I think we should draw up a separation agreement, so the good doctor can get a dose of reality."

I am stung by her words and reject her advice totally. I am waiting for Eros, God of Love. This is how I continue to view Cesar, who is hiding for some unfathomable reason. My strength comes from two places. Both rest in ancient texts. One is the Quran and the other is Greek mythology. One empowers me with faith and the other gives me mythological synchronicity. In fact, at one level I view myself as Penelope waiting for Ulysses.

One afternoon, I go to the Four Seasons Hotel where Cesar often made a lunch date with me. I have no desire to eat, simply to escape the empty house. I am greeted warmly by the manager, who is more than aware of Cesar's generous patronage over the years. Seated by the enormous window overlooking the street, I struggle with a letter I want to write to Cesar. As I stir my coffee, Cesar walks by. His gaze is averted. I jump up and race out onto the street. He is still visible, as he appears to be walking slowly. I am running and I reach him as he turns a corner. I step ahead of him forcing him to stop.

"Hello," says Cesar.

He is wearing dark glasses and his hair has grown, reaching the edge of the collar of his green cashmere winter coat. The flat belt of the coat hangs at the sides. I am aware of the change to his body. There is a marked weight gain. The nose on which the dark glasses are perched appears to be higher in colour. I can smell the alcohol on his breath. While I conduct this relentless inventory of my husband's appearance, my heart beats wildly.

"Darling, I was just writing a letter to you," I say to him.

"I had a cancellation so I am off early. I walked by the house," Cesar replies softly.

"I want you to take me to the place where you are staying." I have moved closer and draped my arms around him.

"All right," he says.

"Can we walk there?" I cannot believe that this is happening.

"No, it's far. I will wait at the hotel. Can you bring the car?"

"Promise." I search his face.

"Promise," he says and starts walking towards the hotel.

"I have left a bill and my coat behind," I tell him.

"I'll settle it. I will wait for you."

I drive into the front entrance of the Four Seasons Hotel on Yorkville Avenue. Cesar is standing there with my coat slung over one arm. There isn't a trace of madness in the air. He opens my door and asks me to let him drive, as I do not know the area where he lives. I slide to the passenger seat and watch him place his briefcase on the back seat, as he always does. Then he pulls out a package of cigarettes from his coat pocket and offers me one. He lights mine first and then his own.

I feel my entire body tingle with fearless excitement. He is permitting me to rescue him once again from an unknown world. I am on a mission, and Cesar is calm and exudes a peaceful air. There is no display of any excessive emotion on either side. It is a new conspiracy I have learned from Cesar. I will make a victorious call to Sharon tomorrow.

The entrance to an older Eastern European neighbourhood depresses me. Cesar takes both the subway and bus to reach here each day. Most of the large homes are rooming houses. The only saving grace is the proximity to the lake and the enormous maple trees lining the streets. I climb the steep flight of stairs, which is in fact a fire escape built years ago. When we reach the top, he opens the door and ushers me inside. I see the expanse of hardwood floor and the mattress on the floor and conceal my shock. The entrance is in fact a little kitchen. I automatically open the refrigerator and see containers of prepared food and the complete absence of fruit or vegetables. A large half-empty bottle of Scotch sits on the counter.

Cesar hangs up his coat and changes his clothes. I stay frozen in the tiny kitchen. Cesar reappears wearing a loose-fitting, worn, navy-blue tracksuit. I think of the large cedar closet stretched across the width of one wall in the basement of our home. It housed both our seasonal clothes but a large part is still filled with Cesar's clothes. He had told me that he gained weight and lost it frequently. So he had a fat and thin wardrobe. I had not believed him then, but now it has different meaning for me.

His manner is almost docile as he pours whiskey into a water glass.

"Sorry darling, there is no wine," he says to me. "It's my tree-top aviary. I sit on the deck feeling like an eagle."

I cannot respond. I am frightened by his apparent physical change and the soft almost exhausted tone of voice he uses. I turn from him and walk into the large room with a sloping roof and a window that looks at the tops of trees and remove my shoes. I lie on the mattress on the floor. It is an overwhelming moment for me, as though my entire body is fatigued. I can see Cesar sitting on a chair on the small landing outside. He has a glass of scotch and it lasts him half an hour. Then he gets up and comes back to the kitchen. I hear the sound of ice being removed from the tray. I get up and walk to him.

"Let's go home please," I remove the drink from his hand.

We have returned home together. I am in the kitchen cooking and Cesar is seated on a stool at the counter near me sipping herbal tea. I continue talking to him. I have been doing this since I brought Cesar home. Pages of my journal are also lying on the counter and I have permitted Cesar to read them. As I slice and stir, I present the most eloquent defence for our life together. Cesar's head is bowed, but he listens intently and sometimes lifts his face and nods. I tell him that medical diagnosis is a pursuit of the truth that he cannot evade. I tell him this is the only way I can test his love for me. There is no reference made to his involuntary commitment.

"I like the title of your journal," is how he first responds.

"Over the Edge?"

"You are not. You are a fortress. That is how my cousin Esperanza described you," he smiles at me.

"Can you save the unicorn?" I ask him pointedly.

Cesar makes a medical decision the next morning. He makes an appointment at the Clark Institute of Psychiatry with a psychiatrist who holds a chair in the study of depression. He asks me to join him. We walk into the glass-fronted building with the pleasant atrium lobby holding each other's hands. For some reason I find the environment to be almost cheerful and I am once again filled with hope. Cesar appears relaxed and he makes me laugh.

"We are all a little crazy, you know. Even the doctor may be crazy. We will never know."

We wait in the tasteful waiting room together. When the doctor opens the door and shakes hands with Cesar, it is with the professional respect each pays to the other. Cesar introduces him to me and I shake hands with him. There is a warm smile on his face as he explains that there will be three diagnostic sessions with Cesar and, on the second one, I will also attend with him. I feel an instinctual trust for him. He is not wearing a white coat but is elegantly dressed in monochromatic clothing. His manner is both self-assured and intelligent. He makes a graceful hand gesture to Cesar inviting him to enter the office first. The door shuts quietly behind them.

When it reopens an hour later, Cesar walks out. I study his face as we head towards the elevator.

"He is fine. He is competent," he tells me.

Cesar's announcement fills me with joy. I consider it a moment of a sweet victory. I believe that this is the tangible proof that my recent dalliance with the sacred text has proven to be successful. I have surrendered to the force of unwavering faith and have been rewarded.

The second appointment takes place within three days. We walk into the doctor's office together. The doctor seats us side by side and asks Cesar why he has deliberately omitted a critical detail in his medical history in the first session. Cesar has neglected to tell him about the involuntary commitment last month as well as his five-month disappearance from Canada. I feel as though a bolt of lightning rents the office. Cesar claims it slipped his mind — which is preposterous. The whole event is discussed and the doctor now takes notes on his laptop computer. Cesar's attitude shifts. He is subtly dismissive about the process. I cannot tell if he is baiting the psychiatrist or simply being evasive. I am asked to describe the behaviour twenty-four hours prior to the commitment. Cesar smiles at me encouragingly, adding to my confusion. I feel as though I am in school and asked to recite a poem whose lines I have forgotten. My head is pounding and my mouth feels dry because I am now afraid.

The third appointment, designed as the diagnostic one, is made again in my presence. There is enough evidence to indicate bipolar disorder with a condition called rapid cycling, where moods can swing between two polarities in a twenty-four-hour period. A regular therapist, medication, and a monthly blood test to ensure compliance is the recommendation of the doctor. Cesar displays no objection, folds both the prescription and the referral to the other doctor, and puts them in his pocket. There is a quiet goodbye. His ongoing care will be in the hands of the referred doctor.

"It is all right, it will be managed," says Cesar.

CHAPTER 13

TORONTO

SOME DAYS IT APPEARS THAT the Endhouse where Cesar and I continue to live and love has been occupied by another entity. The mood disorder has an unspoken presence, yet a power shift occurs. I have become a vigilante, Cesar a subject, and our beloved Endhouse a fortress of sorts, which also needs protection. I am mastering the art of observing Cesar in an unobtrusive fashion. The medication he takes does not create any outward change that I can detect, except that his large capacity for alcohol is now diminished. His therapist is female and he never discusses their sessions, except to assure me she is competent. I cannot invade this privacy and am simply grateful that his treatment needs are being fully met.

When I try to draw Cesar out to describe how he really feels during a mood swing, he is dismissive. On these occasions, I continue to be intimidated by his professional status. I am used to a husband who is a doctor, but the balance has shifted, as he is also a patient.

He alters his practice by working three days at his office and the other two at a busy clinic. He tells me it is a way of rebuilding his medical practice. On Saturday mornings he meditates at a Buddhist temple. He returns home relaxed and often high-spirited. I am familiar with his periodic forays into various spiritualities. When we first met, he had produced a copy of the Quran in English and told me that he had read it all. I had laughed and said he was doing better than I was. His regimen at the health club resumes and he loses the excess weight he had recently put on. My internal checklist appears to be covered with positive strokes. Like a pair of matched horses, we carry the weight of our union with great ease.

I have become a Sunday painter, as I find I need a medium other than language to express myself. My first attempt, acrylic on paper, leaves me fascinated with colours, the texture of brushes, and the abstract images I create. My studio is the large kitchen centre island and Cesar is my ardent supporter. He examines my abstract splashes of colours and makes psychological comments, as though the paintings are a type of Rorschach test. I am obsessed with light and struggle each Sunday to make it rise through colour. I am unaware that the exercise is in fact a metaphor for my entire existence. I am also using memory to see which colours hold me in their sway. Looking through our old honeymoon photograph albums, I try to recreate the red of Marrakech, with its shades of terracotta, in the middle of a white Canadian winter. I am also partial to the colour indigo blue and do figurative work, remembering the fake "blue man" in the Ourika Valley. The colours I am using belong to another environment where days and nights were filled with discovery and happiness. I am surprised at how they emerge with a will of their own. Yet I remain hesitant about the process and am not quite ready to return to my writing desk.

Cesar has told me that his blood test is conducted in the lab of the medical clinic he works at.

"My therapist receives them once a month. So you see, I am being monitored," he tells me to reassure me that all is well.

"It is very convenient, and so is the location. I often have lunch at the Mexican restaurant across the street from the clinic. Join me one day?"

When I do a few days later, and see a small group of nurses eating at another table, he waves to them merrily.

I AM SEATED AT THE dining table and paying bills. I am now directly involved in our financial life. When Cesar's salary is deposited into the bank, I calculate his tax portion and make a deposit into a separate account that is not touched. Cesar's income has almost shot back to what it was and our future is becoming secure again. We have lost our second home, a few paintings, and my investment account, but we have started to address this with humour rather than loss. Another change has also begun to take place. After a few months, there are days now when I go to my study, pull out the journal, and start to rearrange it in narrative form. Hesitancy marks this exercise as I wait for my confidence to reappear.

I notice a change in Cesar in the evenings. He seems to be slightly lethargic and his capacity for alcohol seems diminished.

"Are there side-effects to your medications?" I ask one evening.

"Sometimes a bit of stomach cramps. Nothing serious," his reply is short.

"Are you sure?"

"Yes."

He telephones me the next afternoon from his office and tells me not to cook. He is taking me out for dinner and to catch a film afterwards.

We are seated in a romantic alcove in Sotto Sotto on Avenue Road. It resembles the interior of a cave and is plastered with fat candles dripping wax with artful precision. Cesar orders a bottle of wine and his mood is soft and pleasing. I am giddy with pleasure, for the evening has succeeded in finally chasing away the turmoil of the past eight months. We are back together, gliding in a recovery zone. The conversation between us is animated and we share a meal, feeding each other. I see the light in Cesar's eyes dart and quiver with a sharpness that carries an old and seductive familiarity. The film we choose at the Cumberland Theatre is in the suspense genre. We discuss it when we return home and Cesar points out a few clues in the plot that I remain confused about. His analytical skills are dazzling and my admiration for him soars.

Cesar returns home one evening and comments that his visits to his therapist are quite boring and perhaps they will end soon. He tells me this at the front door, as he gives me a large bunch of roses. The roses are the colour of Marrakech, pale salmon with bursts of coral at the tips of petals.

"Oh! I love them. I am going to try and paint them." I take them to the kitchen.

"Of course you will. You see, you are in recovery." Cesar winks at me.

I have come down from my study and set up my easel on the kitchen counter. I have broken with the Sunday painting regimen. It is Tuesday and my work on the book fills me with a deep sense of unease, as I feel that the story is incomplete. I bring the vase of roses from the dining room and set it down on the counter. The fully opened lushness of the roses is marked by a suspended fragility because the drying base of the petals can detach any second and float to the ground. Even a breath of air can create this state. This suspended state defines my thoughts these days, and I wish to capture this in my painting. I mix white into orange pigment on the palette and draw boldly with the brush. When I look up, Cesar's photograph, which rests against a kitchen window ledge, distracts me. I took it myself a few years ago. He is seated under a canopy of trees on the island. It is a close-up, where the dappled sunlight throws a shadow on his features. Half his face is lit and the other half shaded. The expression in his eyes almost matches the lighting effect. I now see this photograph, which I used to consider simply artistic, to be a true portrait of his life.

It takes another two weeks for the predictable order of our lives to shift. Cesar starts to get up earlier than usual in the mornings. Often I see notes on the kitchen counter, always with the signature heart drawn on them, informing me that he is out walking catching the sunrise. Then there are nights when his sleep is so sound that I feel I could dance on his spine and he would not wake up. When I bring this to his attention, he reassures me, saying that the medication he is on has an effect on his body rhythm.

The snowstorm starts late one night. It turns into a blizzard and I am wakened by the sounds of a car struggling close to the house — whining brakes and churning tires. I sit up and turn on my bedside lamp. Cesar is lying on his stomach fast asleep. I stroke the side of his face turned to my side. He does not stir. Even his breathing is so shallow that I can barely hear it. It is a dead sleep. It frightens me and for the first time I want to know what is responsible for it. I turn off the light and leave the bedroom. Entering the spare bedroom, I close the door softly behind me. Cesar's briefcase is lying on the edge of the bed. From three feet away I look at it with the same trepidation as if a snake were curled on the edge of the bed.

Eventually, I open it and pull out two large vials, almost full of pills. Cesar has not taken his medications for two weeks. I feel as though he has plunged a knife in my heart.

I am brushing away the tears flooding my eyes as I empty the briefcase on the bed. I read every piece of paper I find and check all the calls on his cellphone. It reveals a number that he dials regularly. My sixth sense tells me that it is not the name of a patient. When I scan his appointment book, I cannot find it anywhere. It is a Portuguese name, a female one. I pick up the briefcase and go downstairs to the kitchen. I will stay here until Cesar wakes up a few hours later and appears before me.

I watch the shrubs and trees in our garden imprisoned by sheets of ice. It is dawn and the entire street is buried under mounds of snow. I have struggled to push open the front door only to find a mountain of snow in front. I feel that the house itself has become a frozen tomb where hope has shrivelled within seconds because I have acted like Pandora and opened the box. My judgment is rational and I am now calmer than I ever imagined I could be. However, somewhere in the recess of my mind I hear Albanoni's Adagio playing repeatedly.

You are vanquished, I say to myself, and your enemy is bigger than life itself.

CESAR ENTERS THE KITCHEN IN his dressing gown and halts at the door. He sees his briefcase lying in the centre of the kitchen island counter.

"Did I leave it here?" he asks.

"No I brought it down. I now know everything." My back is turned to him. I am standing by the window looking out.

"I see," he replies gently. "Darling, let me tell you a few things."

"No," I turn around to face him, "you have broken your promise, and I cannot deal with this madness. I don't care about the woman you telephone either."

"Oh God! No! She has just helped me at the lab, that's all." Cesar's face is ashen.

We have spent an hour in the living room, seated before the green marble fireplace where we were married. We are both wearing identical dressing gowns we had bought for each other. This is the only intimacy that is visible, because I am seated on the armchair, and Cesar is sitting on the sofa. Outside the snowplough is clearing the street and releasing cars. This is what I want. I want a powerful force to sweep away the ice encasing my heart.

"Why?" I say finally.

Cesar smiles, crinkling his eyes. It is a familiar smile meant to stroke me with his indulgent love and also to dismiss an absurd question. My eyes are hard, my mouth quivers to suck the tip of the cigarette I have just lit. My habitual response to my husband's beautiful smile is missing. Cesar watches me intently in silence but I do not maintain eye contact with him. He then begins to talk eloquently and builds a skilful argument justifying his actions. It is an arbitrary decision where Cesar does not intend to have drugs alter the chemistry of a mood when he feels ecstatic and alive. He loathes the medication and is not even certain if the diagnosis is correct. He has manipulated the lab technician to assist in falsifying the results of his blood test in order to mislead his own therapist completely. He has done this with both knowledge and cunning. With a confident air, he says that he has successfully subverted his course of treatment. This deception, he tells me, is vital for both personal and professional reasons. He uses his mind to make his living and has done it successfully for years.

This confession, I know, could have been lifted from the pages of the book written by the bipolar doctor I have read. The disease is Cesar's desired companion and his willingness to expose me to its deadly hazard shatters my concept of his love for me. The judgment that results in rejecting treatment is a symptom of the disease itself. I am no longer his wife but an informed partner. I am repelled by all that Cesar admits to, and wish to run screaming from the horror he reintroduces to my life. I get up from the armchair and then cannot move. Cesar also rises, but it is I who have taken the first step. It is away from him.

I AM SIGNING A DOCUMENT at my lawyer's office. Cesar is seated next to me and he will sign this document as well. I make a mistake; I have used my previous married name. Cesar signs the same document without making a mistake.

I get up and whisper, "I am sorry," to no one in particular.

"It's all right darling," says Cesar, reaching for my hand and kissing it.

The two lawyers look on with disbelief.

I am racing down the corridor away from the office. My reflection in the mirrored elevator is alien even to myself. One line from the document I have just signed has changed my life. Cesar and I will live separately and apart. Two synonymous words like beads dangling off a broken necklace are tattooed not on the skin, but on our hearts. I have chosen not to witness the disease ever again, and have tucked love away like soiled clothes in a hamper. I have even betrayed my marriage vows to live with my husband eternally.

Once again, the house is like a museum and I am the curator. Cesar has arranged to have his personal belongings delivered to him. He has no desire to take anything from the house. He does this with great delicacy. I am living alone with the evidence of eleven years of our life together. Even his silver hairbrush lies on top of the cabinet in the bedroom. He told me that I polished it regularly, something he would not do. I am aware that this is his way of leaving a part of himself behind. I have collected photographs of Cesar and put them away in a drawer. My writing desk is clear. There are no books and articles on manic depression in sight. Some mornings when I open the front door to collect the newspaper, I see a cellophane cone of roses lying on the porch. I always bring them in and arrange them in a vase but I do not telephone Cesar.

I search deep within myself daily to examine my notion of compassion. Sometimes I engage a friend I am with, to hear other views, without revealing what has transpired between Cesar and me. An element of guilt still resides in me. My inability to accept Cesar's decision not to take the prescribed treatment for his disease has resulted in lives now being lived separately. I have also chosen another force to justify my abandonment of Cesar. It comes from chapter 17 of the Koran, titled "Israelites," in section 4, titled "Moral Precepts." The injunction declaring the abandoning of a soul for a just cause is as haunting as it is consoling. In my heart, Cesar is part of my soul, yet his lack of responsibility in refusing medical treatment has become an unbearable act of betrayal.

Day by day, I master the art of living alone and become adept at it. I plan a trip to Europe. I choose Italy deliberately, as this is where Cesar was planning to take me for my birthday.

Walking though the streets of Rome, I am drawn to the Coliseum, where I feel as though I am a gladiator who has lost a vital organ while protecting myself. After a week in Rome, I move to a friend's hilltop home in the Italian countryside and write and walk among strangers. In the evenings when I gaze at the mountains of Abruzzi, I feel that they are my guardians. I stop thinking about Cesar using the meditation technique he had taught me when we first met. I note with great irony that it is successful, but when I go to Florence and stand in the Uffizi Gallery before Botticelli's painting, "Primavera," I break down and write a card to Cesar. I write one line. "I am here without you."

CHAPTER 14

TORONTO

I AM WALKING HOME FROM the bank situated in my neighbourhood. Behind my dark glasses, I hide from the world. I have betrayed two vital causes in my life and feel as though I have lost the core of my morality. I am offended at myself. I have taken a loan against the value of the house. This will give me time to work on my new book without worrying about expenses. The decision to keep the house is based on the notion that in a shifting world, it is the Endhouse that is my best friend. When I enter the house, I feel that my life history is spread throughout the rooms. It is also my oasis and I will never part with it. However, taking the loan makes me feel as though I have dug up the foundations of the house. The second betrayal is to my art. I have set the novel aside, and am working on a new book, a commercial venture. I have made this sacrifice to win the missing part of the house back. I regard it as a business decision and a chess move. The castle is in jeopardy but I will flank it with the horse.

I have not seen Cesar now for nine months and am incapable of adjusting to his absence. He lives close by in a high-rise apartment building, but our paths have not crossed. Once, from a distance, I saw a man wearing a dark green overcoat and I followed him only to discover it was not Cesar. I felt like a child who believes that rainbows can be caught. However, the incident had a short life. My biggest secret is that I sense his presence daily in the house. Although his clothes and photographs are missing, the angle of the shower in the bathroom and the position of the chess pieces on the board are exactly where they were placed in our last unfinished game. Sometimes the telephone rings and there is silence. In this silence, I know that Cesar breathes and lives. Words, which flowed in abundance between us, have been outlawed. Occasionally, the roses are also left on the porch. There is no set order to when they appear, so I arrange them and place them on the night table on his side of the bed. His silver hairbrush still lies on the top of the lacquer cabinet in the bedroom.

Leon is a new friend who walks into my life. He lives in the neighbourhood. Our link is Marrakech, where he was born and raised in until he was a teenager, and where I went on my honeymoon. Leon is a loner, but has an intriguing spiritual and holistic philosophy. His artistic temperament and his unconventional behaviour make him a safe companion to be with. We go for rambles through the city, spend hours talking, and sometimes Leon will cook Moroccan cuisine for me. Most encounters with him fill me with positive energy and strength. The only romance we create is built on ideas and a respect for each other's life work. It is a platonic friendship. What I am singularly unaware of is that he is preparing me for the next hurdle in my life. He has not returned to the country that he left as a young man and I pick up both his nostalgia and wonderment for the lost Marrakech of his childhood and convert this into poetry.

I write these poems after we part and I return home. I call them the Sahara Suite poems. Sometimes I will recite one for him, and he is transfixed. Then he simply nods, as though he has given me sanction to enter his private world. I have never been able to gauge his complete approval, but he does strengthen my poetic skills. I feel that Cesar would approve of his presence completely, as Leon fills the empty chambers of my life.

I edit my new manuscript over the summer seated outdoors in a neighbourhood café. I have broken with an old tradition, and left my study at home to work outdoors. The café is situated next to a small park and waterfall. Cumberland Park is filled with carefully selected wildflowers, slabs of black rock that glitter in the sunlight because they are embedded with minerals. The central structure is a huge rock built of Canadian Shield granite and people lie on it to catch the sun and survey the action on the street. The waterfall is constructed of a long steel assembly spanning the width of the park. The water descends in straight lines and one feels as if one is seated next to a wall of water. Sometimes I sense Cesar's presence through the wall of water and wonder why my imagination works overtime. Often Leon walks by and shares a coffee with me and then saunters off.

The day the white legal envelope arrives, I have finished editing the book. I hold the certificate with the embossed seal and study the names on it. A single line of words has dissolved my marriage with Cesar. I know that the intensity of our years of loving can never disappear. I imagined that this document would appear accompanied by the drum roll of a firing squad. I walk to the garden and reach the white rose I had planted for Cesar years ago. I clip a tightly furling bud and place it in the envelope along with the divorce decree. The envelope is placed in an old filing cabinet lying in the basement. It goes into a file marked Cesar, which is filled with dozens of cards he has given to me. That night I am unable to sleep and realize that I am testing a new space in my mind. This space has been created by a ravaging storm that forces the debris of a particular life away. Yet the glory of that same life is resplendent in memory. For the first time in my life, I am completely alone.

I AM SEATED OUTDOORS AT Sassafras, with my friend Evanthia. We are having brunch on Saturday and I allow myself once again to be swept away by her vivacity. Younger than me, she displays a sagacity that is startling and a rollicking sense of humour. Light sparkles in her dark eyes and her strong face, framed by swirling strands of black hair, reminds me of a racing stallion. Like Leon, she is a new friend, but one who showers me with carefree affection. Her Greek heritage lends her a muse-like aspect, and her intuitive forces are sharp and full of prophetic utterances. In this lighthearted space of relaxation, as we still pick at our food, a premonition slowly begins to make its presence felt. I cannot decide what it is; part apprehension and part nostalgia? I am talking to Evanthia but my thoughts fly to the holy man in Marrakech who had sent a drink for my protection. This memory is unsettling years later and I wonder if he knew that Cesar had a mental disease. Had the guide Khadim been privy to it when he had taken Cesar on our last night in Marrakech to some local healer? Suddenly, I have an overwhelming desire to speak to Cesar because I feel that pieces of a puzzle seem to be locking into place.

I go inside the restaurant and find a phone. I dial Cesar's number and hear his message on the answering machine.

"I wish to inform all my patients that they must consult their family doctors for another referral. I have been diagnosed with lung cancer and will not be practising medicine." Cesar's voice is sombre and almost unrecognizable.

Shock wrenches my heart, compassion and fear devastate me to the point where I fly out of the restaurant and collapse in Evanthia's embrace. Her dark eyes turn grave.

"I need to go home," I say to her. "I cannot bear this."

"I know," she replies.

I have called every hospital in Toronto and have found Cesar.

"Hello." He is on the phone.

"What is it? I just called the office. I am so sorry." I am sobbing on the phone.

"I have lung cancer. I will know by this evening if I am elected for lung surgery."

"I am beaming out luck and good vibrations. I am so sorry."

"I know," he cuts me off. "I cannot talk now."

I am certain that Cesar will contact me and when he does not, a sense of oppression enters my life, and I am restless in the house. The weight of my past history makes me feel that I hover on the threshold of some other life without entering it. After a month of not hearing any news of Cesar, I make a decision one August afternoon.

"I will come by this evening with the papers. It is an excellent time to sell," says Monty, who is a real estate agent and a good friend.

"I will be here."

I CAN HEAR THE DOORBELL ring while I pull weeds out of the rose beds. A family of raccoons, perched on the fence, examine me solemnly. Leon had mistakenly placed almonds at intervals of the fence and the raccoons return regularly to look for them. I can see reproach in the black-ringed eyes of the animals I call my sentinels. My neighbour Consuelo is alarmed at their appearance and warns me not to feed them again. I, on the other hand, feel they are a welcome addition to my solitary domain. The sale of the house and investment of the money will give me an income to live on with ease. I know that I clung to the house feeling that familiarity was safety. It has also been a way of enshrining the history of Cesar's and my love. Safety is robbing my life of movement and the desire to be propelled forward becomes stronger than ever. I am tired of being an archivist.

Monty has walked outside to join me. He has left the papers inside on the kitchen table. I turn around and see his blue eyes clouded with anxiety. He has been a cherished guest in my home and is dealing with his own memories.

"I am not ready," I tell him.

"Don't worry. Let's just go for dinner."

"All right, I will change." I am grateful for his sensitivity.

We walk down Hazelton Avenue, meandering through Yorkville, arriving at Prego Della Piazza by the church. Michael, the owner, greets me warmly as so much history is tucked into his restaurant. Cesar has left his imprint as well. He would lunch here in the summertime, often puffing on a cigar. After dinner, Monty asks whether I would like dessert.

"What I would like is your listing agreement. I am ready to list the house for sale." I shock him and myself.

"Sure?"

"Without a doubt," I say, drawing a pen out of my purse.

"Congratulations! Now let's look for your new home tomorrow." He smiles at me.

When strangers file into my home imagining their own lives in it, I walk away allowing Monty to answer their questions. I roam in the neighbourhood looking for a new home, and find it on the first day. I go back after three days and see it again. One of the city's landmark buildings, the Colonnade, is refurbishing its apartments. The sleek and modernized interiors and the enormous living space, ending in a wall of ceiling to floor windows, appeal to me instantly. The eighth-floor location with a long vista down to the museum and rows of exclusive shops makes me feel as though I am perched like an eagle over a prize. The large expanse of bare walls and the gleaming wooden floors are devoid of anyone's history. Here, I feel that I can begin my life again. It is the first time that I will create a home simply for myself. I stand in the middle of the empty apartment and think about colours. And know with certainty that I will choose the rose-tinted terracotta hue of Marrakech for my bedroom.

The house sells within a week, as Monty knew it would. Its Georgian charm has been preserved aesthetically and the location is superb. Agents bring flocks of people to see it. The new owner is a single father of a teenaged son. The son is a musician and I feel that the Endhouse needs to be filled with different music. It is a good omen. The pace of my life accelerates with a welcoming speed. I arrange for movers and check my possessions. I now desire a portable life based on necessity and dispose of the entire contents stored in the basement. From the filing cabinet, I collect two folders holding pages of an unfinished novel

I finally throw away the guest folder from the Hotel La Mamounia in Marrakech, which I had kept for fourteen years. The possibility of ever returning seems remote. It was the playground of a marriage that no longer exists. I fill a small carton with all the photograph albums and loose photographs. I imagine that this is where my life with Cesar will hide for a long time. The moving van pulls out of my street. I follow in my car and have no desire to look back.

I AM DRINKING COFFEE, SITTING on a marble window ledge of the living room in my new home. Instead of raccoons and trees, I watch the street below me teeming with early morning traffic. Behind me, the huge and open living space is flanked by a black marble counter, which separates the open kitchen. I have always lived in homes where doors separate spaces. Here, all the living spaces flow into each other and my entire life is revealed when the front door is opened. There is no mystery, only a wide-open disclosure. There is comfort in this arrangement as it reflects my inner rhythm. I am open to a new life. My study is the space where the apartment curves and creates a niche. I have lined the walls of this niche with rows of glass book-shelves and my writing desk fits underneath. I will now write with a huge window to my left. Although my garden is missing, two pots of white orchids sit on the ledge. I examine them daily and consider them a horticultural challenge. Instead of wrens, sometimes pigeons fly close by outside. Their wings flapping dangerously close to the glass elicits my concern just as the hungry raccoons did.

I AM HOLDING MY FRESHLY published book, *Tea and Pomegranates*. It is small in size and the cover startles me with its romantic appeal. The artist has designed an arched window, complete with an antique wooden ledge. It complements the world I have created inside the book. I write Cesar's name on the first page and put it away. The reviews have been laudatory and I am booked for public appearances for a whole month leading right up to Christmas. The new home and the excitement of having a successful new book keep me busy. It is also a humbling experience for me as I am not comfortable with praise but I cannot resist visiting my local Indigo bookstore to see how my book is displayed. When I receive copies of my taped interviews, I am amazed by the confidence I project. I buy new clothes and change my hairstyle. I hang a small chandelier in my bedroom and have a dimmer switch installed so the lighting creates a baroque pattern on the ceiling. It no longer resembles the room where I slept with Cesar. My life acquires a glossier patina because I am inspired to use a different sense of style and create a new rhythm in my life. With each day, I feel that my life is becoming lighter. The investment company that handles my account deposits a monthly income and I can easily live on it.

I am sleeping on the new bed. I have banished imprints of the weight of mine and Cesar's bodies, but still sleep on the same side of the bed. This side was dictated years ago by Cesar who chose the left side. You are my right hand he had told me, disarming me with his charm. It was an intimacy that followed us on vacations and in hotel rooms. On this night, I shift to the left side of the bed, intent on making yet another change. It is a restless night of tossing and turning and dreaming fitfully. When I wake up in the morning, get out of bed, and head for the living room, I look around, convinced that I am looking for a lost object. My movements are slow as I make a cup of tea and then I remember the dream I had last night.

I am on a mission to find a lost object. I cannot be certain what it is but I remember my actions. Most of my movements are outdoors. I could have been at our home on Manitoulin Island or on holiday somewhere with Cesar. The missing item could have been a piece of jewellery or a book. I am alone and searching, but there is a frantic element to my search. I see a list of places in my hand and know that I am travelling. There is hammering on doors that do not open and folded maps that I cannot seem to read. I even remember digging in the earth with my bare hands. There is a wind blowing incessantly and trees rustle close by. The trees are in a long straight line. The reason why I have not instantly recalled my dream as I normally do is because I have woken up not on the left side of the bed but right in the middle. Although it is mysterious, there is also an edge of excitement to the dream.

The rest of the day is busy. There is a book launch for me at the University of Toronto. It has been organized by the Pakistani High

Commissioner in Ottawa and is a curiously formal affair. When I stand at the podium to read, I wonder if Cesar will make an appearance. I had mailed a copy of the book and the invitation to the clinic where he had worked months ago assuming that mail was forwarded for at least six months. When I arrive at the reception hall, I am shown a magnificent arrangement of flowers. They had been delivered in the afternoon. I quickly rip open the envelope of the small, attached card with trembling fingers. The flowers are not from him.

Later, I return home with the flowers and a few friends who are still in a mood to celebrate.

"What is the next book?"

"I don't know as yet," I reply honestly.

"I thought authors had books raging in their bellies."

"There is nothing in my belly," I say.

The two manuscript folders lie on top of the front hall closet and I have ignored them. Nothing will persuade me to look at the past because I have embraced the future. I toy with the idea of inserting both Leon and Evanthia into a novel set in Yorkville, where I have lived for seventeen years. Their lives hold immense fascination for me and this fascination invariably piques my creativity. This quality is like the embers scattered in the hearth of a dying fireplace. A sudden infusion of a combustible substance can turn the embers into a roaring fire. This is how I view my creative output and the birth of all books. I will simply wait for this to occur.

"Did you ever drink the champagne I bought?" Monty is asking on the telephone.

"I can't have it alone."

"Yes you can. It is called a private celebration. If you cork it well, it can stay for a day or two."

I AM OPENING THE CHAMPAGNE late in the afternoon the next day. I was taught by Cesar years ago not be frightened of the cork. He always used a pair of oversized yellow rubber gloves and gently eased the cork in a circular motion. The cork would pop out without flying to the ceiling. I have always kept the gloves and pull them on. I ease the cork in the motion taught to me. My shoulders stiffen with fright but the cork pops out with ease. I pour some in a glass flute and cork the bottle with the spare cork as instructed by Monty. I stand before the bookshelf and salute the new book lying on the middle shelf. When I raise the glass to my lips, the telephone on my desk rings. I lift the cordless telephone with the other hand and move away from the desk.

"Hello, I am calling from Dr. Jones' office. As he has died, I want to know where to send Dr. Cesar's records. His office number is not working."

"This is not his residence number," I reply. "Please call the clinic. They will have a contact address for him."

It is an awkward moment. When the telephone rings again, I have just taken my first sip of champagne.

"He died at the end of August."

I AM LYING ON THE carpet near my desk. The carpet pressed close to my face feels damp and I can see shards of glass around me. I am now a stranger to all that I feel. The news that Cesar has died has made me weep an entire life away and all this has taken place alone, without a witness. When I stand up I am uncertain whether a great burden has been lifted or that I have suffered the most immeasurable loss that I can imagine.

There are days when I cannot decipher my true feelings. Cesar's death, almost three months ago, occurred on the day that I listed the house for sale. His cremation and lack of funeral service or obituary was his own wish. I have been deprived of the finality of his death, and more than anything in the world I wish to give him a funeral. I keep my secret closely guarded.

I have decided to leave the new home and life I have just created for two months. It is not possible for anyone to understand that I wish to perform a ritual in a foreign country simply to acknowledge Cesar's death. My mourning for Cesar will only end when I have done this. It will be the final release from all memory. I arrange the trip and leave within two weeks, taking a manuscript and two objects in a small blue felt bag. I have also opened the sealed carton of photograph albums and pulled out four photographs. Finally, I have understood the symbolism of the haunting dream where I dug out earth with my bare hands.

The overnight flight is across the Atlantic and while others sleep in the plane, I am writing in a small notebook with a maroon spine. It has been given to me as a travelling gift. During the journey it becomes my companion, even when I fall asleep the notebook is in my lap. I change airports in Paris and board another flight. Three hours later when it circles over a small airport, I am filled with a wild excitement because I feel Cesar's presence very strongly. After landing, I walk down the ramp to the tarmac. The noonday sun caresses my face and I begin to relax. The people around me have benign and smiling faces. I accompany the porter carrying my luggage outdoors and see the barren surroundings, a line of ancient taxis, and hear the throaty vowels of the foreign language swirling around me, and I pray fervently that I have made the right decision to come to this completely alien environment. It is a land of strangers and my only link with them is a fourteen-year-old history.

CHAPTER 15

✿ Marrakech, 2006

I AM SITTING IN THE square leather armchair facing the massive floral arrangement in front of me. There could easily be two hundred coral-tinted roses shooting from the blue ceramic urn. The gigantic crystal chandelier overhead has a similar air of opulence. The lobby of the grand Hotel La Mamounia is unchanged. I am acutely conscious that resting within the silence of its glistening interior, both time and personal histories are suspended.

The photograph held lightly in my fingers was taken fourteen years ago and when I show it to the concierge at the entrance, he asks me to wait until he can make some inquiries. I cannot decipher his expression but take him for his word. It is enough that I have returned to Marrakech and reached the only place I am familiar with.

The apartment I have rented is a five-minute taxi ride away. It flanks the corner of a wide road studded by a palatial convention centre, new hotels, chic pavement cafés, and lush greenery. Looking down its length, one can see the snow-capped range of Atlas Mountains rise majestically. This part of Marrakech bears no resemblance to any place I have previously visited during my honeymoon with Cesar fourteen years ago. Only the monochromatic colour of all the structures identify it as being the environs of a developing Marrakech.

Here, I think, I can live in complete anonymity for a month and accomplish my mission. My accommodations belong to an international banker who had not only described it well on the telephone but is delighted to rent it to a writer who has come to do some writing. His ingratiating mannerisms on my arrival are overwhelming so I collect the keys and escape, pleading jetlag. Within minutes, I unpack my bags and walk outdoors to hail a taxi to take me to the Hotel La Mamounia.

The sensation of having floated into a turn-of-the-century film set returns with the same hypnotic lure. A mixture of Art Deco and Moorish craftsmanship is how I described Morocco fourteen years ago. The theatrically attired doormen of the hotel positioned at the pillared entrance seem uncannily familiar. Their mahogany faces becoming pointers on a map. I have returned to the salmon and gold wedge of North Africa, as though a honey-sweet slice of cantaloupe slithers down my throat. Yet now I have come on a mission without any surety of what the outcome will be. All I know is that I am completely bereft of tourist defences and alone.

The comforting folds of the armchair and the silent contemplation of the forest of roses in front of me confine me to a meditative space. So when the sound of an exchange somewhere in the lobby floats towards me, I slowly turn around. The tall figure incongruously clad in a beige winter jacket and a baseball cap moving towards me makes me rise. I move towards him, wondering if the concierge was successful.

I utter his name and he looks down at me from his great height. I can see the look of inquiry on his face and am certain he has not recognized me. Yet he acts as though he has, while I study his face in shock. It is as though fourteen years have become the edge of a surgeon's scalpel. The flesh from his cheeks, missing and marked by deep furrows and one side, is more depressed than the other. His complexion is darker than I remember. Glasses with thin round frames cover his eyes and the hair is close-cropped, revealing a sprinkling of grey at the sides. I want to see pages of my manuscript dance off his face. In fact, what I imagine is that he will simply step out of the fourteen-year-old photograph lying on top of my handbag. The photograph shows him standing before the rented car holding the door open for me.

Cesar had taken the photograph.

Khadim of the clownish black suit, shock of dark waving hair, and dazzling smile is nowhere in existence. For a moment, I panic wondering if the hotel has made a mistake.

I lead him to the chairs and he chooses the one closest to me. He immediately inquires about my husband, the doctor, which changes my mind about his not recognizing me. There is a passive neutrality to his manner, as though somewhere in the recesses of his mind memory slowly uncoils.

I tell him that Cesar has died and a gentle sigh escapes from his lips and an expression of empathy moves across his face. Then I add that I have come to work on my book and want to ask him a few questions. He offers to take me to a peaceful place.

I follow him out of the hotel where he collects a bicycle and we walk along a road that flanks the minaret of the Koutoubia Mosque. It is not until half an hour later, seated on the rooftop terrace of Café de France nearby and looking down on the massive public square called Djemaa el Fna that I question his choice of a peaceful place.

This is Khadim, the guide, in whose hands Cesar would press folded one-hundred-dollar bills. He showed us the city of Marrakech for a period of five days and had not only insinuated himself into our honeymoon but also into my writing. He had invited us his home for dinner and we had accepted. When we left Marrakech, he shyly presented me with a cylinder of white hyacinths. Sitting in the shaded alcove of the terrace and watching him pour mint tea for me, he has no idea that he exists in the pages of a book that has sat for fourteen years in a drawer.

He has no way of knowing that I recorded the words and actions of our bizarre ménage à trois simply to move a narrative along in which I questioned unexamined parts of my spiritual life. His nationality converted him into a prototype for a certain theme. Yet in a prophetic way, I now feel that it is more than an artistic sleight of hand. A careworn pensiveness to Khadim's features no longer resembles the vibrant younger man who had impressed Cesar with a smattering of history learned by rote about the sites he took us to. Cesar was convinced that he appeared to be a cut above the pack of wolves masquerading as guides. Perhaps the badly cut yet quaintly formal black suit and neat white shirt lent him an air of respectability. Cesar appointed him as our de facto guardian during the rambles into souks and, in fact, had left everything in his capable hands.

I remember my resistance to his presence and the discomfort that I often stifled during the honeymoon. Yet the national language of Arabic, and the predatory response of the local community to foreigners, was a formidable barrier for both of us. Cesar's French, better than my schoolgirl rendition of disconnected vocabulary, was handy but not enough to communicate effectively. So I learned to stifle the touch of discomfort that I experienced in Khadim's presence. I also remember the tinge of judgment in his watchful eyes. Beneath the almost servile courtesy, his eyes betrayed him. They could easily have been the eyes of a predator, and sometimes I detected a hint of lechery as well.

When I aired this notion to Cesar, he laughingly dismissed it by saying, you are a beautiful woman darling, of course men will look at you. Now this subdued and rapidly aging man before me appeared to be someone else.

Hours go by as we chat about Morocco and Canada and he points out landmarks along the skyline of the city. I am so relaxed in his presence that a sense of euphoria seizes me. Cesar's ghost is dancing around us. I am not ready to talk about my book but marvel at the ease with which I communicate with him.

He exudes a peculiar familiarity that has a soothing effect, and speaks English with a studied precision. He is wearing cheap clothing with an air of dignity. His trousers are paper-thin and the beige sweater has seen better days. The tan baseball cap and the dark glasses give him the air of a man who has adopted touches of American culture. When I inquire about his family, he informs me that he has married and divorced three times and has an estranged son who lives in France. A melancholic note enters his voice and I have a rush of sympathy for him.

The wave of humanity beneath us in the Djemaa el Fna throngs around jugglers, musicians, snake charmers, and storytellers. The hypnotic tattoo of drums and cymbals spirals upwards to the terrace. The square has a visceral quality as though the city of Marrakech is split open to reveal its throbbing heart. The veins and arteries are the paths winding into the labyrinthine souks spread around it. The blood supply comes from the tourist wallet as clean and crisp dollar bills flow into outstretched hands.

Yet the medieval ambience hovering around exudes a power that seems to mock the newly installed mobile phone booths and vigilant tourist police vans dotted in the great square. Men wearing floor-length hooded robes called djellabas sit as ancient custodians on the paved floor. Their expressions are remote and unfathomable as they examine the flashes of exposed tourist skin.

The streaks of sunlight recede to herald a flame-coloured sunset and I am mesmerized by the beauty of the city. We sit quietly watching the transformation of Marrakech and the questions I want to ask Khadim remained unuttered. The first awareness of sleep deprivation makes me ask for a taxi. He leads me down to the square shielding me from a sea of people by walking ahead and then gives me his mobile phone number. I sense that he wants to escort me home but is trapped by his bicycle, and I ask if it is convenient to contact him again.

"Certainly," he replies, enunciating the word with great clarity.

He then switches to Arabic and gives the taxi driver my address and opens the door for me. When I am seated inside, he bends down and simply offers his hand. I clasp it lightly and wave with the other one. He smiles, transforming his face completely, a hint of the old Khadim tugging at the contours of his face. We say goodbye.

The taxi shoots forward in the maze of traffic pouring out of the square. Tourist buses, calèches, cyclists, and taxis converge from three directions. The fumes of diesel make me lightheaded, as does the notion that the man I have spent time with seems to have comforted me in some indefinable way. Is it because my memory of him is associated with Cesar's presence? Yet I know that I am in a country where courtesy to foreigners is zealously entrenched in social encounters, as it invariably leads to lucrative compensation. Khadim, true to his calling of a guide, wears this courtesy as a mantle of grace integrated effortlessly into all his mannerisms. However, although I treat the encounter as being social, I wonder if he views it as being professional. This is the world of illusions and mirages and all that the outsider is capable of seeing is an imagined reflection. My landlord, the banker, has cautioned me about this and warned me that Morocco is not Europe. He has also warned me that it is not possible to have friendships with the locals. I am offended by his comment.

I walk through the apartment chilled by stone floors. The walls are lined with Moroccan ceramic plates and garish paintings. The living room has a massive television set and stereo system and two couches. Through the violet-tinged dusk, the front window displays an exotic vista of palm trees and terracotta buildings dwarfed by the outline of the minaret of the Koutoubia in the distance. I have changed continents and surroundings with lightning speed without permitting myself to question anything. The faded blue folder containing the fourteen-year-old manuscript sits next to my computer. It is my incomplete novel. In the bedroom, a felt cloth bag fastened by a drawstring lies on the night table. I lie across the bed and clasp this bag to my chest just as the call to prayer echoes from the opened window. Once again, there is apprehension about being in this foreign country by myself.

The telephone rings. Nobody knows that I am in Marrakech so I do not answer it. This is a new habit I have painstakingly acquired. I regard the telephone as a dangerous instrument with the potential to truncate life. That is how Cesar's death was announced to me two weeks ago in another continent. Lying on this bed in a strange apartment in Marrakech, I question my judgment about being here. Hearing the intrusive tones of the telephone, I fly backwards to the event that has brought me here. This act of revisiting is almost obsessive behaviour, where I search for errors in my judgment and then finally cling to the validity of a decision. I must smell, taste, and savour repeatedly until the event or situation becomes a blueprint stored in my mind. I often use this as a writing technique as well.

So I recreate the scene in my apartment in Toronto. As champagne bubbles exploded under my nose, a phone call had become an invisible body blow where I felt my heart collide against my ribcage. Later I find myself lying on the carpet unaware that hours have gone by. All I could remember is that when I knelt to pick up the glass I simply collapsed on the floor. When my swollen eye opened, I knew that the carpet under my face was damp with my tears. The sun had set and the apartment in Toronto had become shadowy while memory played cruel tricks.

Was it Cesar sitting on a couch holding a glass of scotch in one hand? Had I actually heard the ice cubes tinkling?

They burned your body, Cesar, and never informed me. I wept for hours. I had also realized that the day he died was the same day that I chose to list the Endhouse for sale. I kept reliving our first experience in the house. When it was purchased fifteen years ago and the keys delivered to us on a cold December evening, we both raced to the house. Four logs of wood sat in the fireplace. Cesar lit the fire instantly and within seconds, the unopened flue of the fireplace flooded the living room with smoke. We doused the fire with the bottle of champagne Cesar had brought with him. Then we made love on his green cashmere overcoat on the wooden floor. The smell of cashmere, wood smoke, and Cesar's sandalwood-based aftershave lotion burrowed itself into my olfactory memory. No other fragrance ever succeeded in replacing it.

I tortured myself wondering if in some telepathic fashion he knew of my decision and viewed the selling of our only haven the ultimate act of betrayal and so died in protest. Diagnosed with lung cancer, he permitted the removal of a lung but refused further treatment. Was he depressed when he made the decision or did he simply resort to his exquisite gallantry and decide to spare me all the pain? I listed the house for sale determined to make us both part with our best friend. I wanted to change the history sewn into a particular room of the house. It was the room where Cesar's physician's bag lying on the edge of the bed had became a Pandora's box late one night. Months later, guests slept in the room only to comment that they had never slept so peacefully. There is blood on the walls I wanted to tell them, but never did.

He chose a solo exit designed to halt our vivid history, which did not end even after a year-old separation. He never knew I recorded this life for years in an attempt to understand both of us. These were my field notes into our life.

THE WEDDING RING CESAR PLACED on my finger and the silver Tiffany hairbrush I gave him for our first wedding anniversary lie in the cloth bag lying across my chest. They have travelled from the top drawer of my bedroom cabinet in Toronto to Marrakech because I finally read something I kept hidden for years.

Later the same night when I heard of his death, I pulled out the blue file folder entitled "Moon over Marrakech." The pages were the only copy that existed and the print was light. When the first band of light poked through the bedroom blinds, I knew it was dawn. The pages scattered around me fluttered softly like the wings of doves. I felt that morning that I could be content for a lifetime to lie motionless surrounded by what I captured years ago.

The first seeds of Cesar's undetected mystery were sown in these pages. Before his death, Cesar was taken away from me by his mental illness. I calculated that after Cesar realized he was critically ill he stopped his contact deliberately. I was busy changing my life. There was a terrifying synchronicity to what was happening in our lives. The manuscript had a searing effect as well, for it carried the seed of a prophecy I could not seem to forget. This seed had its roots in the city of Marrakech in Morocco. I viewed it all as a life mystery then, as I was disinclined to step out of the charmed circle of my exotic honeymoon. This is how the decision was made to arrive here without informing anyone about my real objective and sudden travel plans.

I intend to give Cesar a burial in the olive garden of the Hotel La Mamounia by burying the two items I have brought with me. The garden was Cesar's personal oasis within the confines of the hotel. I plan to wander into the garden one day and do just that. In the shadow of my first night in Marrakech, I think that the burial of inanimate objects will be the ritual necessary for me to both salute and wave farewell to Cesar.

By some improbable stroke of luck, I have found Khadim as well. I have all the skills to interview him about certain events, as he was a witness to them. He has mentioned that it is a low tourist season in January and there isn't much work for him. I am aware that this comment indicates that his services are available. Finally, it was what Cesar would have done himself. Check the terrain and use local resources.

Sleep becomes elusive, as I am unable to halt the montage of scenes where I remember my only lived history with the city of Marrakech. I am also reliving my honeymoon and travelling fourteen years backward, entwining the past with the present. The transformed Khadim has piqued my curiosity in ways I cannot seem to comprehend. I feel energized and almost excited, as though an adventure has suddenly presented itself and I will embrace it willingly.

CHAPTER 16

❀ *Marrakech, 2006*

I AM ESCORTED TO THE billiard room on the ground floor of the Hotel La Mamounia. It is a room panelled in gleaming wood and separated into two sections. One half has a large billiard table and the other half has dark leather armchairs and a large regency-style writing desk with striking leather accessories. The spirit of the legendary guest Winston Churchill, who painted outdoors in the grounds of the hotel, hovers in the room. Or perhaps this notion is a product of my overworked imagination?

The hotel has offered me this room as a writing space as there is no use for it at present. It is a gesture of touching generosity. They are aware that I have retuned to Marrakech after fourteen years and am using the hotel as a location for my work. The public relations manager, Anissa, is a trouser-clad elegant woman with an excellent command of English. She displays an interest in me and is more than willing to accommodate my request. I have told her about Cesar's death and my desire to bury my wedding ring in the olive garden of the hotel and she becomes a charmed accomplice. In her mind, there is an element of romance and drama associated with me.

I walk out of the hotel and engage a horse-drawn calèche, and instruct the driver to head for Djemaa el Fna. He has a wizened face underneath the tattered straw hat perched on his head and dark eyes that examine me with curiosity. Late January does not see tourists in Marrakech and I am aware that he is calculating what he will charge me. I throw him a smile and do not discuss rates with him. The carriage moves down the street leaving the hotel behind and flanking the garden besides the Koutoubia Mosque.

The mobile phone my landlord has left for me in the apartment vibrates in my pocket. I do not answer it. It continues to vibrate without stopping. So I answer it.

"Hello. Hello. Where are you?" Khadim's low-pitched voice catches me by surprise.

"I am going to the square."

"In a taxi?"

"No in a calèche," I reply.

"I will be there when you reach the square."

The telephone goes dead before I can respond. I am not certain if I want to see him on my first day of discovery. There is an intrusive element to his joining me. I simply want to wander through the square and attempt to go down one of the winding lanes in the medina by myself. There is also an objective to the exercise, as I want to pick up some fresh flowers for the apartment. More than anything, I want to hear my own thoughts and gauge my feelings for a city that has occupied a mythical space in my heart for all these years.

The carriage leaves the tranquil space beside the Koutoubia gardens and turns to the main avenue towards the square and the roar of sound pierces the air. Cars and buses lumber perilously close, but the horses are guided expertly by the elderly driver as they move towards the calèche station beside a cluster of palm trees flanked by a park.

Standing on the pavement where the calèche stops is Khadim. His appearance has altered as he is wearing black trousers, a maroon sweater, a white shirt, and a tie. The absence of the baseball cap and the eyes masked by dark glasses give him a gentrified look. He flashes a broad smile and helps me down from the calèche with a flourish, bowing his head. There is an expectant and excited energy to him that I find both amusing and infectious.

"Come, I will show you my streets in the medina," he says.

"Your streets?"

"Magic." He raises both his hands and eyebrows theatrically.

I am amazed by the intimacy he creates instantly.

"I don't really want to do any sightseeing, Khadim. I just want to relax and wander around and pick up some flowers before I go home."

He looks down at me and smiles, then nods and starts moving along a small and busy street that runs parallel to the square. Within a few minutes, we reach a small arched brick gate. Over the left side of arched brick passage is a white signboard with the word "Stylia" written on it. Stepping through the gate, a long and winding lane lined with high walls unfurls ahead. Behind these walls lie the homes and shops of people who live in the medina.

It is quiet, with very few people and the overwhelming presence of the colour of Marrakech. The uneven ancient paving stones and thick plaster walls studded with closed wooden doors make me feel as though I am moving through a sand-coloured tunnel. Khadim, by my side, is silent and his gait is light as though he is aware of every changing contour of the stone floor. I walk beside him mesmerized by the allure of the lane and the instant departure from a remembered Marrakech of opulent hotels and fountains.

I have never seen a street like this before. When he takes sudden turns that lead to other lanes, I am in step with him. Tiny opened doors reveal local handicrafts with shopkeepers seated placidly outside. He is greeted by most of them and he nods his head imperiously and places one hand over his chest. This exquisite gesture implies that one carries the sight of the other in one's heart.

Without warning, the heavens open up, and through the hazy sunshine a misty rain descends on us.

"Come, we will find a dry place." He suddenly grasps my hand.

We race through the winding lanes. Khadim has a large hand and his grip is both light and firm. It's his way of ensuring that I do not slip on the wet cobblestones. He jogs lightly with me to a stone and stucco passageway that ends surprisingly at a wooden door. He steps inside pushing aside a curtain made of a tribal wool rug and greets a man who ushers us into a large covered atrium. We are in fact in the covered central courtyard of an enormous carpet shop.

He leads me to a padded bench and says, "They will bring you tea, I have to pray."

Again, before I can respond, he abruptly moves away from me to a corner of the room. I watch him slip off his shoes and stand on the bare floor facing east, hands raised to his ears. In the next four minutes, I watch him go through the motions of the Muslim prayer. Whether he adopts the seated posture, or the one of prostration, I am drawn to the serene and yet vulnerable expression on his face.

Under the vaulted ceiling, with carpets descending like streamers from balconies, Khadim becomes an *objet d'art* himself. I am oblivious to my damp clothing or the tea tray assembled in front of me because a flash of memory lances me. I know that this is the same atrium where I choose a carpet fourteen years ago while Cesar sat on the same bench I am now sitting on, sipping mint tea. Khadim's choice of shelter halts time and swiftly deposits me back into the life I am finally disassociating from.

When we leave the carpet emporium and step outside he casually tells me to look up. A rainbow arches overhead, disappearing behind the rooftops of homes and high walls. I gaze at the sky enthralled by a particular joy that I have not experienced for a long time, because I have become a carefree child and could have well drawn the rainbow on the sky myself. In the purity of this childlike moment, there comes another blessing, the ability to return to my remembered self has been weighted down for so long. Khadim's concept of magic and his ability to gauge my responsiveness to it is faultless. It has taken two years for this effervescence to resurface in me. I gaze at Khadim and see the painful shadow of Cesar's death disappear in the glittering sheen of his dark eyes. I become tongue-tied walking beside the man who has chased a ghost away and succeeded in making me experience a spontaneous lightheartedness.

Later that evening when I am home familiarizing myself with the apartment and going through the music CDs by the stereo, the doorbell rings. When I open the door, Khadim stands in front of me with a cascading bunch of wild crimson roses in his arms.

"You forgot your flowers." He extends them formally, not stepping closer.

"I am making chicken soup. I think I have caught a cold. Would you like to have dinner?" I am enchanted by the offering.

"I will go to the mosque to pray then I will come." He turns on his heels and swiftly walks away.

I switch on the electric heater in the living room of the apartment. The roses sit on the circular Moroccan table in front of the couch. I have massed them in a large ceramic water jug as the sharp thorns prevent any tidying manoeuvre. I place two soup bowls on the table. The garish paintings and crude ceramic plates are an irritant, so I turn off the overhead lights and bring a lamp from the bedroom to soften the ambience. It is an attempt to entertain with grace in makeshift surroundings.

Half an hour later, he arrives with a white box in his hands. He silently hands it to me and carefully enters the apartment. His movements are like some jungle creature treading warily in unfamiliar terrain. I motion him towards a couch and open the box. Seeing the four chocolate pastries, I cannot resist scraping the icing off one and promptly licking it off my finger. He throws me an amused grin as I take them to the kitchen to serve after dinner.

When I return to the living room, he is standing fiddling with the remote control of the large television set. A soccer match is on the screen. Seeing me, he hastily switches off the television.

"Do you like sports?" the inane question slips out of my lips.

"Yes. I was a sports teacher in a school," he tosses off casually.

"Before you became a guide?" I am curious.

"We will eat?" He ignores the question.

I place the bowl of clear chicken broth garnished with a few carrots on the table. For a moment, I am a little embarrassed at the simplicity of my offering to a man whose native cuisine is heavily starch- and meat-based. However, Khadim sits as if before a banquet. He instantly adopts the posture of host, and ladles soup into my bowl first, dropping more chunks of chicken than I can possibly eat. Then he fills his bowl. We eat in silence and I remember the gift of Moroccan wine in the refrigerator.

"Would you like a glass of wine?" I ask him.

"No alcohol. I do not drink. I gave it up. I used to drink a lot. If you must, it is no problem," he replies with a polite smile.

"What did you replace it with?" I ask mischievously.

"God. I practise my religion."

His comment is smugly self-righteous. Is there a barb aimed my way because I decide not to have any myself? In the softly lit room, Khadim sits upright on the couch. The gaunt face and semi-anorexic frame poised like the blade of a knife. I view him as being utterly foreign and yet familiar. He mistakenly assumes that I wish to spend time as a tourist and talks lightly about places I should go to. I inform him that I am invited to Rabat for the weekend as the guest of a diplomat and, en route, I will stop at Casablanca for lunch at the home of friends Cesar and I were introduced to on our first trip.

"I can drive you there and back," he offers.

"I am going for the weekend, and I have been told that the train takes the same time. Thank you, but I will get to see the countryside in the train."

"I can get a car. You will like it better than the train." He smiles as though my going by train is a travesty.

"You mean you will borrow a car?"

"No, I will rent it. It is no problem."

I refuse again, finding his manner both ingratiating and oppressive, and I rise from the couch. Khadim springs up as well.

"I have to say good night, Khadim; I am still a little jet-lagged. Thank you for the pastries. They are delicious."

He stands by the door and looks at me silently. I walk up and turn the door handle, opening the door. He is by my side, silent and waiting. I turn to him and say goodnight the second time and he reluctantly steps out. I shut the door immediately and feel a peculiar tension. Although the room is empty, his presence lingers.

I AM SEATED IN THE first class compartment of the Marrakech Express en route to Casablanca. The endless sea of sand-coloured terrain rolling beside the train sometimes shifts its colour to deep ochre-tinted soil. When clumps of vegetation appear, an element of hope redeems the unrelenting and barren landscape. The sun gleams everywhere cascading though the glass window of the train catching the dance of dust particles swirling inside.

My Moroccan travelling companions exhibit curiosity about my nationality and my inability to speak Arabic. When the train halts at Casablanca and I walk outside the terminal, Ali and Zohra Ben Jelloun's chauffer, Ibrahim, recognizes me easily, in the way most of the locals detect foreigners. It is a short drive to the wall-encircled villa. Fuchsia bougainvillea cascade over the small wooden door hiding Zohra Ben Jelloun, whom I have not seen for fourteen years. When she steps forward to embrace me, although time has taken its toll on her face, her grace and welcoming charm are undiminished. The arresting face is alive and animated. There are now silvery strands in the gleaming jet hair caught up in a long ponytail and she mentions that she has suffered a cardiac ailment.

Seated in a living room lifted from the pages of a French country home, my eyes repeatedly study the space behind us, which is a more traditional Moroccan-style salon. Zohra presides over a trolley set with French wines and snacks. We share cigarettes and catch up with our lives. I tell her that Cesar has died and that I am visiting Morocco to do some research on a book I set in Marrakech years ago. I also mention meeting Khadim. A look of concern mars Zohra's face.

"You must be careful not to associate with anyone from a different milieu," she says.

"He was our guide in Marrakech."

"Particularly a guide," she says with apparent distaste.

I remain silent, debating at which point I would have to inform my aristocratic friend that the guide could well arrive to drive me to Rabat. He telephoned me the night before and said that he had a car and would reach Casablanca two hours after my arrival. His skill at dispensing with my resistance made me give him the address of the Ben Jelloun villa in Casablanca.

"How do you like Morocco after all these years?" Zohra asks.

"I feel very comfortable, as though in some way I belong here," I smile at her.

"Of course you belong. It is always your home," she says cryptically.

"I am carrying a gift for your King, a copy of my new book," I tell her.

Zohra throws her head back and laughs. "Perfect!" she says in French.

"I think the ambassador has already sent it, and the palace asked if I wished an appointment to present it myself but it could take a few weeks, and I said I will have probably left by then."

Wearing an old navy-blue striped wool suit, Khadim arrives at Zohra's doorstep within the hour. Initially I am a little perplexed by his formal attire but then realize that he wishes to impress us. His modest background does not permit him entry into a home such as this, or even the residence of an ambassador in Rabat. However, I am a little irked by Zohra's attitude and decide to defend his status. When I introduce him, it is done with the ease of introducing him as a friend. Zohra murmurs a greeting, rakes him with her eyes, but does not have much conversation with him. When we leave, I am aware of how Khadim shrinks inside his suit, almost tongue-tied in the presence of a member of one of the leading families of his country. It was in the palatial home of Ali Ben Jelloun's grandfather that the declaration of Morocco's independence from the French was signed. This social division inflicts a small wound in my democratic stance and leads me into making a decision that dramatically shifts the tone of the weekend in Rabat. From the car, I call the embassy and ask if I can include the friend who is driving me to Rabat. Her secretary informs me that it is a formal dinner for eighteen, however, if a guest declines the ambassador will be happy to include my friend. Within ten minutes, I receive a call on my mobile phone saying that I can include my friend.

I am excited at the prospect of attending a diplomatic dinner in Rabat and wonder whom I will meet. The ambassador had once served in Canada and her warmth always impressed me. I am also equally excited that I will give Khadim the sort of experience that he has never been exposed to. It is a revolutionary act intended to break down social barriers in an etiquette-prone society, yet it is made with the confidence that Khadim's innate sense of dignity will make him sail through dinner at an ambassador's table.

Rabat, perched on the edge of the Atlantic Ocean and nestled in gardens, is an important city. It is the capital and houses the long sprawl of the imperial residence of the new young King Mohammad vi. Khadim drives expertly through the city heading for the diplomatic enclave in an area called Souissi. We drive up to the enormous cream-coloured home with a green-tiled roof.

I am swept into a warm embrace by the ambassador, and then she greets Khadim graciously. We step into the sumptuously appointed residence filled with flowers and a mélange of both Moroccan and European furnishings. The dining table is laid for eighteen guests and both of us will be seated at this table in two hours. Khadim is led to a bedroom where he can freshen up or rest. I am taken upstairs to my room, which is close to the family area.

Before we part, she asks Khadim if he has made arrangements for spending the night in Rabat.

"No. Not as yet," Khadim replies.

"I am not expecting any other houseguest. You are welcome to stay here if you like," she responds.

I am amused by this development and notice how graciously Khadim thanks her for the hospitality.

A few hours later seated for dinner, I notice Khadim's fixed stare across the length of the dining table. I am having a frivolous conversation with the two diplomats I am seated between. Khadim's place at the far end of the table between a foreign office official and a Moroccan technocrat could well be the other side of the moon, yet his eyes move to my end of the table constantly. The power of this gaze is intense and my senses are filled with confusion. It is as though I am seated in a bathtub filled with scented oil and every now and then a scoop of silky water rolls off my body. My friend the ambassador, who is a single mother and a career diplomat, seated at my right at the head of the table is quite perceptive.

"Is this a Moroccan romance?" she whispers to me.

"Don't be absurd! I hardly know him."

"What does he do?"

"He is a guide."

"Ah! Then I made a mistake, I though he was with the Ministry of Tourism. But then you have always been adventurous." She smiles at me reassuringly.

The next morning after breakfast Khadim volunteers to show us Rabat.

"I am taking the Saturday off and going to relax with you," says my hostess.

The three of us are walking up a steep incline half an hour later. We are exploring Rabat and walking through a village of small two- and three-story homes perched over the ocean. An ancient retaining wall flanks the small community. However, the most enthralling aspect of the houses we walk beside is the colour. All the exteriors are painted in two colours. The top half is white and the lower is a deep azure blue. The doors are also painted blue. This is the surprise Khadim had mentioned at breakfast half an hour ago. I have just invited both my hostess and Khadim for lunch and he suggested that we should see a certain part of Rabat before lunch.

The overwhelming beauty of the blue keeps all three of us silent. I walk alone ahead of the other two feeling encased on both sides by a band of colour that separates me from all my realities. I am heading towards infinity, shedding every aspect of the life I was leading. I think of paint palettes and large canvasses. I feel the presence of the blue Touregs and the miraculous artistic sensibilities of a largely impoverished society that endures in a constitutional monarchy. It is a luminous moment because it bonds me to the people of Morocco in an indefinable way. I wonder if I am truly in a magical kingdom and Khadim holds the keys to this kingdom.

The perfection of the day continues through the evening and the night. At about 2 a.m., I am sitting in the dark on a small couch in a small open area. Khadim is standing in front of me, shutting the main door to the ambassador's residence. The house and the staff are all asleep. We have just returned from attending an extravagant party at a small Moroccan palace in Rabat. The ambassador has declined the invitation but insisted that Khadim and I will be accompanied by a married couple who are good friends of hers. Steven and Mariam Guyer are the fashion couple of Rabat. He is the blond, blue-eyed member of the American Rockefeller family who has converted to Islam, and she is the daughter of a Pakistani ambassador who served in Morocco. They have settled in Rabat with two young children, are part of Moroccan society, and have a close friendship with the new king. They are a vivacious and brilliantly educated young couple and inform me that I shall have a taste of the private Morocco tonight. They accept Khadim easily and do not question me about him. From their faces and attitudes, I learn that it is quite easy for Europeans and Americans to lead happy lives in Morocco.

In the ballroom of the palace, marble columns are draped in shimmering gauze and roses cascade from ceilings and huge copper urns perch on pedestals. The party is to celebrate the birth of a son and the hosts greet us effusively. Our companions point out a few cabinet ministers who are also guests. Champagne flows from a long linen-covered table and a multi-course meal is expertly served by white-gloved waiters. Musicians and dancers congregate on a stage performing. Groups of young female guests wearing sumptuous caftans cinched at the waist with jewelled belts sway to the music, while the men stand and simply watch them. They pull me up with them and Khadim remains seated at the table watching the scene.

It is a heady night and I am aware that the enclave of privilege we inhabit bears a close resemblance to some of the social life I have been exposed to in Pakistan. However, the Moroccan motif differs in both the dress of the women and the behaviour of the men. Khadim, I am also aware, is nervous and out of his social milieu but presents a dignified attitude.

A few hours later when we have returned to the residence, I walk into a small salon and sink on a couch. He kneels at my feet in the darkened room. I feel his fingers slide inside my evening shoe and he slips off one and then the other. His large hands encase my foot and he strokes it delicately. In a graceful movement, he rises and buries his lips at the base of my throat. My entire body surrenders, and I lift his face with both palms and return the kiss he places on my lips.

"Come," he whispers in the dark, pulling me up from the couch.

My evening shoes stick out of the pockets of his jacket. We glide along the marble floor towards his room. He leads me to the room lit only by the light spilling in from an opened window. My clothes lie on the floor where he has undressed me.

I see his body poised over mine in the dark room and am reminded of the African Masai tribes. His naked chest is so narrow it could belong to an adolescent child, and the stomach flat, ending at narrow hips with long tapering legs. Even the shape of his face changes when he is naked. It is more elongated but the eyes glitter in his face. He has undressed me with speed and I, lying on the bed, sense his urgency and his hunger. I will mate with a cheetah.

From the first leap to the pressure of his movements until the shuddering breath of his release, I am aware that I have permitted some powerful force of nature to enter me.

I embrace his offering, am stunned by a music felt in the solitary chambers of my body. Not a word is spoken. I rise from the bed, scooping my pile of clothes and racing naked out the door to the marble staircase leading to my bedroom on the second floor.

Halfway up the stairs I hear movement and turn around. He pursues me, also naked, holding my forgotten shoes close to his chest.

For a second we halt and he places the shoes on top of the pile of clothes in my arms. I cannot look at his face but continue moving up the stairs. His hand trails over my hips and thigh lightly and he races down the stairs on his bare feet.

I am standing by my bedroom window. The intricate wrought-iron grill reveals the wide expanse of lawn outside. The city of Rabat winks intermittently like a glow-worm. I am sifting my emotions. Not a trace or imprint of Khadim's body marks my own body memory. There is a sensation of being the victim of a hit and run accident. Yet there is also a larger and more conflicting sensation of having experienced a force enter my body. It challenges the realm of my entire sexual experience.

Remorse also enters this state, because I have surrendered to desire without extending and testing familiarity. But I also sense danger, and it is not until the morning that I realize that the danger only comes from myself. My brief association with Khadim under fairly controlled circumstances has continually evoked emotions that I have sublimated. I am also now aware that he has pursued me with a single-mindedness that has not wavered. The prospect of this being simply a sexual encounter in a foreign country fills me with revulsion.

We meet over breakfast the next morning at a formally laid table. He is already seated, chatting with my friend the ambassador who has just pressed an omelette on him, which he eats with great relish. I sit away from him and greet the ambassador.

"Sabah el kheir." He gives me a sweet and gentle smile.

The classic Moroccan morning greeting, "May the morning go well for you," which I am drawn to, sets my teeth on edge this morning. I look at Khadim noting that the eyes that linger over my face now hold a new expression. It is one of heightened intimacy and almost indulgent confidence.

CHAPTER 17

❦ Marrakech

MUSIC AND A PUNGENT HERBAL odour fill the car. Khadim drives the
rental car at high speed and the city of Marrakech disappears behind.
I am listening to the throaty articulation of the Lebanese male singer
on the car radio. The Arabic song is piercingly beautiful as a man
declares his eternal love. I cannot understand all the words but absorb
the emotional resonance. Every phrase of the lyrics is a barb sinking
into my heart. Every song is Khadim. When he smokes the untidy
hand-rolled cigarette I am unaware that it contains hashish until the
aroma rises, and I question him about it.

"It relaxes me and it is part of my culture." He looks straight
ahead.

"Can I try it?" I ask.

"No. It is better that you smoke your cigarette," he replies.

I do not require anything for relaxation because I am riding a
wave of ecstasy. No further enhancement is necessary. In a space of
ten days, Khadim and I have become inseparable lovers. The novel
that I am writing is moving towards a different ending.

The city of Marrakech becomes the exotic setting for our romance.
Therefore the seduction is orchestrated faultlessly both by the man
and his city. I am incapable of separating one from the other, feeling
as though I am seated at a never-ending banquet of delights. The

seed of my receptiveness to all aspects of Moroccan culture, and to Khadim's persona, were planted years ago in childhood fantasies.

I begin to feel as though the pages of Arabian Nights have come alive. It is no longer the text of print and exotic illustrations but a felt and seen reality. My Canadian existence and the ethnic imprint of the country of my birth are totally submerged in the floodwaters of a passion that ensnares me completely. Like some medieval sorcerer, Khadim leads me to visual horizons of beauty by day and to the enclosure of his arms each night. I am recording this daily in notes and on the side columns of my manuscript.

At nightfall the terrain changes to the rolling hills leading to Agadir, a seaside resort town rebuilt after a great earthquake. We do not break the journey but at one stage, he pulls into a roadside food stand. Sides of freshly slaughtered meat dangle from iron hooks at the stall. Khadim searches for the perfect cut and supervises the man putting the chunks of meat into a meat grinder. The meat is then fashioned into patties and barbecued on the grill. He places this between two pieces of bread and offers it to me with a scalding cup of black Moroccan coffee.

We eat seated on a little crude wooden table and when I finish eating, he produces a small paper bag filled with tangerines. The miniature-sized fruit still has leaves attached to the stems as though it has just been plucked from a tree. The juice that floods my mouth is honey sweet. It is infused with the sun, the red soil of Marrakech, and the cool waters of the steams running down from the snow-capped Atlas Mountains. Ultimately, what heightens the pleasure of eating the fruit is the delicacy with which Khadim peels the orange and places perfect segments in my mouth. The erotic elements of this exercise create a languor within me that even slows my movements. I live in all these moments without ever wanting them to end, and my lover has seen to it that they never do.

The journey continues in the night away from Agadir and towards the town of Tiznit. When we reach Tiznit, a fork in the road leads to a gravel road. The night air changes, carrying a hint of the ocean, but the headlights of the car reveal nothing except the winding dirt road ahead. Our destination is the village of Aglou. A cluster of small homes begins to dot the road. Khadim brings the car towards a small structure set apart from the rest and halts the car. Then he reverses the car and aims the headlights towards the house.

The block-like structure is covered in white stucco with windows and door painted the deep majorelle blue of Morocco. It appears as though a postcard has come to life. In front of us, the ocean makes its presence visible by presenting a white line of sea foam extending for miles. Khadim watches me, gauging my delight at the surprise he has orchestrated by bringing me to his brother's beach home.

I jump out of the car and race to the blue door. He follows and opens the door with a set of keys. We enter the dark open-air vestibule illuminated only by the stars studding the dark sky overhead. The interior of the house is guarded by another door made of wrought iron. I wonder what delights await beyond it, but when we step inside and Khadim switches on the light, I am shocked. The naked lightbulb dangling overhead reveals a dirty clutter of cartons, cheap furniture, shoes, and old mattresses piled half way up the room and covered with a thick layer of dust.

The beauty of the exterior of the white stucco home is shattered by the unkempt almost slum-like interior. The toilet and washbasin in the crude bathroom are encrusted with grime and the overhead shower with exposed pipes releases a trickle of cold water. There is another room with a bed covered with a faded and stained pink satin bedspread. I mask my revulsion by remaining silent.

He enters the room behind me, jerks off the satin coverlet, and spreads a clean blanket on the stained bed sheets. Then he undresses me and makes love to me. The wind-filled roar of the ocean muffles all our sounds of pleasure.

The next morning he leads me away from the house to a small seafront café. He is instinctively aware of my feelings about the chaos and lack of hygiene in the house. The café sits on a promenade facing the ocean. As the morning sun casts a glittering turquoise hue to the water, Khadim talks of marriage. This is the second time he mentions that he wishes to marry me. The spiritual order of his life must be valid, he mentions. He repeatedly uses the Arabic word "Halal," which means sanctified and made pure by God in the Muslim faith.

My mind swirls as I try to find some delaying tactic. Khadim's desire coupled with his proposal is like an avalanche poised over me. I have given no thought to my future with him except that I receive and return his love in an equal intensity. My home lies in Canada across the Atlantic, but the sensation of standing at the threshold of a new life is overwhelming. I am happy and I am able to love again.

"All right, let's have a Moroccan wedding!" I say recklessly.

"Here?"

"Yes," I reply. "I love everything here and I want to experience your traditions."

"Can you live here?"

"I am a writer, Khadim, I can live anywhere. My publishers are in the West, they will get my manuscripts from here."

"I want to show you my dream, my future in my country."

"Where is it?"

"Very close by. I will take you there."

The oasis is breathtaking. The tall royal palms clump together in a strip of land that straddles two villages. Moss and rocks surround the base of the trees. There are clusters of desert flowers tucked into the wild foliage around the palms. In the centre of the oasis is a clearing where two huge palms rise majestically with a small platform of rock beneath them. I can visualize us dressed in blue seated on this small embankment on our wedding day. I see the soft earth around lined with Berber rugs and a Moroccan feast spread on low circular tables. I am certain we will spend the night in a tent lit by brass lamps. At this moment, I know that I will marry him.

A man from the village appears at the oasis. He is an elderly bearded man who has a conversation with Khadim. During the conversation, his eyes repeatedly stray to me. His exchange appears to be hostile and, although he walks away abruptly, he does not leave the area. Khadim tells me that he wants to get permission from the administration of the region to make the oasis a tourist site and the revenue generated would assist the villagers in learning how to conserve the oasis. This is the dream he shares with me, and I respect his progressive ideals. The ecological elements of his dreams also fill me with admiration. Given the place of his small country, which battles with poverty, illiteracy, and social injustice, I view him to be a progressive man. The commercial aspects of his dream are his desire to improve his financial status of being a guide. He tells me that although his income is a quarter of mine he is bound to be successful if I am by his side.

We return from the weekend trip late in the night. I fall asleep in the car and wake up as we reach my apartment in Marrakech. I discover that he has covered me in his jacket while I slept. As Cesar disappeared from my life so did many small gestures of tenderness. Khadim's gesture makes me acutely aware of his protective nature and this brings him closer to my heart.

I wake up the next morning to an empty bed. When I turn my head, I see him kneeling in prayer by the side of the bed. A long bath towel is draped at his waist and his hair is still damp from the ablutions he performs before prayers. The bent head reveals the nape of his neck and I am flooded with the desire to press myself against his back. In fact, it is the act of worship that I find to be erotic beyond belief. This daily act of cleansing and offering prayers five times a day are tucked so seamlessly into his life that they become inseparable from his other activities. I am conscious that at this moment I am being courted by two forces simultaneously, one spiritual and the other sexual. But I cannot reveal these emotions to Khadim.

"You do not pray?" he asks after he finishes.

"No."

"You have to practise the faith if you are Muslim." He tweaks my nose.

"I just believe and feel," I respond defensively.

"You should pray."

"I do when I see something beautiful, in my own way. Arabic is not my language so I am uncomfortable just repeating prayers I cannot fully understand."

"I will translate for you." He sits by the bed and embraces me.

"I question everything, Khadim. For me this is an ongoing intellectual exercise. You should know this, I have told you before." I struggle out of his arms and face him challengingly.

"It is your life," he says with a grave smile on his face, "you must do as you wish."

The next day we walk into the Hotel La Mamounia together. Khadim gets curious looks from the reception desk, as guides are supposed to stay outside and not enter the hotel. The public relations manager waits for us. I introduce Khadim to her and she waves us towards the garden. She has asked me to come before 9 a.m. so that the gardeners who tend to the grounds are not present. We walk outdoors towards the pathway lined by olive trees in the garden adjoining the swimming pool. I am carrying a plastic bag in which the small blue felt bag and a large cooking spoon rest. We walk along the path. Beds of white roses are sprinkled in the grass behind the trees. Halfway down the walk is the bench that Cesar used to sit on fourteen years ago, smoking a cigar, and waiting for me. I instinctively choose the olive tree to its right. I walk to the base and kneel down. With the spoon, I dig the earth close to the trunk. Khadim kneels with me and takes over the digging. The kitchen spoon is quite efficient and within a couple of minutes, a narrow but deep hole has been dug. I place the bag in the hole. It contains my wedding ring and Cesar's silver hairbrush with his initials embossed on it. Then I rise, pluck two white roses, and place them on the bag. We pack the hole with the dug up earth and Khadim cups his hands and recites the Muslim prayer called "Fatiha" softly. I repeat it in my mind and say goodbye to Cesar forever. We both rise silently and Khadim plucks another rose, hands it to me, and I place it on the spot and take a photograph of the base of the tree. I have performed a rite that has brought me across an ocean to the tip of North Africa. In fact, I have just given Cesar a funeral.

"Do you know what the date is today?" asks Khadim as we walk towards the hotel.

"It is Tuesday," I reply.

"Yes," says Khadim, pulling the local newspaper out of his jacket pocket, "it is February the twenty-first, and you choose the twenty-first olive tree. I counted the entire line of trees."

There is a mystical, almost glazed expression in his eyes and I wonder if he is into numerology.

I am home at the apartment packing as four weeks have gone by and I am flying home tomorrow afternoon to Paris and then to Toronto. This will be our last evening together but Khadim is planning to visit me within two weeks. He disappeared in the afternoon. The telephone rings.

"I have planned a surprise for dinner and you should wear one of your pretty dresses."

"Where?"

"Magic," he laughs on the phone.

"Magic," I repeat, knowing he is fully capable of holding something back until the end.

I am wearing a green chiffon cocktail dress and Khadim is wearing his faithful navy pinstriped suit. The taxi in which we are seated is headed outside the city of Marrakech. The small road seems to travel through the wilderness until we reach a set of large stucco gates. A paved courtyard greets us. He holds my hand as we walk up a flight of steps where a photographer with a Polaroid camera takes a picture of us. As it develops, we both look at it silently. It is as though we have been married for years. An air of known familiarity clings to the way I lean against him. Khadim tucks the photograph into his breast pocket.

Another vestibule leads towards a large pavilion that has a roof but is open on the sides. It is a large restaurant with circular tables and Moroccan divan seating. The walls and ceilings are draped in tapestries and the ambience is baroque bordering on the theatrical. Oversized Moroccan handicrafts are sprinkled everywhere. The place is called Chez Ali. Khadim orders Moroccan wine for me and a three course traditional meal is served at a leisurely pace and at one point Khadim gets up to greet the manager of the establishment and introduces me as a Canadian writer who is visiting Marrakech. A troupe of Berber female dancers and musicians perform at the tables adding to the festive air. Most of the guests are foreign tourists.

After dinner, we walk towards another structure. The enclosed stadium lies a short distance away from the dining area. We enter through a special entrance and I am seated with Khadim in the middle of the first row of seats facing the Chez Ali amphitheatre. The stadium in front of us is dark and Khadim holds my hand. Suddenly a spotlight throws a beam at the far end of the stadium. A white camel carrying an elaborately decorated and curtained seat is visible. Instantly music swells up in the darkness.

"The bride is going to attend her wedding," Khadim whispers.

Lights are turned on and the stadium is illuminated to reveal a semicircle of musicians and dancers fanning out on either side of the white camel. Overhead trick lighting creates a "son et lumière" effect and a carpet floats in the air. The procession moves slowly towards the centre of the stadium where we are seated. I am transfixed by the picturesque tableau unfolding before me and the perfect silence maintained by two hundred people in the dark.

"Where is the groom?" I whisper to him.

"It is the bride and she is the queen today," he arches an eyebrow and grins at me.

"Will he also ride a camel?"

Khadim shrugs his shoulders. "It can be a white horse."

"Would you?"

"Anything you want."

"I want to get married in the oasis riding a white camel."

"Everything can be arranged," he smiles at me, setting fire to my imagination.

When the procession reaches us, the white camel carrying the cloistered bride kneels. It is right before my seat, and I know this has been arranged by Khadim. As legions of women before, I allow the fantasia to seduce me utterly. When the procession moves away and a pack of stunning equestrians race their horses in the stadium, the rider on the white horse becomes Khadim for me. In the enchantment of this moment I realize that I am returning to my home in Canada only leave it. Not even the presentation of the bill for the entire evening, which Khadim slides towards me saying he has arranged for a discount, mars the occasion. I throw down my credit card without glancing at the bill, paying for both of us without a care in the world.

I want to see Khadim's home. He has been living with me for the past three weeks at the rented apartment, returning home only to change or bring clothes. Initially, my request is met with reluctance but as I am leaving, I insist.

"I am a simple man. I live in my mother's home."

"It does not matter. I need to find out who you really are," I am intrigued about his reluctance.

He does it the next morning before my flight. The twenty-minute ride away from the affluent district where the apartment is situated leads to a broad avenue lined with shabby apartment buildings and shops. The neighbourhood is new and devoid of any charm. The taxi enters a small lane infested with shops selling cooked food, then an unpaved road heads towards a house barricaded by high walls and an iron gate painted green. We get out of the taxi and Khadim opens the smaller metal gate to the side and asks me to wait. He returns within minutes and leads me inside.

"My mother will receive you now," he says hesitantly with a formal air.

I walk beside the tiny front garden overflowing with weeds and an orange tree. I am returning to a house where Khadim had entertained Cesar and me fourteen years ago on our honeymoon. It does not look familiar as I remember a white, block-like, two-storey home.

The young bride is missing, as she was divorced years ago. As we step inside the front door, the interior is also unfamiliar. I follow him into the front hall and he turns into the first room on the right. It is a typical Moroccan sitting room with all four walls lined with upholstered plank style seating. It is a tasteless room filled with a decaying air. Three women and a teenaged girl wearing Moroccan caftans and headscarves concealing their hairline sit in a line on one side. The short elderly woman rises and moves towards me.

"My mother," says Khadim, looking tense.

"Salam-aleikum," I say using the Arabic greeting.

The woman with soft brown eyes embraces me and kisses my cheeks three times. The other two women have impassive faces and say *bonjour*. They are Khadim's older sisters and a niece. There is no communication between us and I am examined with curiosity. I try to use a few words of Arabic and snatches of French vocabulary. The young girl responds in French but I do not have the skills to have a conversation. I notice a row of metal utensils placed on top of a cupboard near us and question her about them. The mother returns to sit across from me and simply gazes at me. Khadim walks in with a tray of Moroccan mint tea and six glass tumblers. His mother pours the tea and speaks to Khadim in Arabic, gesturing at the utensils I had pointed to.

"She wants you to have the tray," Khadim tells me.

"Oh no! I was just wondering what they are used for. Please thank her for me but tell her it is too large to put into my suitcase." But I am charmed by her offer.

Tea is drunk in silence. Khadim rises and tells me we must leave. His mother gets up to embrace me and says something softly to her son.

"What is she saying?"

"She is telling me to take care of you."

We walk towards the front vestibule and he leads me towards a concrete staircase that curves up to the second floor. When we reach the landing, he pulls out a set of keys and opens the heavy wooden door. We step into the second-floor balcony shrouded by a heavy metal grill. In front is another door that Khadim unlocks with a key. I am mystified about the locked doors in his mother's house.

"Why is everything locked?"

"Because they come up and take my things away," he replies angrily.

Khadim's second-floor apartment has a long hall. The salon on the right has the same four-sided Moroccan seating. There is one rectangular wooden table piled with old newspapers, empty plastic bottles, an overflowing ashtray, and odd bits of clothing. A gigantic television set lies in the middle of the otherwise bare room. Naked bulbs dangle from one wall. I walk down the hall to the miniscule kitchen with a large window that looks down to the courtyard below. The bathroom has ancient stained fixtures and a tub. The bedroom is bare with the exception of a large white armoire. The room next to it is cluttered with a broken bedstead and shirts and trousers hanging from a pole rack. There are jumbled piles of shoes and stacks of cartons. I am both devastated and depressed by the forlorn and shabby surroundings, which do not reveal a hint of Khadim's personality.

We then walk up to the third floor, which is stunning. It is a sun-filled enclosed terrace with three rooms surrounding it. All the doors to the rooms are locked. When I ask Khadim what they are used for, he says they are filled with junk.

I have already redecorated Khadim's home in my mind. I see the rooms painted the terracotta rose of Marrakech with all the doors and windows painted in majorelle blue, the heavy wooden doors removed and replaced by stucco archways. I place a fountain on one wall of the terrace and shrubs in pots and vines that will create a canopy overhead. More than anything, I see myself speaking in Arabic to his mother. My nesting instincts make my fingers immediately itch to clean the Aegean stable that is Khadim's home. The absence of the bed brings his confession that he sleeps on the divans in the living room watching television.

"It is not a home. I just sleep and change my clothes here," he tells me when we leave.

I AM CLOSING MY BULGING suitcases filled with gifts for friends in Toronto. The ring on my finger gleams. It is made of silver with two bands that overlap in the centre and then part to form the band. I call it the crossroads ring and Khadim is wearing his as well. I had bought the identical rings in the shop of a Berber jeweller in the medina of Marrakech and given Khadim his a week ago on Valentine's Day. He had walked into the apartment that evening with a small brown paper bag and casually tossed it on the bed. When I shook the bag, an exquisite blue velvet caftan with a hundred miniature silk buttons fluttered out. He had helped me expertly sliding the miniature balls of silk into the loops. Then I had given him the ring and he slid it onto his finger saying that he would never take it off.

I telephone the Hotel La Mamounia and make a dinner reservation at their Italian restaurant. We arrive by taxi, enter the hotel, and head towards the restaurant. The European manager at the front desk gives Khadim a cold look as she checks the book for my reservation.

"I don't like this woman," whispers Khadim to me.

"Would you prefer the Moroccan restaurant?" I ask.

The restaurant has very few diners and the searching for the reservation scenario is being delayed by the female manager. I sense tension. Moroccan guides are not encouraged by places like the Hotel La Mamounia to enter the dining rooms.

"I think we will dine at the Moroccan restaurant instead," I tell the manager coolly and turn away. I am a foreigner and can obviously afford to dine here. The maître d' at the Moroccan restaurant does not pose too great a problem and Khadim has a whispered conversation with him. We are led to a table and have a wonderful meal. At the end of the meal, a procession of musicians, headed by a woman carrying a plate with a candle on it, walk around the restaurant and eventually stand before our table. "Happy Birthday" — *bon anniversaire* — is sung in French to me.

"It's not my birthday, Khadim," I tell him in surprise.

"I have told them that it is the anniversary of your return to Marrakech," Khadim grins at me.

I realize that this is how he has managed to dine with me without being subjected to hostility by the staff. Although it is a cheap trick, I realize that he has done this for me. His admission does not rob the evening of its delight and we even have a photograph taken to add to our memory book.

The drive to the airport is silent. He sits in the front with the taxi driver as I watch my home for four weeks disappear behind me. When my baggage is checked in and I am issued a boarding pass, he takes me to a little kiosk in the terminal and buys coffee for us and a chocolate bar for me. He carefully spreads a paper napkin on the counter and places the paper cups of coffee on it. The he lights a cigarette, takes a puff, and hands it to me. It is as though we have lost all powers of speech. The rings glint on our fingers and the enormity of what we have created between us is a new frontier in our lives. The plans and strategies of sharing a life together remain unuttered.

When he escorts me to the security barrier, my steps falter. I look at him as tears gather in my eyes. A small muscle quivers in his jaw and he raises a finger and presses it to my lips. I turn away and walk through the barrier carrying the cautioning pressure of his finger. Before I clear the barrier, I turn around and am shocked to see his head disappearing behind a column. I wonder, "Will I ever see him again?"

CHAPTER 18

TORONTO

KHADIM WALKS THROUGH THE GLASS doors at Toronto airport and I am first in line at the arrivals lounge. His face lights up with joy when he sees me. He leaps forward and his kiss collides into my teeth almost throwing me off balance. He has brought the force of his entire continent with him. The sun of Morocco is the light in his eyes, the velvet night sky of Marrakech imprisoned in his black hair, and the mystery of Africa in his loping stride. We walk outside together as though the three-week separation does not exist. I am so excited that I leave the car behind and arrange for an airport limousine to take us home. I want to observe his face during the drive on the way home, as he has never been to Canada. He watches the traffic and the skyline of the city with avid interest, holding my hand tightly. In twenty-five minutes, we reach the plush glass and chrome lobby of my apartment building. The doorman and concierge beam at us and assist with his oversized red suitcase. When the elevator door closes and I am pressed to him, relief floods me as though I have regained the use of a limb I had lost.

I unlock the door to my apartment and hold it wide open for him. He enters quietly and places his suitcase against a wall. Then he treads delicately through the entire living, dining, and open kitchen space.

"It is very beautiful. Magical," he finally whispers in awe.

I have filled vases with white lilies and roses. The white-walled living space with cream-coloured furnishings is accented only by the colours of the art hung on the walls. He examines everything, including the fourteen-year-old carpet from Marrakech under the glass dining table. When he reaches the end of the living area, he halts before the huge plate glass windows and looks down at Bloor Street below.

"It is not Marrakech," he grins at me.

"Do you want to see Marrakech?" I say mischievously, and lead him to my bedroom.

We enter the bedroom painted in the rose-tinted terracotta with the oriental furniture and silk carpets. I have kept the chandelier on dimly so that it throws the geometrical design on the entire ceiling. He looks around silently and then pulls me into his arms as the telephone rings incessantly and the answering machine switches on.

"I have been lost without you," he finally whispers into my ear.

Later that evening he pulls out gifts from his suitcase. He brings me freshly ground spices, natural perfumes in small glass vials, braided leather belts with large metal buckles, and a matching handbag with ornate metal fixtures. These are the treasures of his souks where he leads tourists for shopping expeditions. I do not know at this point that he has lied to various shopkeepers in Marrakech that he is going to do business in Canada and takes these items as free samples.

I am overwhelmed by his generosity and delighted with his choice of colours. He hands the items one by one to me quite casually, as though it is nothing worth making a fuss over. The last gift is a bottle of perfume called "Soir de Marrakech." I immediately press the spray and a mist of fragrance settles around us. The heady top-notes of the fragrance take me back to the night air of Marrakech redolent with the scent of flowers. It also makes the moon shine on cue over the tower of the Koutoubia and the ancient rampart walls float in front of me. Words fail me but I know I will always use his fragrance. Later, I feel as though I have been courted in the most sophisticated manner. He has delighted all my senses with a methodical list of items chosen with precision.

Within a week, his presence permeates my entire life. I introduce him to my life in Toronto, and all my excited friends entertain him lavishly. He walks through my city carrying a delicate and exotic air of displacement with him. It is as though he secretly doubts the purity of the very air we breathe. The luxurious storefronts of shops, the tall buildings, and the architecture of the city overwhelm him. Even the mosque he locates in the east end of the city and visits regularly makes him feel alien. He drives my car expertly, weaving through the traffic-laden City of Toronto with the instincts of a hunter. He never gets lost bringing us home, never misses a street. Compared to his, the luxury of my appliance- and convenience-laden home makes him say repeatedly that I must bring everything with me so I do not miss anything. I take him to Niagara Falls where a rainbow obligingly loops itself across the sky and the roaring falls. Eventually what succeeds in exciting him is attending his first ice hockey game. This is where his athletic sensibilities are saturated with admiration, and he says he would like to play.

Often I find him stretched on the couch in front of the television gazing in fascination at the glass bookshelf that stretches across an entire wall. The nights we are home, I serve dinner on the square, low coffee table in front of the living room couch, and place large cushions on the carpet for us to sit on. I add this touch, as it resembles the Moroccan style of seating he is used to. He removes his Western clothing, wears a pale yellow caftan, and eats gracefully with his fingers, lifting choice bits of meat or vegetables from his plate and putting them on mine. When I try to pour a beverage for myself, he imprisons my hand, and pours it himself. He slows my pace, except when we make love; then his desire transforms him into storm lightning crackling across the plains of my welcoming body.

I take him to see a provocative and psychological Woody Allen film. He catches every aspect of North American relationship dilemmas and we discuss it for a long time over coffee at Sassafras. I sense that his intelligence, which is essentially streetwise, is also flavoured by a mystical quality. Although every aspect of his gentle and measured behaviour is graceful and appealing to me, I notice him shrinking in stature in my environment. It convinces me that my decision to live in his country is wise. Against the backdrop of Marrakech, he towers over people, his dress and colouring merge harmoniously and his knowledge and pride in his country give him a status that here is slowly being reduced to a non-descript anonymity. In Toronto, he is simply a tall, thin man wearing a shabby, black wool coat and shivering in the blast of a capricious Canadian winter. I think of magnificent wild animals imprisoned in zoos where they pace listlessly, and lose the gloss in their fur.

He makes telephone calls to Morocco daily to arrange the wedding. I ask him where we will live.

"I will take you home," he responds quietly, "but can you live there?"

"Yes I can. Just paint it. I can furnish it easily."

It is the last week of his month-long visit and we design our wedding card together. He takes a felt pen and draws an oriental design. He covers the entire white page with a complex design drawing freely with a spontaneity that makes me realize that he has artistic tendencies.

"We will paint together, on the terrace of your house," I see myself there already.

"One canvas. You will paint one side and I will do the other side," he laughs with pleasure.

He examines my free-floating glass shelves holding close to four hundred books daily, it is as though he is measuring the dimensions in his mind. He is fluent in both French and English. We play chess together and he wins easily, offering to teach me how to improve my game. I even take him to my health club one day where he views the army of equipment. He smiles telling me that he will take me into the Moroccan desert for a trek and I will not need machines. Looking at his lean muscular frame, I am half inclined to believe him.

Like any woman in love, I shower him with gifts. I choose elegant silk trousers and shirts in pastel colours and shockingly expensive ties. He is fearful of the prices but accepts my offerings with pleasure.

The impression he makes on my friends is more than favourable as they are comforted by the protective manner and loving devotion he displays towards me. We select a wedding date together, five days after my birthday in the month of June. I have roughly seven weeks to join him. The day he flies back to Morocco, I cling to him and start to cry.

"I must go to prepare our nest," he whispers to me softly, delicately flicking my tears away with his long fingers.

I arrange for him to be driven to the airport because I cannot bear to say goodbye. When the taxi moves away he does not look back, but he calls from Paris the next morning and leaves a message on the answering machine while I am still asleep.

"I am lost without you."

A month later, I get a call from Federico.

"There are some visitors from the World Congress of Psychiatry in town and I am having a dinner party for them. I would like you to come," he says.

"Why?"

"Morocco's leading psychiatrist will be coming; you are going to live in that country he may be a good social contact for you. I have told him all about your Moroccan wedding."

I am intrigued. So I attend the dinner party. Dr. Driss Moussaoui is a slight man with a gnomish charm and he expresses great delight when we are introduced. I am drawn to his vivacity instantly. We talk non-stop about my fascination with Marrakech. He tells me he was raised there, although he now resides in Casablanca. I impulsively invite him to my Moroccan wedding and he informs me that I must visit him in Casablanca when I arrive. He offers me his card and Federico observes this new alliance with a beaming smile. I suppose in Federico's mind I will at least know someone other Khadim in Morocco. When I leave this dinner party, I have no way of knowing what part this encounter will play in my life.

I am just folding my tent, I say to myself. There isn't an element of betrayal in my heart for abandoning a country I adopted thirty-eight years ago. With a speed that leaves those around me breathless, I terminate all my living arrangements in seven weeks. The contents of my home and my car are shipped to Morocco. I dispose of most of my furniture with the exception of my writing desk and leather couch from my study. I leave my income-generating financial investment intact in Canada, and take six months income with me. I also include expenses for the wedding as I realize Khadim's modest income will not be able to provide for the wedding in an oasis. I establish a mailbox address and stock up six months supply of vitamins and toiletries. Eight of my friends will fly to Morocco to attend the wedding in an oasis. I upgrade my computer. I talk to Khadim daily, who says his life is hectic as well, and sometimes there seems to be a frantic edge to his voice. The city of Marrakech is full of tourists and he is working and having the house painted. I feel that I cannot get there soon enough.

Finally, when my home disappears in cartons that are taken away, I realize that even my unfinished manuscript is sailing from Canada to North Africa. Will my novel, I wonder, be influenced by the new life I am about to embrace? My writing life will disappear for a time because I will be getting used to married life and settling in a new country. However, stories do not just disappear; if they are good ones they wait. I check into the Intercontinental Hotel for my last two nights and walk around the familiar streets of my town alone but do not say goodbye, for I plan to return each year. When I am seated on the plane and it lifts off, I am reminded of Isak Dinesen who had endured life in another part of Africa, had suffered immensely, and had written a novel, *Out of Africa*. I tell myself that I am going into Africa to be loved eternally and to write the best books of my career.

I spend two days in Paris and then fly to Marrakech. At the airport, my two enormous suitcases filled with wedding clothes, presents, and all my legal documents are wheeled out by a porter. I search the crowd for his face and do not find it anywhere. I do not leave the terminal but am rooted to the spot and waiting for him to appear. After twenty minutes, I walk out and follow the porter heading towards the exit. The June sun of Marrakech scorches my face. I am blinded, so when a hand on my waist spins me around I am disoriented. He stands in front of me wearing a blue shirt with an enormous cellophane-wrapped bouquet of white lilies and a head full of boyish curls. His face is thinner than before and I can see the outline of his collarbone jutting out from his neck. He appears to have lost weight so his entire appearance has an unfamiliar delicacy. I feel as though I am looking at the face of a starving ascetic in some medieval icon. He lightly brushes my cheek with his lips and then motions to the porter to bring my luggage to the car he has rented. Then he opens the car door and seats me inside. I sit in a cauldron of heat holding the flowers in my lap, my excitement swept aside by a nameless tension that grips me.

We are back in the same apartment, as I have rented it again from the banker. I shall stay here right until the wedding then shift to his house. The container from Canada has been scheduled to arrive a week after the wedding and honeymoon. It is going to be a small and intimate wedding with eight of my friends coming from Canada and his immediate family of six siblings and his mother. We have twenty days in which to get all my documents translated and filed for the marriage licence granted by the Moroccan government, and my wedding dress stitched. I have decided to wear a Moroccan caftan in majorelle blue and silver. I insist that Khadim retains the car he has rented for a day right up until the wedding and that I am happy to pay for it.

The next day we are standing in a crowd of people at a government office. The goal is the desk of a bureaucrat who will stamp one of my documents. Pandemonium erupts around us as there is no system of queuing and the official ignores most of the documents on his desk. The heat is unbearable and the odour from sweating bodies clothed in long robes pressed around me makes me nauseous. Khadim, beside me, is arguing in harsh, strident tones with people around us. The cords of his neck muscles are distended and anger robs his face of its customary grace. I am shocked at his behaviour, as I have never seen this before. When I try to restrain him, he bellows at me and I draw back in shock.

"I can't handle this. I am going out until the people before us are through," I tell him.

"No. You will stay here," he shouts at me and clasps my arm.

I feel as though a band of steel encircles my arm. Before I can shake myself free, Khadim has pushed us towards the desk of the official. The man holds my document and studies it for a long time, and then with a vulgarity bordering on contempt, focuses on my breasts beneath my summer blouse. Finally, he pulls out a shabby ledger and begins to enter the information by hand. His pen moves and halts periodically, and I have the sensation that he has difficulty reading. When he finishes he stamps my certificate and asks for my passport, making a great show of studying my photograph. Finally, he hands it back to me. I find his manner highly offensive. We return exhausted and dishevelled to the car. I feel as though I am suffocating in the brutal tide of culture shock. The non-computerized bureaucracy is obsessed with documentation. It is both ill-trained and corrupt, wielding a controlling power over its largely illiterate population. I am distressed by the resigned passivity of people who have travelled for hours from rural areas, who are ignored for hours, and then told to come back. They lie in the public waiting areas, faces marked by hopelessness, bodies slumped in fatigue.

This exhausting regimen continues for eight days under the scorching June temperatures of Marrakech. I am a foreigner and every Canadian document of mine has to be translated into Arabic and then submitted. I am also filled with anxiety about the unfamiliar transformation in Khadim's personality. He is belligerent with motorists on the street when he drives, sometimes uncharacteristically brusque with me, and his entire body ripples with a nervous tension I find undecipherable. He also disappears regularly for ten or fifteen minutes when I think he is by my side. When he reappears, wraithlike, he seems calmer and more relaxed. I wonder if he is taking a break to say his prayers but can never be certain. When I open a bank account accessible in foreign currency to foreigners, he wants to fill out the cheques for me in case I make a mistake in French. If I open my purse to pull out my wallet, he roughly grabs it and tells me never to take it out in public.

"Please don't do this," I protest and take my wallet back from him.

"I don't want you to have a bad experience. Then you will want to go back," he pleads, his face contorted with some anguish.

"This is where I keep my money and cards. I have to take it out and nobody can just grab it out of my hands." I am surprised at his behaviour.

"There are pickpockets everywhere," he says darkly.

"I will never go back darling," I reassure him. "We are getting married next week."

We eat out most nights in the neighbourhood restaurants as the days are spent running around government offices. I pay the bills for all the meals, thinking that I have chosen places where most of the tourists eat and Khadim's modest budget cannot accommodate these prices.

My birthday is the most exciting day since I have landed in Marrakech. All my Canadian friends have arrived, checked into their hotels, and will meet us at my apartment in the evening for drinks and then Khadim has arranged to take us all out for a birthday dinner he is hosting for me. As always, he says it will be a surprise and that I will love it. I bathe and say I will be at our little café having breakfast. He joins me and then disappears for some errands he has to run. I return to the apartment to find white lilies, another bottle of "Soir de Marrakech," and a card written in English. The card tells me that his love for me is larger than the tower of the Koutoubia! I feel that my happiness is complete. The rest of the afternoon is spent meeting my friends, who are all excited to be in Marrakech for my wedding.

Later that evening, a fleet of taxis drive us to the Kasbah section of Marrakech and the La Rotunda is the most beautiful restaurant I have ever seen. It is owned by a Venetian antique dealer who has created a magical combination of Moroccan and European furnishings.

Our table is in the covered courtyard and there are three other men invited by Khadim who sit at another smaller table. His brother from France and a friend of his have also come to attend the wedding. The third man is Italian and has some business connections with Khadim.

It is a charmed evening as my Canadian friends are exposed to the finest ambience in Marrakech. Federico has come along with his wife; he has always wanted to visit Morocco. All of them are thrilled to combine a week's vacation with my wedding. They are all seasoned travellers but, more than that, it is my exotic love story that they have come to witness. Even my family doctor from Toronto, who literally invited herself to my wedding, has come with her husband. Her presence lends an air of confidence to our little Canadian group. They drink the local wine and select local cuisine. I am too excited to eat anything and at one point get up to go the toilet. Khadim follows me.

"You have to collect the money from them," he says to me.

"From whom?"

"Your friends for the dinner," he replies.

"This is your birthday dinner for me and they are our out-of-town wedding guests. All these people entertained you in their homes in Canada. I will never ask them for a penny." I am furious at his suggestion.

"Sshhh," he hisses at me.

"This is the biggest insult. How dare you suggest this?" I head for the toilet stunned at the exchange we have just had.

When I return to the table, he is talking to my fiends, jovial and smiling. I simply erase the moment and enjoy the rest of the evening. He does not bring up the subject again when the evening ends and neither do I.

Two days later, we are all in the capital of Rabat for the henna ceremony. My friend the ambassador has offered her stunning garden for this event and has handled all the table arrangements. In a fit of generosity, or skilled public relations, she has invited half the foreign office of the government of Morocco. My brand new Moroccan friend, Driss Moussaoui, is also attending with his wife. The Ben Jelloun's from Casablanca have also been invited and so has Khadim's only friend, Chafiq.

I am stepping into the saffron-coloured long skirt encrusted with turquoise beads and crystal embroidery. The weight of beads drags the skirt a few inches behind me. I then slip into the short waist-length tunic, identical to the skirt, and drape the turquoise chiffon shawl around one shoulder and tuck the other end into the waistband of the skirt. I am wearing a clump of gold bracelets on one wrist and my sliver "crossroads" ring on my left hand. The ambassador's maid helps me to get dressed and then goes to the window and watches through the curtains. The ambassador's guests and my friends from Canada are assembled outside. The ceremony will begin when Khadim, accompanied by his family, arrives bringing henna for me and platters of sweets and flowers. Then I will be escorted outside to sit next to Khadim on a decorated dais and the ceremony will begin. The wedding will be Moroccan but the henna ceremony three days prior to it will follow Pakistani traditions.

Forty minutes later, I am still inside waiting for Khadim to arrive. The ambassador comes in a few times to remind me that she is also serving dinner to all the guests and the delay is discourteous. I call Khadim on my mobile phone, and he tells me that his mother was delayed arriving from Marrakech and they are just getting ready to leave. I am distressed by this, but realize that punctuality is not a local value. Twenty long minutes later, I hear the sound of music and voices outside and I peek from behind the curtain only able to see the top of Khadim's head as he is surrounded by his four sisters wearing flowing djellabas with their heads covered in scarves.

I walk the length of the table-strewn garden escorted by the ambassador herself. It is a June evening and the lawns have been decorated with a festive touch. Khadim is sitting on a small dais dressed in a Pakistani cream silk outfit of trousers, a long tunic, and a waistcoat with gold edging. It is my gift to him, as the henna ceremony will reflect my culture of origin. He is smiling broadly, watching my slow progress across the lawn towards him. His sisters and mother sit at a table close by looking like a cluster of jewelled butterflies. They all wear the double Moroccan robes fastened by stone-encrusted metal belts, and coins and necklaces flutter around their headscarves. Next to them is another table of my Canadian friends dressed in evening dresses and formal suits. There are at least another fifty people whom I do not know. But I spot the beaming presence of Driss and his beautiful wife Khalida. Most of them are dressed in Moroccan evening clothes. The tables are covered in white tablecloths with floral centrepieces. When I reach the dais, Khadim stands up.

"You look gorgeous." He lifts the long heavy skirt and helps me to sit.

"So do you," I whisper, holding back the tears of joy that threaten to spill out.

Flashbulbs explode as we sit together and faces beam at us.

"Why are they taking so many photographs?" I whisper to him.

"If you could just see yourself," he smiles at me and I notice the dreamy expression in his eyes. It is as though his iris glides across the cornea.

ON TWO WHITE SQUARES OF linen placed on the palms of our hands, people dab bits of henna paste. Then the cloth is removed and a woman hired for the event draws designs of henna on my palms and feet. That is when I discover that Khadim and his family have come to the henna ceremony empty-handed. However, the ambassador has also prepared platters of henna, decorated with flowers. When dinner is served, Khadim brings a plate of food and feeds me so that the henna dries without being disturbed on my palms. I dance with him a few minutes later barefoot on the grass with henna encrusted on my feet. He twirls me around elegantly, always disentangling my long skirt so I do not trip. I spread my arms and embrace the entire universe to the beat of Moroccan music. His smile extends towards infinity, folding me into its generous expanse.

TWO DAYS LATER, WE DRIVE to the resort town of Agadir and check into a large suite in the Palais des Rose Hotel. An imprint of my Visa card is taken for this reservation. The wedding site is about an hour's drive away from Agadir. Both of us hide our wedding outfits as though we are children who wish to surprise each other. The day before the wedding, a crisis-laden telephone call makes us fly out of our stunning hotel and drive to the oasis where the wedding will take place, but we halt well in advance of our destination. The villagers of Ras Mouka have blocked the route to the oasis by placing huge boulders across the road. Khadim stops the car and I get out as well. The waistband of my thin cotton trousers is damp and pools of sweat ring the T-shirt I am wearing. Dust settles in clumps over the sunblock on my face and my eyes sting. My throat is parched and the relentless afternoon sun of Ras Mouka scorches my skin through my clothes. I feel a profound hatred for the clump of men standing by the truck on the dusty rock-strewn field.

My outrage is also heightened by Khadim's terse request that I stay in the car while he speaks to the people. In the all male preserve, I watch the negotiations conducted with flying hand gestures and raised voices. Khadim and his brother return after a while, faces slumped with dejection.

"They are prepared to make trouble. I have the permission of the governor of this region and he can send guards," Khadim tells me.

"A wedding surrounded by angry people and armed guards?" I look at him in disbelief.

"If you wish it," replies Khadim.

"I do not wish it. Let's go to the top of the mountain then." I remember the beautiful spot overlooking the lake of the barrage above the oasis.

"Yes. It will be as beautiful." Khadim nods his head.

"It's called crisis management," I say, giddy with the sun and relief.

His brother walks over and we tell him of our decision to move the wedding site and he also regards this as a perfect solution. The man from the catering company is also present and he is told about the change of location. He seems responsible; after all, he has been paid forty thousand dirhams by me for the wedding dinner for twenty people. I sit in the car with the air conditioning on and let Khadim handle the arrangements.

"They are ignorant people," Khadim says returning to the car.

"Is it their land?"

"They own the land around it. Not the oasis," he replies.

"It doesn't matter," I reassure him.

THE NEXT MORNING, ON THE day of our wedding, I am lying on the marble ledge of the "Hamam." Heated water pipes underneath the marble are more effective than the steam. The female attendant scrubs my body with a black abrasive mitt and the flying dark specks in the air are parts of my skin. Then my hair is washed in the Rasul clay of Morocco. It is filled with rose petals and rose water. A mixture of henna, rose petals, and Argan oil is massaged into my skin and rinsed off. I leave the Hamam and go to the hairdresser, who sets my hair with tiny rollers and, after drying it, he separates each curl and sprinkles silver dust in it. An hour later, I am seated in a rented hotel car with my wedding double caftan resting on the front seat. My toilet bag contains my wedding necklace, perfume, and silver wedding shoes. I will be driven to the wedding alone. Khadim has left three hours earlier with his wedding clothes, which I have not seen. I have chosen to go alone and not with my friends or his relatives, as I want privacy. Throughout the day I am consumed with a tension I am unable able to shake off and think it is simply my nerves. I believe that I am facing the most significant and last solitary journey of my life. I will change in the small tent Khadim has told me will be put up for me, away from the wedding tent.

The driver of the car is exquisitely courteous but troubled to be carrying the bride to her wedding alone.

When we reach Ras Mouka, the car turns on the Barrage Road leading up to the mountain. In ten minutes, we reach the huge artificial lake and begin the ascent up the winding mountain road. At the first turn, the white wedding tent is visible. It floats like a white pavilion and I feel my heart hammering with excitement. My Moroccan fairytale wedding is just five minutes away. When the car reaches the top, the driver halts it before the other cars and the catering truck where shabby looking men wearing long robes appear. I can see my small cluster of Canadian guests standing outside the tent with members of Khadim's family. There is no smaller tent for me to change into my wedding clothes. The small parapet jutting out of one side of the mountain, which was to be covered with carpets, roses, and a bench for us to sit on, while the Muslim wedding ceremony called the "Nikah" is performed, is bare. Khadim is not near the car to receive me. In fact he is nowhere in the small space and neither is the car he drives.

I ask the driver to retreat down the mountain and ask him to search for a place where I can change. I am furious with the man I am about to marry as every detail discussed between us, which he had assured me would be managed, seems to be missing. In the barren surroundings by the edge of the lake, a small guard post is found. It is in fact a small wooden hut with a corrugated iron roof. I walk to it carrying my wedding dress and my toilet bag. I open the door and am confronted by a small space filled with metal tanks of gasoline. I shut the door and change in the darkness. I know that silk caftan brushes the dirt on the floor and my fingers tremble as I try to fasten the clasp of my elaborate necklace. I have no idea how I look. When I open the door and step outside on the rocky ground both the driver and the guard are transfixed.

"La Reine," is the whisper floating in the air.

I look up at the mountain plateau and see once again the white tent floating like a magical pavilion in heaven. Instead of excitement, it is now a sense of foreboding that fills me.

CHAPTER 19

✿ Marrakech

THE ELABORATELY DECORATED WASTEPAPER BASKET next to the long dressing table overflows. It appears to be filled with silver. Into this basket are stuffed my wedding caftan of blue silk encrusted with silver embroidery, the inner white caftan made of chiffon with a silk lining, cream lace lingerie, silver shoes, and wedding necklace. Late at night, I drop these items one by one into the garbage can. The silk and lace wedding negligee sits unworn, folded in a bed of tissue lying in the armoire. Two empty velvet jeweller's boxes lie on the carpet near the bed. A trail of silver cosmetic powder emerges from the marble bathroom leading up to the bed where it dots the bed sheets and the pillows.

I am asleep in the oversized bed curled into a fetal ball. My hands are tucked into my stomach but the left hand displays a small gold band gathered into a deep blue stone. Khadim, also asleep, lying on his back, is wearing the same ring on his outstretched left hand. A huge bouquet of roses sent by the hotel manager lies shrivelled in their cellophane tent. A white hotel bathrobe with a torn sleeve trails off the edge of the bed.

This is my memory of what I saw around me when I opened my eyes the next morning. The trauma of the preceding evening only evoked a survival plan in my head. I spent the next two hours in an act of deception that was designed simply to escape from an unimagined horror. Perhaps it was the spirit of my father who had insisted that I had to climb back on the horse that had orchestrated my response. Or that I simply refused to acknowledge the warrior within me. But I have become a cold and unflinching machine.

A taxi speeds along the Agadir Road heading towards Marrakech. I am sitting in the back seat, writing on a notepad. I am itemizing expenses. In twenty days, I have spent 86,000 dirhams in Moroccan currency on my illegal wedding. Khadim had left the hotel this morning in pursuit of some document that prevented the cleric from attending the wedding and performing the "Nikah." I drown in a sea of mistrust and uncertainty as every version of his story rings untrue.

The man I know and love is lying to me and I am trapped in a foreign country without a person by my side. The trauma of the fiasco on the mountaintop has made me shut a portion of my conscious mind. I have blanked it out. At no point is Khadim aware of the extent of my devastation. He makes no mention of the honeymoon he indicated, which would be a complete surprise for me. This is the fourth day of our stay in the bridal suite of a luxury hotel. He disappears each morning on a document-collecting mission to town while I hide in the hotel and say goodbye to my departing friends, lying to them that we had a private wedding ceremony. When I ask him if the house is ready in Marrakech, he casually tells me that there is nothing in the kitchen.

"What do you mean, nothing?"

"There is no cooking stove."

"I see," I am having difficulty digesting this information.

"You can use my mother's kitchen downstairs," he replies dismissively as though I have uttered something foolish.

This statement is like a cannon aimed at my heart, and I am speechless with rage. I wait until he leaves the room and dial Driss's number in Casablanca.

"I think I have been swept into some joint family system without my permission."

"Just wait and see how it works out," he responds.

I do not tell him about the entire fiasco and he assumes that the wedding has taken place and I am having some last-minute jitters about life in Khadim's family home. I do not find any solace in this comment. It is nobody's fault but my own and I spring into action.

I hurriedly pack my bag, walk down to the reception desk of the hotel, and clear my personal bill. I inform the manager that we are registered under both names and that Khadim will settle his own portion. I then immediately hire a private car and driver. I am removing myself from chaos and betrayal in the only way I know.

In the speeding taxi, the events replay in my mind despite all my efforts to control this exercise. The silent three-hour wait on top of the mountain in a white tent devoid of all the lavish arrangements I had paid for had brutalized me to the point where shock prevented me from uttering a sound. Khadim, smelling of sweat, with a disconnected smile, dressed in a diaphanous cape worn over cropped pants with long white socks and slippers, a red Fez cap perched absurdly on his head, had appeared by the side of the car, told me that I looked beautiful, and helped me walk towards the twenty guests who had already waited for two hours. We stood for a few moments for photographs to be taken. It was only months later that I realized that I could not smile.

Khadim had seated me at a table in the tent and proceeded to float around as though he was in charge of a group of tourists and not a groom soon to be married. The arrangements I assumed he had made for our meticulously planned wedding were non-existent. The tables in the tent were devoid of the flowers I had ordered. The appetizers and wine were noticeably absent. The musicians were two old men who strummed on discordant musical instruments. His family seated at another table also waited in silence. Dressed as a bride, I waited with my guests for three hours in the tent without any legal wedding ceremony or any festivities. Every now and then Khadim would appear and sit by my side and murmur that everyone was waiting for the Adul, or cleric who performed the wedding, to appear. I remained speechless with shock. My confused and disturbed friends huddled in silence, and left for their hotels after hardly tasting the rough fare presented as the wedding dinner. I finally rise and simply walk to the car I had hired as fifty villagers from the Ras Mouka oasis below take over the mountaintop and eat the food the guests had difficulty consuming.

Khadim appeared in front of the car and stopped it. He opened the door and sat with me. In the silent ride, all he did was hold my hand. We reached the hotel before midnight and I swallowed a sleeping pill that I used for jet lag. I have very little memory of what transpired in the night as I unconsciously blocked a great deal out.

Now, as I sit in the racing taxi and make a list, I permit myself to recall the utterly bizarre events. I remember lying on the bed wearing the hotel bathrobe and Khadim kneeling on the bed looking down at me. He spoke words like love and protection and then slipped the wedding ring on my finger. He then held his hand out to me, and I followed suit in a robotic fashion. He said we were now married in the eyes of God and the paperwork would be completed soon. He then told me that he used the address of the beach house as his residence, and as this was an out-of-province wedding, perhaps some mistake was made. He appeared both confused and disoriented himself.

I have protectively shut away the nightmarish events and, at this moment, I am consumed with flight and escape. The driver of the taxi keeps receiving calls on his mobile phone and tells me that it is Khadim, instructing him to turn the car back to Agadir and bring me back.

Then the manager of the hotel also calls and I take his call. He informs me that Khadim refused to pay his half of the bill, made a scene in the reception area, and claimed that I ran away with all his money and they should call the police and the Canadian embassy.

I refuse to take any further calls and tell the driver to proceed to Marrakech. My own phone rings incessantly and I no longer answer it. My survival mechanism operates faultlessly.

I reach the apartment in Marrakech. My two bags lie unopened. The smaller bag contains all the wedding clothes that Khadim had retrieved from the wastebasket in the hotel and carefully packed. The apartment shows signs of our whirlwind days and nights before we left for the wedding a week ago. There are wedding gifts bought by my friends from Canada lying unopened. By tomorrow noon the apartment has to be vacated and the shift to Khadim's house has to take place. I keep turning the wedding ring on my finger.

I am also playing another desperate game with myself. With shock, I realize that I am desperately seeking a way to separate Khadim from the hideous events that have transpired in five days. The first sense of being in completely alien surroundings re-enters with accompanying fear. In fact, what I want is a second opinion on what has transpired but there is no one I know in the city of Marrakech. I am too embarrassed to call Driss in Casablanca again, for fear that I may be judged. I am completely dependent on Khadim. My only strength lies in my financial mobility. I cannot call anyone in Canada because I do not want to reveal that the Moroccan fairytale has turned into a nightmare. In a week's time the container from Canada will land in Casablanca. In fact, I am so inexperienced that I do not realize that all I had to do was call the shipping company and tell them to reroute the container back to Canada. I am convinced I have burned my bridges behind me. I have already lied to the friends from Canada who were taking flights home and said we got married in a private ceremony much later that night. I have done this to save face.

In the middle of the night, the phone rings. I hear a guttural voice using obscenities ask me in English if I am looking for an adventure in Morocco. The phone disconnects and my feeling is that the voice is eerily familiar, but I cannot place it. The next day Khadim arrives before noon. He opens the door and walks in.

"I left the ring and my watch to settle the bill." His manner is subdued.

"Why didn't you pay the bill?" I am shocked.

"I cannot afford such an expensive hotel."

"Did you tell the hotel manager horrible things about me running away with your money?"

"Darling," he places his hand on his heart, "how could I say such a thing?"

"How were you planning to pay for the honeymoon, Khadim?" My voice is breaking.

"I didn't plan anything."

"You mean you lied to me?"

"No. We would decide together where to go." He gives me a gentle smile.

"Then I misunderstood," I falter, wanting all the madness to stop.

"Certainly. Come let us have some lunch in the café downstairs." He embraces and kisses me.

"Your ring. They took it?" I look at his bare finger.

"I ordered another one. He will have it ready in two days. But why did you run away from me? I went to fix the paper in Agadir and it was not ready. We have to go back for it."

"Never. I am not going back," I say slowly, leaning away from him.

"We have to get married officially now," he smiles at me indulgently as though I am a wayward child.

"In Marrakech where we are going to live," I reply.

"If you wish, but it will take more time. We have to fill new forms," he says reluctantly.

"It doesn't matter," I say, wondering what I mean, "I just want to go home. I am sick of hotels and apartments."

The rental car I have paid for is missing. We meet the landlord of the apartment and hand over the keys. He loads my luggage into a taxi and, within minutes, I see the familiar part of Marrakech disappearing as we head towards the long broad avenue called Allal Fassi, dotted with shabby highrise buildings and shops. The taxi turns into the unpaved road beside the Pharmacy Asif. The men operating the food stands study the taxi with interest. The driver takes a sharp left and then swings right and the iron gate with the green design becomes visible.

Right opposite this gate another unfamiliar scene greets my eyes. A huge used clothing kiosk is open just in front of the house. In the night, it is lit with kerosene lamps. The clothing spills over the pavement in paper cartons. Two burly men at the stand, stare at us unabashedly, as Khadim lifts my suitcases out of the taxi. He then opens the small iron gate and pulls me inside. The house rises in darkness before us as I stand in the front garden. There is no light visible either inside or at the door. The fragrance of jasmine rises in the heat of the July night in Marrakech, and I am flooded with a sense of foreboding as I am about to enter the space that is meant to be my home in Marrakech.

HIS MOTHER IS NOT PRESENT to greet us. In fact the door to her apartment is shut. Khadim tells me she is asleep. We climb up the stairs to the second floor in darkness and halt before the door that he has had painted in blue. He opens the door and turns on the light in long bare hall. The air in the closed apartment is musty and stifling as temperatures are high even in the night. I walk to the dark bedroom.

Khadim switches on a tiny lamp sitting on the floor. It reveals that the colour of the room is terracotta and the window is painted blue. The room is bare except for a large white armoire set against one wall. I walk into the room adjoining it and see that, although it is painted, it is still filled with the clutter of the broken bed, cartons, and masses of clothes hanging off a wooden pole I saw four months ago. The kitchen has no stove, but the old refrigerator hums quietly in the corner. Dirty glasses sit in the tiny steel sink and garbage sits in a plastic bag on the floor. The room adjoining it, meant to be my study, has a large brown metal desk in it.

On the wall behind it, aluminum strips for a shelving assembly are nailed in. One small glass shelf lies on two metal brackets. Gazing at it, I become oblivious to the various empty rooms and ignore the fact that Khadim had done nothing whatsoever to prepare the house. I regard the solitary bookshelf a symbol of Khadim's attempt to recreate the home I have left behind. In my shattered condition, I cling to this as an act of love, and compassion floods me, strengthening my resolve to accept the lack of amenities in the house without reacting. I am being challenged to accept the primitive conditions facing me and my innate sense of adventure rescues me.

I open my eyes the next morning conscious that my body feels stiff. We have slept on the floor of the empty bedroom, on a thin mattress. The window is shut; I have woken up in a sauna. The heat swirls around me in the room, which has neither an air conditioner nor a fan. Khadim is missing. One of my opened suitcases lies on top of the other closed one. I find a robe, walk to the bathroom, and open the hand shower mounted above the bathtub. The cold water wakes me up. There is a green towel hanging on the hook, I wrap it around myself and head towards the bedroom. The hall door opens and Khadim walks in with a tray of tea. I move towards him.

"Good morning, room service. I am being spoilt," I smile at him.

"Cover yourself," he replies curtly and walks into the salon with the tray.

His words are like a bucket of cold water tossed on me. The man who spent half the night making love to me on a mattress on the floor and spread a rug covered with sequins on the floor beside me, is displaying the mannerisms of a monk in the morning. I wear a light robe and join him in the salon. He is waiting for me seated on the long couch.

"Sabah el kheir," he says formally and pours tea for me.

"Lovely," I respond, taking in the breakfast on the tray.

There is a pot of mint tea, a circular disc of Moroccan bread, and a saucer filled with a dark green oil and another filled with thick dark honey. He adds the honey to the olive oil, breaks a piece of bread, scoops it in the mixture, and offers it to me first. I chew on the bread, finding the mixture smeared on it to be unpalatable. But I eat it, chasing it with sips of mint tea.

"We should have breakfast on the terrace," I suggest.

"You can be seen from the terrace," he responds.

"By whom?"

"People on the street; they are watching all the time."

"From the grill?" It is on the third floor. "Darling, don't be ridiculous."

"Don't shout." He jumps up and puts both hands on his hips.

I also stand up, "I am not shouting. What is wrong with you?"

His leans over and places both hands on my shoulders and presses me down on the couch.

"I am going to pray. Eat your breakfast," he commands and walks out of the room.

WE ARE WALKING OUT TOGETHER an hour later. I am wearing a cotton skirt with a camisole and linen jacket. Sweat pours down my back and I am aware that the nape of my neck is wet. The heat is unbearable and the linen jacket makes my skin prickle. The jacket is required in the seedy neighbourhood filled with rough-looking men who simply lounge against walls and leer at women. Khadim is impervious to the heat. His tan face is smooth and dry, and his short-sleeved shirt crisp without a trace of sweat. He locks the two doors, and when we reach the first floor, his mother is standing in the hall. I greet her in Arabic and receive the three kisses on the cheeks. For a moment, I cling to the older woman in confusion wanting to say something but the words dry up in my mouth. Khadim speaks to her in Arabic and I know that I am being discussed.

"Wait, she wishes to welcome you to the house," says Khadim.

The mother goes to the kitchen and brings out a tray with two glass of milk and a dish of dates. I stand in the vestibule drinking the milk and eating the dates. I find the local custom to be charming and see the warmth in the mother's face and am certain that we shall be friends, but why didn't she bother to see that there was a bed to sleep on in the bedroom upstairs? When we step outside I look at the jasmine vine Khadim has planted for me and it is wound around a thin rope leading to the second floor balcony. His mother, who has stepped out with us, plucks a flower and offers it to me. I inhale the tiny flower and feel as though my universe will balance itself again.

When I step out onto the street with him, it is alive with vendors and a huge pile of garbage sitting twenty feet from the house. I conceal my shock, stepping carefully over the potholes in the street until we reach the main boulevard and he flags a taxi.

The taxi takes us to an enormous shopping complex. He leads me inside to the large supermarket called the "Marjane." I race up and down the aisles in excitement tossing familiar grocery and cleaning items into the cart. This touch of domesticated normalcy sweeps all cultural barriers away. Khadim is balmy and relaxed, patiently walking besides me as I examine new food and packaging. When I ask him his food preferences, he smiles and says, "Whatever you serve me will be fine." When we reach the checkout and I pay the bill, which is enormous by local standards but in keeping with what I would spend in Canada, he simply looks away.

When we return home, he says he needs to go out and will return in a short while. I busy myself tackling the kitchen. There are a few items of cheap Chinese crockery in the shelf. Two plates, a bowl, and a set of green acrylic-handle cutlery. A battered saucepan and a few cooking spoons. I clean out the empty refrigerator and stock it. When he returns, we head out again, this time to buy a stove. The taxi leads to a busy neighbourhood in the heart of the city. We enter a store where he buys a two-ring gas burner and collects a canister of gas. All I see is cheap aluminum cookware, so I pick up two cooking pans, a garbage can, and wastepaper baskets for the house.

When we return home, he places the burner on the kitchen shelf, hooks up the gas, and shows me how to light the pilot with a match.

It's like I am camping and I know that I can manage. But when I try to light the gas ring, the flame jumps up and singes my fingers. He pulls my hand away and gives me an irate look. I try again and am just not quick enough, this time he pulls me back and shouts something in Arabic.

"Do you want pasta or fish for dinner?" I ask him gaily, wanting to dispel the tension.

"Both," he shoots a broad smile at me.

"Both!" I laugh.

"Why not?" he smiles and walks away.

I spend the entire late afternoon and early evening cooking in the ill-equipped kitchen. I have not even unpacked my clothes, only my toiletries. Cooking is one of my strengths and I prepare a large meal and arrange the tasteless plates on the only table in the house in the living room. Then I walk down to the miniscule garden and pluck hibiscus from a vine creeping up the wall. I arrange the flowers in a water tumbler, but realize there are no serving platters or bowls for the food. I walk down the stairs to the ground-floor apartment looking for Khadim's mother.

I enter the kitchen. Khadim's mother is sitting on a small stool with a wooden table in front of her. She is diminutive woman and practically buried in her clothing. First, there is an under-caftan covered by a gauzy over-caftan fastened by an embroidered belt and a cord holding back the double sleeves. The misshapen feet are stuffed into socks and open sandals. A necklace of worn beads and shabby earrings with missing stones display her innate penchant for adornment. Yet the effect is one of stolid dignity.

Hunched over the stool, her air of being the long-widowed matriarch of a clan of seven children is undeniably present. A stack of vegetables lies on the table and she is peeling carrots. I drag the other stool next to her, find a small paring knife in the jumble of cutlery, and sit beside her. Then I lift a carrot and silently start peeling it. Fatima Zohra smiles, raises her eyebrows, and then gives me an approving nod. I hold up the carrot towards her with a look of enquiry and she is gives me the Arabic name.

For the next fifteen minutes, a delicate bonding takes place between us. My objective is to convey that, despite cultural or social inequalities, we are two women cooking together. The hilarity caused by my mispronunciation in Arabic fills the kitchen with merriment. My mother is no longer alive but a mother is being gifted to me, and she is the one who will teach me how to speak Arabic to her.

Khadim and I sit side-by-side eating dinner. He brings me a stubby white candle, lights it, and places it next to the tumbler of Hibiscus. The huge cavernous salon with the sinking blue upholstered divans and a riotous blue floral carpet has a different ambience to it now. In the candlelight, his features soften and the pleasure he displays by complimenting and devouring the food placed in front him transport me to a familiar and safe zone. This is who he really is, I say to myself. After dinner, he helps me take the dishes to the kitchen and assists in washing up. We walk through the empty rooms and discuss my plans for furnishing the house and the excitement of my container arriving at the end of the week. He defers to my tastes and preferences, saying, "You can do whatever you please in the house."

I am lying in the tub filled with oil of Argan and rose essence. Khadim has lit incense and it wafts in through the open door. The lyrical love songs of the Lebanese singer float through the apartment. When I finish, I wear a delicate chiffon nightgown and walk into the salon. He is rolling hashish into the tobacco from an open cigarette. I now realize that this is part of his relaxing ritual. I have been told that is a common indulgence just as a glass of wine would be for someone else. In fact, what he has done is dupe me completely. I am told this is a herbal relaxant and not the harmful chemicals ingested by Western cultures. He puffs on it leisurely and throws me a hazy smile. I blow him a kiss and go to the bedroom to find a cigarette from my purse. I light it and walk to the front hall and step on the grill-covered balcony to smoke it outside. Through the wrought-iron grill, I peer at the dark street outside. I am utterly relaxed and gaze upwards to see the crescent moon surrounded by stars pasted on the clear night sky. I am excited and ready to begin my life in Marrakech.

A hand grasps my right shoulder and I am spun around with such force that my slippers are torn off my feet. In the dark, Khadim looms over me, propelling me with a monstrous force down the hall. I scream struggling and he pulls me into the bedroom where he puts both hands on my chest and sends me flying backwards to land on the mattress on the floor. I shout at him to stop, and spring up but he pushes me back again. I get up again panting and enraged.

"I am getting out of here. You cannot treat me like this! I am leaving you."

I take two steps forward and he steps closer, closing the distance between us and pushes me with both hands again. I tumble backward but rise again. He is completely silent as he does this. My equilibrium is shattered and my outrage makes me disregard any physical injury I may suffer. I am determined not to back down. He stands like an impassive column intercepting all my efforts and silently pushes me back with measured force. It is as though he has calculated my body weight and knows exactly the right amount of force needed to send me tumbling back on the mattress.

In the dimly lit room, we continue like gladiators from another era. The mattress that bears the physical imprints of our love transformed into a deadly arena. The delicate fabric of my nightgown strains around my body and the skin across my chest becomes sore, but I do not give up. Khadim's bullying aggression spills into a previously unrevealed stance of domination that revolts me. I battle in vain with his force for half the night, until exhaustion and his unwavering strength make me collapse on the mattress not to rise again.

He leaves the room and I hear the door being locked from the outside. I am so stunned at what has happened that I lie in the darkened room questioning my sanity until I fall asleep. Later, in some fatigued twilight zone, I find myself cradled in his arms, my back massaged with long sure strokes.

"They must never see you from the street," he says.

"You are mad. It was dark and no one can look into the balcony. There is a grill." I am fully awake now and try to move away from him.

"You must never refuse me," he whispers to me.

CHAPTER 20

❀ Marrakech

I AM WATCHING THE STEEL container carrying my car and the contents of my Canadian home roll out of the Casablanca shipyard. I am torn by conflicting emotions because the excitement of finally claiming the conveniences of a familiar life are shadowed by the turbulent existence of my new life in Marrakech with Khadim. Within days, my tenuous status in the three-storey Marrakech home reveals itself. My movements are both subtly and aggressively controlled by Khadim. His complete shift from the liberal attitudes he had displayed during courtship to a startling conservatism bewilder me.

Khadim has an obsessive need to be informed of my movements on an hourly basis, and the names of the shops where I have picked up items for the house. Deep within the core of his assertion is the notion that I am in a foreign environment and need this type of protection but I detect a chameleon streak in his personality. Moment by moment the new series of complexities of his temperament are also displayed. He vacillates from amorous lover, protector, and artistic companion to a robotic ascetic and a harshly judgmental man riddled with a paranoia levelled at his own society. I have always prided myself on my resilient adaptability and feel that although the environment poses no great challenge, Khadim is testing my spirit in many ways. I am also beginning to wonder if I have made the biggest mistake of my life, yet there is no one to discuss this with.

A few days ago, we were both seated in his sister Ruqaiya's home. It was a spontaneous visit and not an invitation to visit formally. His three other sisters are also present and over the traditional mint tea, a heated argument breaks out. Khadim addresses his sisters in loud, angry tones.

"What is it darling?" I break in and ask him.

"They want to sell the house," he replies angrily.

"You mean where we are living?"

"It belongs to all of us. There are seven parts and my mother has one," he tells me wearily.

"Tell them I agree. They must sell it immediately. I do not need their house." I am shocked at the revelation and the hostility.

"We shall see. They are only women. My brothers and I have bigger parts than them." He gestures to me that we are leaving.

"This Ruqaiya is not a sister," he says bitterly in the car.

"What do you mean?" I want to understand his relationship with his sisters.

"She did black magic on me. A sister! I was so shocked. Never eat anything she gives you," he warns me.

"You are joking. Black magic. I don't believe in it," I laugh.

"It is in the Quran. It was done to the prophet himself. You are to believe me."

"Ridiculous! There is an acknowledgment of the darkness and negativity that exists in people. These are the last three verses of the Quran. That is all." I refuse to back down.

"As you wish, but I am serious about Ruqaiya." He gives me a worried look.

"Too late, darling. She came to visit your mother yesterday. I was in the front and greeted her, and she opened a handkerchief and offered me a candy."

"Did you eat it?" he screams at me.

"Of course I did. It was a candy. I was being polite. After all, she is your elder sister."

Khadim starts reciting verses from the Quran and drives the car as though he is being pursued.

"This is absurd. It was dark, made of honey or some sort of molasses. I didn't like it much and just swallowed it," I tell him nervously, surprised at his behaviour.

"Are you feeling all right?"

"Of course. It's just the heat I can't handle but I am fine." I lean over and kiss him on the cheek.

"Don't. I have to pray." He draws back as though he has been stung.

"What do you mean?" I am equally stung by his repelling gesture.

"I have to stay clean or my ablutions will be spoiled," he replies, turning to look at me.

"I see," I reply, amused. "Ablutions required before prayers refer to sexual intercourse and not to a kiss." I also remember that this taboo did not seem to concern him overly when we first met.

WE HAVE RETURNED FROM CASABLANCA. When the customs officers opened the seal of the container and I saw my car, at that bizarre moment my heart leapt with excitement because I was transported back to my life in Canada. My car still has its Ontario registration plates on and I consider this a reassuring touch in the middle of the chaos of the shipyard. Khadim had told me that I was not to let the international shipping company make the land arrangements for transporting the container from Casablanca to Marrakech.

"I have an agent and he will do the customs clearance and take care of it for just three thousand dirhams."

The agent spent four hours with me at the port marching me to various offices where I wrote a series of cheques for fraudulent taxes and duties that were not applicable in my case. However, I was the last to know. Then the car was registered and insured by a company that only dealt with foreigners. When we left for Marrakech with the container and the truck it was hitched to following us, another payment was demanded instantly. It was double what Khadim had quoted. When I protested, a sheet of paper was put in front of me that quoted the rates. Khadim told me not to complain; this was his country and he knew all the regulations. I write the cheque and pull into a gas station. I go to the toilet and telephone Driss.

"There is something wrong Driss, I have paid a fortune."

"You are not to take your belongings to his house," said Driss.

"Why?"

"I see trouble ahead. Store your belongings outside until you feel comfortable to make this move."

"You mean a public storage facility?"

"How far are you from Marrakech?"

"Maybe an hour's drive. But Driss it is almost eight in the evening."

"I have relatives in Marrakech, I will call them, and they will store your items. I will call you back with their address."

When he does, I am driving but I take the call and repeat the address for Khadim, who dutifully writes it without knowing anything.

Luck is not on my side. When we reach the city, I tell Khadim it is very late and I have arranged to have the cartons stored somewhere else until the morning.

"The men have to take the container back tonight, or you will pay another day's charges."

"I know."

Even the weather conspires against me. An unseasonable rain falls that night in the city. The house we drive to is small. Driss's cousin is a charming woman and shows me a strip of space in a bedroom not realizing that that there are forty-two large containers. Then she suggests storing everything outside in the courtyard. I tell her I have fifteen large cardboard containers where my art is stored. It is a doomed project. In exhaustion and complete disorientation, I drive behind the container headed for Khadim's house.

In the morning, I see that the forty-four containers have filled the room meant to be my study in the house, which I now know does not belong to Khadim. However, he has told me that it is my home as long as I want it and his other two brothers are aware of this. Even though I plan to furnish each room before I open items that will be placed in them, I am conscious that it is a temporary arrangement. I wonder if the sisters will march up the stairs and invade our privacy.

Dust and heat swirl through the house in the searing month of August. Khadim's brother donates a portable air conditioner and it is brought up to the apartment on the second floor. Khadim positions it in front of the bedroom door and it offers some relief while the rest of the house is a cauldron. Yet I wake up each night bathed in sweat because somewhere in the middle of the night Khadim has switched the cooler off.

Our days are spent chasing craftsmen and electricians and bringing them home. I do not unpack anything until the house is furnished to provide shelving and items of furniture. The constant dust that fills the cavernous apartment terrifies me. Khadim's minimalist existence in the barren second-floor apartment is slowly being redesigned by me. This is the one area in which he gives me complete autonomy and is pleased with my fascination with Moroccan décor. When we are together, he drives my car, racing through the narrow streets of the medina of Marrakech, dodging donkey carts and motorcyclists with expertise. His personality changes when he drives. He waves to his acquaintances and adopts a lordly posture. When I drive alone, I sometimes escape the dusty city and head up the Ourika valley road that splices farmlands and rolling hills leading to the Atlas Mountains in the distance. This is when I can listen to my thoughts and wrestle with the new demons that plague my life. I am drawing large sums of money from my account weekly to cover all the living expenses. Although I can afford this, Khadim's inability to cover even modest expenses is based on the assumption that he is short on funds because he has taken time off from work to help me settle in. It makes me wonder if he will ever show some sign of a regular income. He has been using various delaying tactics for the past three weeks when I ask him for my own set of house keys. Because of this delay, my movements have to be co-ordinated by his presence. I am also aware that I can modernize the house but it is joint family property, so I tolerate the primitive conditions of both the kitchen and the bathroom. Despite these unsettling elements in my life, my love for him has not diminished. In an unknown world, his presence is the only known reality and I cling to it.

Day by day, I discover the city of Marrakech and its inhabitants. Khadim introduces me to the craftsmen in the medina who will make furnishings for the apartment. I have only brought my writing desk, a leather couch for my study, and my glass dining table from Canada. I still have not unpacked. Khadim rips open a large carton one day while I am out. I return to confront my writing desk, a gift from Cesar, sitting in the middle of the room like some stranded passenger on the tarmac of an airport.

We spend time in the fascinating Jewish quarter called the Mellah where the glasscutters measure and cut shelves for a bookcase. He smiles at the mock ferocity with which I bargain over prices and he tests my resilience by leading me for lunch to food stalls where men in tattered clothing eat bowls of lentils and stews. Here, he always pays the bill with crumpled twenty-dirham notes and I am stunned to see him receive change back. I suspect he wants to introduce me to the simplicity of his life and I am determined not to let him down.

His mother, Fatma Zohra, silently climbs the steps to our apartment one afternoon, surprising me. She stands hesitantly in the hallway and I welcome her with an embrace. In my eyes, she is the only mistress of the home purchased by her late husband. I lead her by the arm and show her the newly installed kitchen shelves and the local ceramic dishes I have purchased. Her eyes linger over the glass shelves in the bathroom displaying stacks of towels and my toiletries.

"Mizian," she says repeatedly.

This word in Arabic means good. When I show her Khadim's jumble of clothes converted to neat piles on the shelves of the armoire she smiles and makes a comment. Although I cannot understand what she says in Arabic, I sense her approval, and in the universal world of women, she acknowledges that I am doing what women do naturally, domesticate their men. She embraces me and gestures me to follow her down. The destination is her bedroom, which I have simply glanced at but never entered. It is an untidy room bursting with furniture. Her bed is heaped with faded blankets and ringed by tables covered with fraying fabric. A vintage sewing machine sits on one of the tables. A large wooden armoire takes up half a wall and she unlocks it and returns with a small bag. She empties the contents of the fabric bag on the bed. A few pieces of artificial jewellery roll out. In a heartbreaking gesture, she conveys that this is all she has to offer to me. I shake my head and pick up a necklace made of beads with a red glass pendant. The pendent has Arabic script etched into it. I fasten the necklace around my neck and thank her. Khadim is standing in the doorway. He says something to his mother harshly.

"Tell her that I will never take it off," I say to him picking up the flicker of distress that dims the light in his mother's eyes.

Khadim turns on his heel and walks away, leaving me puzzled by his discourtesy.

When the defining moment, which alters the course of our life together, arrives, I discover that my survival instincts are stronger than the sum of all my passions. We decide to go to the Aglou beach house to escape the stifling heat of Marrakech for the weekend. The Italian, who wants to run a travel agency with Khadim, if they are able to get a licence from the government, also joins us. When we arrive at the beach house late at night, it is occupied by seven relatives who sprawl on the couches in the living room. The sole bedroom has a padlock attached to it.

I insist that Khadim and I check into the tiny neighbourhood hotel. It is a tense and disappointing weekend. The next day Khadim takes my car and disappears, saying he will be back in half an hour. I sit on the hotel terrace and wait for more than three hours. When he returns, I complain about his lack of punctuality. He tells me we are expected for lunch at the beach house with his relatives and he has brought a fish that they will cook. The beach house is cluttered with people and dirt and the communal meal that we are expected to share is an unpalatable experience. A large Tagine, fish stew, is placed on the table and eight pairs of fingers lift sections of fish and heap the bones onto the bare table. The absence of cutlery and napkins make my hygienic North American sensibilities recoil. Although I have shared meals with Khadim like this, the forest of fingers that are raised to mouths, licked, and dipped again makes my gorge rise. I lose my appetite and am aware of Khadim's displeasure.

On the drive back to Marrakech, I take over the driving from Khadim. It is the first time that I am driving outside Marrakech on the single-lane road. After two hours, I see that gas gauge is close to empty. I pull into the first gas station and ask Khadim to pay for the gas as I cleared the hotel bill and thought I was short.

"I don't have any money," he says.

"Marco, can you let us have some cash please?" I say to his friend sprawled in the backseat.

"I left my wallet in the beach house."

"You are joking." I remember his small knapsack that always stayed shut.

"It's all right, he does not have money." Khadim looks at me irately, as though I am misbehaving.

I pull into the gas station and stop the car, pull out the keys from the ignition, stuff them deep in my pocket and get out of the car. Both men also get out of the car.

"The ride stops here gentlemen, please take a taxi to Marrakech," I say to both of them.

"Darling, give me the keys," says Khadim softly.

"I mean it," I reply furiously and back away from him.

"It will take a long time to find a taxi," he smiles at me and steps closer.

"I don't care. I am getting a little tired of paying for everything," I watch the gas station attendants looking at us from a distance.

"Beat her, Khadim! Who does she think she is? Take the keys away from the bitch if you have to," Marco shouts at Khadim.

"If you come near me, I will tell the men to call the police." My body stiffens with rage and shock at Khadim's passivity.

I walk rapidly towards the men.

Khadim races after me and grabs me. "Give me the keys and I will get rid of him," he whispers in my ear.

"No. I am not comfortable doing this," I reply.

"What is the matter with you?"

"You are two men in your fifties and I do not accept that you have no money in your pockets. You are humiliating me. He is a crude and abusive man, and he will never sit in my car again."

Khadim moves away and talks to the other man. They have moved away from the car and are standing near the edge of the road. I can hear the sound of the roadside tirade. It is laced with obscenities directed towards me. I race to the car and lock the doors from inside. Then I lower the window two inches, start the car, and drive towards them.

"I am leaving. Are you coming?" I shout to Khadim.

"No," Khadim shouts back.

"It's me or him. He will never sit in my car again," I say loudly through the small opening.

Khadim turns his back to me and at that moment, his choice is clear to me. In an avowedly patriarchal society, he will save face at all costs. I press my foot on the accelerator and swing out of the gas station. The dark road stretches ahead. The headlights of a lumbering transport truck blind me from behind.

My hands on the steering wheel tremble, as I am both shocked and outraged. I use one of them to rummage through my handbag and find a crumpled one-hundred-dirham note. I have no idea if there is another gas station on the road or whether I am on the right course heading towards Marrakech.

Suddenly, a small taxi overtakes me and I see both Khadim and his friend in it. Neither one of them look back. I drive in fear and in shock. The forks in the road are unfamiliar and I am praying for another gas station to appear. When it does after a harrowing ten-minute drive, I watch a few litres of gas being pumped in and find it difficult to grasp my predicament fully.

When I reach Marrakech and drive to the darkened house the doorbell is not answered. I keep dialling Khadim's phone number but he does not reply. I wait for an hour and then I drive away and head for a hotel on the broad avenue I am familiar with. I drive inside and park the car, pull out my handbag and walk into the front desk and register for a room. Mercifully, I find my Visa card but when the front desk manager asks for my passport, a requirement for all foreigners, I find the leather folder it sits in missing. The handbag sat on the floor of the passenger seat in the car. I know without a doubt that Khadim has removed it. Without hesitating, I tell the man that my passport has been stolen. The manager immediately tells me this is a criminal offence in Morocco and asks if I know who has taken it. I give him Khadim's mobile phone number. The manager calls and tells Khadim, who has answered the phone, that the hotel will send its car to collect the passport. Obviously it is a mistake. Then he hands the phone to me.

"How dare you remove my passport? I want it back now," I say.

"Come home darling. What is the matter with you?" he says softly on the phone.

"I have waited outside for an hour and I have been calling you. I have checked in and I need to make some decisions. I need to think things through. I am going to drive down myself. I am going to park the car across from the pharmacy."

"Madame, should I send someone with you?" says the desk manager.

"No, I can handle it," I say, walking out in my beach sarong and T-shirt.

I am driving down Boulevard Allal Fassi and then make a U-turn and park across from the pharmacy. The car is pointed in the direction of the hotel. It is about two in the morning. The car is parked under a streetlight. The street is empty, lined with closed shops and no visible traffic. I do not see him anywhere as I keep watching the lane next to the pharmacy. After a while, a shadow appears on the passenger side window. He materializes like a spectre. Looming over the car with a thin smile pasted on his face. I start the car in fear and roll the automatic window down an inch.

"Push it through the window, please." I turn my face away because his expression terrifies me.

"Open the door," he says leaning over and placing a hand on the window.

"Push it through the window, Khadim, or I will go back to the hotel and they will call the police."

He holds up his right hand and the passport folder is curled into it, the hand in a fist. He peers closer to the window with a calculating look that changes the expression on his face.

"Now!" I scream in fear. "I want it now!"

"Let's go home. Open the door. I will drive."

"No. I want my passport first. This is my identity in this country. You cannot take it away from me," I am sobbing.

He smiles again, changing the expression on his face and slides it through the opening. Instantly, I floor the accelerator and the car shoots out of the parked space. I am terrified of the man I call my beloved.

I wake up at ten the next morning, stunned at how well I have slept, knowing that it is the air-conditioned room that has added to the comfort. I pick up the phone and ask Khadim to bring me a change of clothes, saying we need to talk. He does not respond the entire day. I am trapped in the hotel room without clean clothes. He appears the next morning in the lobby holding a small plastic bag. I walk towards him and he simply hands it to me and sits in a chair in the lobby.

"I am going to change; I will be back in five minutes."

When I reach the room, I discover all the bag has in it is a brassiere and a white linen blouse. I race back to the lobby to discover that he has disappeared.

I HAVE BECOME HOMELESS AND all my personal possessions are lying in a house I have no access to. It is a condition I have never experienced in my entire life. I have abandoned my Canadian home and cannot return to the Marrakech home, as I have no keys. This bizarre turn of events has taken just two months. Even the vitamins I take daily are lying in the home of a man who abandoned me on a road I had never travelled before. Although he has never struck a physical blow, the quiet menace to him now terrifies me. It is as though he has become a complete stranger. My devastation does not permit me to view him either as a husband or as a friend. I am marooned in a city that is as alien as it is exotic.

I am driving in the exclusive Hivernage area of Marrakech, ringed by the best hotels of the city. My mission is to buy a change of clothes and I turn into a street where a four-storey apartment building with balcony has a sign on the second-floor apartment. I stop the car and inquire from the guard standing outside. He tells me to wait and makes a phone call. Within moments, I walk through the air-conditioned two-bedroom apartment with a wide balcony overlooking the tree-lined street. It has a large modern kitchen with a window, arched corridors, and bedrooms with wall-to-wall closets and the two bathrooms with marble appointments. In the middle of chaos, it represents a pocket of sanity. The rent is affordable and I have the option to create a home closer to the standard of the life I have left and miss desperately. The landlord tells me that it will take three days to paint it and then I can move in. I choose the terracotta hue of Marrakech and ask that all the woodwork be painted majorelle blue and give him a deposit cheque.

I drive back to Khadim's house. The iron gate is shut. I ring the doorbell and even his mother does not appear. The food vendors outside the house eye me curiously. The open mound of garbage sits on the concrete square close to the house and the sun blasting down on it releases the odours of refuse. The T-shirt and three-day-old beach sarong I am wearing are soaked in sweat. I feel the insane tide of hysteria rise within me. I dial Khadim on the mobile and he keeps disconnecting the phone. I return to the car and drive back to the hotel.

"Hello, hello. How are you today in beautiful Marrakech?" inquires the handsome young man I had spoken to over breakfast at the hotel in the morning.

"In crisis, Idrisse. I have all my things from Canada sitting in a house. I need to get them."

His eyes cloud with concern and he leads me to a private alcove in the lobby. He is an architect educated in Paris and comes from a wealthy Moroccan family. I tell him about what has transpired with Khadim and his face becomes solemn.

"We will arrange for a truck and men and we will take your things out of this house in the morning. This man is not behaving properly."

"The apartment will not be ready for another two days. I need storage facilities. I am told you have no such thing here in Marrakech."

"My family owns this hotel and another one. We will store everything there and my manager will organize the move. Please smile now," says my brand new friend.

I drive to the house again in the evening. Khadim hears the bell and opens the door. He gazes at me silently and we walk up the stairs together.

"I am packing some clothes and taking them. I have found an apartment. We need another place, somewhere neutral. Our own home, if we can work this out. A home to which I have the keys at all times," I tell him, walking to the bedroom.

I hurriedly pack clothes in one suitcase and lift my jewellery case. He is in the salon and does not come near me. I walk past the salon struggling with both cases. He rises.

"All or nothing," he yells and grabs both cases from my hands and sends them flying across the hall.

I look at his rage-distorted face underscored with pain and the aggression of his bullying stance and back away from him. The same defensive fear rises in me and I will not risk a physical altercation with him. I race down the stairs and walk outside to my car. I call him later that night from the hotel room and tell him I will be there at ten in the morning with the movers and if he does not open the door, I will have it broken down.

"It is my property," I say finally.

He disconnects the phone without saying anything.

The next morning I drive to the house followed by a large, crude moving truck. Five burly men sit in the truck. I park the car on a side street and allow the moving truck to reverse right up to the gate. The men are labourers but aware that I need some protection. I am a foreigner and not legally married to the man in whose family home my belongings are stored. The house is silent and I ring the bell. There is no answer. There is movement behind me and Khadim materializes. He opens the smaller gate with his keys. We walk in together and I unlatch the larger gate and swing it open alone. The men file out of the truck and follow me up the stairs, and I tell them to wait on the balcony. Khadim goes to the salon and I follow him.

"Do we have to do this? What is wrong with you? I don't know who you are anymore. This was to be my home but you have driven me away." My voice breaks.

He stands silently, an unfathomable expression in his eyes. I stare at the man who has broken my will. This is my moment of defeat because all the seemingly planned aspects of our life together have ceased to exist. At this moment I pray for a miracle.

"Please give me an explanation for your behaviour. Anything? I can stop this move right now. I love you Khadim."

He stands in front of the wooden table with a remote expression. The section of the couch behind him has a pillow and sheets on it. I know he has not slept in the bedroom. I walk to the kitchen and open the refrigerator. Nothing has been touched. I walk back to him and the only thing I can say is, "What have you been eating?"

It takes an hour for the men to remove the cartons one by one into the moving van. When they enter the bathroom with a carton, the simple act of removing my toothbrush from his makes my head spin and I sink to the floor grief-stricken. He stands in the doorway watching me coolly and then walks away. I rise from the floor and regain my composure. I instruct one of the men to put the entire contents of the bathroom into a carton.

Fatima Zohra appears at the balcony, moves rapidly to me, and holds me. I cling to her, devastated by the tears in her eyes. I look into her face and try to reassure her using English. Khadim moves towards us rapidly and tears his mother away from me. He shouts to his mother in Arabic and pushes her towards the steps leading down.

That night I am seated at the front of the hotel near the fountain. I watch six columns of water cascade and the August roses spill their fragrance in the night air. The full moon floats over the top of the Koutoubia and the four balls of gold on the minaret are visible. The legend surrounding the fourth ball is mired in Moroccan history. An angry sultan had punished his wife, who had missed observing one fast in the month of Ramadan, by having all her gold jewellery melted and fashioned into a ball for the mosque.

Forty-four cartons lie in the basement of the Islane Hotel facing the Koutoubia. Idrisse, the young architect, has had a fan installed so that the cartons of my art are protected from the heat. I am completely detached from my surroundings and the unpredictable life journey that faces me in the morning. I feel as though my soul has been wrenched from me, and the only reality I cling to is that my boxed-up Canadian life is both safe and close at hand.

I see Khadim in the cascading water of the fountain, in the fragrance of the roses, and in the unearthly perfection of the silver moon. Unknown to me, Khadim, wearing a beige djellaba, his face totally concealed by the deep folds of the hood, hides behind the cover of palm trees, watching me.

When I return to the hotel room, I open two things. First, I pull out my jewellery case and discover that four gold bracelets are missing. Then I open my manuscript bag and discover that the file folder containing the only printed copy of my work in progress is missing. I grab the telephone and call Khadim. My rage at his malicious theft has me screaming.

"I don't have your jewellery or your book," he says and hangs up.

My next call is to my friend the ambassador in Rabat. I tell her what has happened.

"Is your laptop with you?" she asks.

"Yes."

"Write an official complaint to the governor of Marrakech and go the office tomorrow and hand deliver it. I shall send him a fax in the morning as well."

I AM DRIVEN TO THE governor's office the next morning. I sit in the reception area and wait for the secretary. My telephone rings. It is Khadim.

"I am not going to speak to you. I am sitting in the governor's office with a formal complaint about what you have taken."

"Don't do that darling. I will be right there," says Khadim.

I have waited for ten minutes and then a man motions to me to follow him through a set of glass doors. I rise and see Khadim running through the reception area towards me. I look at him and see that he is empty-handed. I have declared war now so I ignore him and follow the man. He shuts the door behind us. I hand him my letter and explain that there is also a fax sent from Rabat to the governor. He takes the envelope from me and I return to the reception room.

"I don't have your things. What have you done?" Khadim looms over me.

"This is your way of hanging on to me Khadim. How dare you touch my personal belongings? Particularly my manuscript."

"Let me look at home. Maybe you left something behind."

"No. You find them and give them back to me." I walk away towards the door.

He appears the next day while I am having lunch at the hotel.

"I am giving you twenty-four hours to produce my bracelets and my manuscript," I tell him.

He nods and orders some coffee and casually places a plastic bag on the edge of the table. He sits across from me in the booth-style seating as though nothing has happened between us. I find it difficult to eat or converse with him.

"Those bracelets are part of my wedding jewellery. They are part of my family history," I tell him.

He gestures to the plastic bag. I pull it towards me and open it. The bracelets are in a small transparent plastic bag and the green file folder sits underneath.

"Why are you playing these stupid games?" my voice rises in the hushed dining room.

"My mother said they were lying on the table in her living room."

"They walked out of my jewellery case and my manuscript just walked out of the book bag by itself?"

He gives me a cool shrug, as though this is no concern of his and somehow I am responsible for this. For a preposterous moment, he almost succeeds as relief overcomes me.

"How were you raised, Khadim? You cannot take something which does not belong to you."

"You are careless and I have kept this safe for you."

"Without informing me?"

"Yes."

I return to my hotel room and call the ambassador in Rabat.

"I think we frightened him. There would have been a police investigation and he cannot afford that," she says briskly.

"Well, it's over."

"Is it?"

"He is behaving so differently. I cannot believe what is happening," I tell her.

"You have to be very careful. Social justice for women is an issue in this society, particularly as you are a foreigner. Also, please remember you are not married to him legally."

Nothing is over between Khadim and me and I am more than aware of this. Although every life plan we had made so casually four months ago in Toronto has been disrupted, we are still bound together by the power of our emotions. The vast cultural abyss that has risen between us is as elusive as smoke. I am made conscious of its presence day by day and yet I am unable to make a final and critical judgment. I am still in love with the man I imagine I know, and feel as though an imposter has inhabited Khadim who is revealing aspects of his personality that were not present either during our courtship or his visit to Toronto.

CHAPTER 21

🌸 *Marrakech*

I AM STANDING ON THE balcony of the apartment, drinking coffee and watching the line of olive trees on the street. This early morning ritual is only observed by the guardian of the apartment building. He is a modern-day sentinel holding his post all night long in a chair and keeping a vigilante eye on the entrance of the building. When morning breaks, he stretches his body wearily and walks around the building. He raises his arm in greeting to me and I wave back at him. This exchange carries a comforting predictability and restores my faith in the stability of my life. The lush foliage of the trees turns silver at night and I have appointed them as my sentinels as well. I feel that the trees are steeped in mystery because they have been here for a long time. Within days, they have also become the focus of meditation where I only listen to my breath and sense my mind detaching from all thought. I am leading a life that is as mysterious as the olive trees

I feel that I have burned my bridges and can never return home to Canada. I also want to have every opportunity possible to salvage my relationship with Khadim. As I cannot leave until this is accomplished, I shall make the best of the situation.

The city of Marrakesh has become my domain and the apartment a tranquil home. Naima, the Berber maid, will arrive in an hour's time and clean the apartment, do laundry, and prepare lunch before she leaves. Each day we offer one word from our respective language to each other. We hold the word between us as though it is a talisman for the day. Naima embraces me and kisses my cheeks when she arrives and slips into a guardian niche. She views my presence in her country to be an honour of sorts and conducts her cleaning chores as though she has been chosen to unlock the doors of her culture to me.

I am living in the city of a million roses planted on streets and in parks. Even my apartment has roses in every room. I go to the flower market each week and return home with an armload full of them. One single rose is always presented to me by the flower seller. It is invariably the most scented one, and this is his way of telling me that the men of Morocco know how to be gallant. The walls of the apartment are hung with all my art and my ornate collection of silver sits in a Berber metal-and-bone-inlaid cabinet. My silk Bokhara rugs compliment the three Berber rugs I have carefully chosen. A dozen majorelle blue, star-shaped glass light fixtures illuminate the apartment. The second bedroom is my study. This room is a complete replica of my study in Canada. The only difference is that the writing desk faces a window from where I can catch the occasional sight of a calèche. The hoof-beats of the horses halt time and reassure me that the pageantry of Marrakech, which continues to enthral me, is still intact.

Two days after I shifted into the apartment and unpacked all the cartons, Khadim appeared at the door and silently walked through all the spaces I had organized.

"Of course it is better than my home," he says with a dejected expression.

"No. It is just another home. I have created a home for us. All parts of this home belong to us if you can share this," I answer, never taking my eyes off his face.

He walks up to me and holds me silently. I rest my head against his chest and know that his silence deafens me with the sound of promise. We walk to the study where the leather couch opens up to a bed. His tall, angular body folds over mine with familiar speed and his eyes are luminous with desire. Later we shower together and he scrubs my body gently and tells me if I am happy here, so is he. We get dressed, go to a bedding store, and spend half an hour testing mattresses only to be told that the bed will take four weeks to be delivered. When I write the cheque, he spells out the amount in French slowly as a teacher would do.

"Do you realize I have not had a bed for three months?" I laugh.

He holds out a paper bag of deep purple figs to me. I bite into my favourite fruit and regard the succulence of the fibre and the tang of flavour on my tongue as offerings that are richer than promises. Day by day, his personal objects appear in the apartment and he inhabits the space I have created with ease. He also begins to establish a protective ring around me. He does this subtly and does not display the volatility that took place in his mother's home. I must not wave to the guardian. This is his culture and the man may get too familiar. Naima, the maid is not to be taken out to lunch; it will encourage her to become demanding. He makes disparaging comments about two friends I have acquired in the bank lineup. They are a gay British couple who are opening a Riad Hotel in the Marrakech. When he notes my annoyed reaction, he quickly adds that he understands my desire to speak in my own language. He tells me he is also beginning to process the marriage application in Marrakech. There is no progress on his receiving a government licence to operate a travel agency so he is beginning to work at his regular job as a tour guide. However, he has chosen a hotel close to the apartment.

Within the circle of this charmed domesticity, the weeks slip by and I establish a writing regimen. I join a health club at the hotel adjoining the apartment and start each day by exercising. Khadim, whose day starts later, waves goodbye to me from the study where he is watching television. He takes breaks for lunch at home and we eat outdoors on the balcony. His arrival punctuates the day with his unwavering regimen of saying his prayers first in one corner of the living room, then expressing delight at the lunch served to him and his immediate adaptation to the Western style of eating with separate place settings, cutlery, and napkins. Often in the evenings we drop in to see his mother, who serves us glasses of sweet mint tea and seems remarkably complacent about the new living arrangement. I am waiting for the couch I have designed to be delivered before inviting her home for a visit.

I AM STUDYING THE BANK statement that has been delivered by the guardian to the door. This is my account in the local bank and I am surprised by the alarming dip in the balance. I am aware of the amount of money I draw weekly on my card and the telephone and electricity bills that I pay by cheque monthly. There have also been occasions when I sometimes find less money than I expect in my wallet. I do not discuss this with Khadim and make arrangements for more money to be transferred from my investment account in Canada. My portfolio manager cautions me that I am coming close to drawing from the principle sum and it will affect my income, but I am optimistic that Khadim will soon contribute to the expenses of our life together. As I am entirely self-sufficient, I decide simply to wait for his gesture. There is a new excitement in my life as I have opened my book and have started writing in the afternoons. A very critical part of my identity is being restored.

IT IS FRIDAY AND THE call to the noonday prayer resounds from the tower of the Koutoubia nearby. I am expecting Khadim after the prayers that he offers at the mosque in the neighbourhood. The maid has gone home after preparing lunch. I stand on the balcony watching for Khadim to appear on the road. Two hours goes by and then I dial his phone. Instead of hearing his voice or his own answering message, a bizarre Arabic message plays in a strange voice that I have never heard before. Late in the evening, I drive to his mother's house. She has no news of his whereabouts.

Four days have gone by. I dial the telephone in vain to be greeted by the same message. I let other people who speak Arabic hear it and they are equally puzzled, and suggest it appears that the voice has been deliberately distorted and it mentions dialling another number, which is not a valid one.

In five days, my Marrakech fantasia unravels. Once again, a partner has disappeared. My functioning capacities diminish to the point where I spend hours pacing the apartment and leaning over the railing of the balcony looking at the corner where Khadim usually walked home from. I have sleepless nights and barely eat, stunned at the realization that my dependency on Khadim is bigger than I had ever imagined. The city I live in is still foreign and I have no friends with whom I can discuss this disappearance. I cannot call my friend the ambassador in Rabat because she had cautioned me about life with Khadim, and I have not told her that in fact we are living together in my apartment. I exchange emails with Driss who is also unaware that Khadim is living with me in the apartment. Yet Driss is canny and he is a psychiatrist and continually warns me about any association with Khadim. Naima appears daily with a rose for me. She coaxes me to eat and leaves with a sorrowing shadow to her eyes. She lingers that day not wanting to leave, drawing out her cleaning chores. I come in from my command post, the balcony, pay her, and tell her to go home when the front door opens silently and Khadim steps inside.

I feel as though a vise encases my ribcage and I cannot breathe. Finally, what escapes from my mouth is not breath, but a cry, and I have hurled myself at him. He catches me as my arms encircle him.

"Sssh. She will hear you," is the first startling whisper that emerges from his mouth as he jerks his head towards the kitchen.

We are seated at the dining table and a meal is set in front of us. I have dropped a note on his dinner plate that says that I expect this never to happen again. He cannot disappear without informing me, and I need to hear his voice wherever he is. He reads it silently and stuffs it into his breast pocket.

"Where did you go?" I ask.

"Sometimes, I just disappear," he says slowly.

"Where?"

"I just disappear," he repeats.

"You mean you take time out, for yourself?"

"Yes, when there is too much happening," he adds.

"You mean here. With us? Are you referring to our life together?" I am stunned.

"No," he states calmly, without helping me in any way.

"I don't handle disappearances well. You have to tell me when you are planning to disappear," I smile at him thinking of Cesar. "Is there a problem that I need to know about?" I still haven't given up.

"There are many things. But I will take care of them," he ends the conversation by rising and heading to the kitchen.

He returns with a bowl filled with fruit. I look at it and say I wish it was chocolate instead. He holds the bowl in front of me and grins, and then slowly lowers the bowl in front of me on the table. A second before he sets it down he makes a sliding motion with the bowl and holds up his palm. The bowl of fruit is on the table in front of me, and there is a bar of my favourite chocolate lying on his palm.

"Magic," I am laughing.

"Yes. I can make things disappear and then appear." He gives me a cocky smile.

A week later, I am opening the top drawer of the long cabinet in the bedroom. It holds my jewellery and I am looking for one item. When I lift the black silk ring box and slide the catch open, the box is empty. I feel as though I have been punched in the stomach. I methodically search the entire drawer and every handbag that I own with a sinking heart. The eleven-karat rose-coloured gem tourmaline is my favourite possession. The baroque stone had decorated an imperial Japanese garment and the jeweller had given me the history of both the stone and his setting design. I had purchased it with the first royalty payment of my first book twenty years ago and added my own history to the stone. I often wore it on my right hand for days and always stored it carefully in its case. Even Khadim had expressed admiration for both the colour of the stone and its appealing antiquity. When I straighten up from the drawer, I am filled with shock and anger. The removal of the ring constitutes a violation not only of my home but of my personal history. I race to Khadim and inform him immediately.

"It is your maid," he announces flatly walking into the bedroom and seeing the drawer.

"Never. She is so honest she picks up all the change I drop, collects it, and gives it to me, even beads of a necklace that I broke. Impossible!" I reply heatedly.

"We have to report it to the police at once," he replies, ignoring my agitation.

"I will not do that."

"They will get if from her, don't worry," he says coldly.

"She is cleaning the balcony. I shall ask her myself."

Naima is on her knees, her long caftan hitched between her legs as she scrubs the flagstones on the balcony floor. Her concentration is acute as she washes away imaginary specks of dirt. I call her name softly and she turns her face around and smiles at me through the curtain of dark hair surrounding her face. I gesture to her to follow me, and she rises immediately and releasing the folds of her caftan. In the sunlight, her statuesque physique, flowing garments, and arresting face imbue her with a presence that makes me only want to photograph her rather than lead her to my bedroom for an interrogation. I can see Khadim standing in the living room watching us and I head towards the bedroom followed by Naima. Silently I open the jewellery drawer, lift the empty box, and open it in front of Naima.

"It is gone. Have you seen it Naima?" I ask with a trembling voice.

Naima stares at the box and raises her face to me. She shakes her head from side to side and keeps her gaze fixed on me then her lips begin to quiver and she backs away from me.

"No, Madame. I have not taken it," she breaks into a sob.

It is a devastating sob of anguish. The tall sun-filled woman's beautiful face flinches under the subtle accusation. Then her posture shifts to one of supplication and she holds her arms out to me. I see the carefree ease of our relationship vanish before my eyes and I am filled with a sense of intense disloyalty. I turn to Khadim who stands tall in the doorway.

"Darling, I can't bear it. I don't think she would ever do this," I tell him.

"She would not feel this, if she was in your place. She is the only person who enters this house. We have to let the police handle this," he roughly gestures to Naima to follow him.

We file into the living room together and Khadim talks to Naima in Darija. With Khadim her manner changes and Naima appears to be putting up a spirited defence.

"Tell her, if by any chance she has it, I will give her anything she wants in return," I break in desperately, hating every second of the predicament.

"You are mad. She will never admit it. I have told her to go," says Khadim.

"I have to pay her."

Khadim lifts his eyebrows ironically.

THE LATE AFTERNOON CALL TO prayer resounds and I am locked in my study. I have pulled out the Quran my father gave me. Again, I indulge in an ancient practice called "stitchomancy" a form of divination. I meditate for a while keeping Naima's name in my thoughts and open a section randomly. The page I read fills me with dread as it discusses moral judgment and the consequences of straying from the path of belief. I regard Naima as my friend despite our social division. My instinct tells me she has not stolen anything but Khadim says that theft by domestics is an everyday occurrence in Marrakech; the temptation is too great. His arguments are compelling and I find myself weakening in my resolve to prevent a police investigation. I am not prepared to lose my ring and if this is the way to get it back, I have no choice but to proceed. I have never had anything stolen from me before, and I am disturbed at the anger that fills me. The results of the investigation, which require a court sanction before the police can take any action, leads to no results. Both Naima and the ring disappear from my life, inflicting a wound I cannot fully reveal. Naima's replacement is another maid with whom I maintain a formal relationship. The door to my bedroom is locked when the maid comes to work.

The month of Ramadan begins and with it comes another cultural shift that alters my life. Khadim fasts daily and leaves the house each evening after breaking his fast and saying the last prayers of the night. He returns in the early hours of the morning, lies in the study, and then watches television until it is time for the meal before sunrise. During the daytime, he is listless, irritable, and judgmental. I only keep three fasts on Fridays. One night after Khadim leaves, I pull out the car and drive in the city. Every café in Marrakech is alive with hordes of men drinking coffee, playing cards, and socializing. When I question Khadim about this, he says their day begins at night. One night I insist on accompanying him, he smiles and tells me that I may not enjoy this. I insist and he takes me to a café where he is meeting two male friends. He introduces me and the men greet me and then ignore me. Within twenty minutes, I leave him and drive home alone.

I am seated at my favourite neighbourhood haunt, Jad Mahal. It is a large restaurant with an indoor pool of water and walkway running though it. The appointments are opulent and candles and roses are arranged in great profusion. Women carrying trays of candles on their heads appear at 10 p.m. and dance through the tables. They are followed by a string of belly dancers who dance on the walkway on the strip of water. Khadim is working late at night with tourists and I am familiar with the owner and staff and feel comfortable being here by myself. The patrons are all European tourists and this environment makes me feel as though I am still connected to the Canada. I stay for an hour and then walk home. Khadim walks in the minute I enter the apartment, surprising me by his timing.

"You never dress for me like this," he screams at me.

I am stunned by his outburst, but I ignore it and walk towards the bedroom. He races behind me, grabs the waistband of my skirt, and jerks it down to my knees. Fear returns like a hammer blow as I struggle to raise my skirt back up.

"Are you crazy? How dare you behave like this?" I shout at him. .

"You are meeting men," he snarls, jerking my skirt down again.

"You have been smoking hashish. Stop it. I think you need some help." I am backed into one corner of the bedroom.

"There will be conditions if we are to marry," he looms over me.

"You mean that piece of paper," I reply scornfully.

"I want everything to be *Halal* between us." He pushes me back against the bed.

"It was *Halal* the minute you put the ring on my finger," I retort.

"Sometimes I can kill. But I resist," he tells me in a softer voice.

"Then you need help." I am terrified of this statement.

"A psychiatrist, like they do in your country?" His smile is sinister.

He turns around abruptly, ripping his jacket off the hook of the bedroom door and charging out of the bedroom. I collapse on the bed and hear the front door closing behind him.

I drive to his mother's house in the morning. The small iron door is open and I walk through it. He is kneeling by the front door easing an empty gas canister onto a metal dolly.

"I think we need to talk," I say, walking up to him.

He straightens up and pushes the dolly past me and out the gate and I follow him. We cross the street together. He turns and gives me a silent, furious look.

"We have to talk Khadim, you cannot behave in this fashion," I say again.

"I will break your face with this." He pulls a metal wrench from his pocket in holds it in a threatening gesture.

"Stop it, Khadim. You are not frightening me," I say, throwing caution to the wind.

He leans the dolly against the wall, grabs my hand and my entire arm, and drags me across the street, back into the house through the open gate. Pain shoots up from my finger where the nail has been half ripped by his violence. I hear the front gate slam shut behind me as blood appears on the nail bed I am examining. I run to the kitchen and hold my finger under the running water to stop the bleeding. Fatima Zohra, his mother, is in the kitchen. Her eyes widen. Khadim enters the kitchen and shouts in Darija to his mother. I hold my finger under the water and know he is talking about me. I turn around.

"I need a bandage, I can't stop the bleeding."

He walks out of the kitchen without looking at me. Fatima Zohra stands silently at the stove without moving towards me. I sense that the entire fabric of my connection with this family has ended. I turn the faucet off and curl my fingers into a ball. Slowly I walk upstairs but the door is locked and Khadim has disappeared. Marching down the stairs, I do not look backwards but walk out to my car and drive to the neighbourhood pharmacy.

The next morning when I wake up, I head to my exercise club and run on the treadmill for thirty minutes. I am drenched in sweat as I sit doing a set of weights. I am tired and once again devastated by the reappearance of Khadim's bizarre volatility. I rise and lift one leg across the padded seat and trip. The first fall makes me dizzy because I have bumped my head on the padded bench of the adjoining machine. I disentangle my feet and step over, again missing clearance, and come crashing down towards a projecting metal bar. At the last minute, I lift my right arm to protect my face from the metal ledge I am falling towards.

I AM LYING ON MY back with my right arm folded across my chest and the screams ricocheting off the ceiling of the gym are mine. A ring of faces gazes down at me curiously. I am screaming words like "ambulance" and "morphine" in between the waves of unbearable pain shooting from my right forearm. My body is cold with shock and the knife-edge of the double fracture does not abate. I tell the face peering into mine to call Khadim and they tell me there is no answer from his telephone.

Two hours later, I am being wheeled into surgery at the Polyclinic du Sud and my British friend Robert is walking beside me. I cannot talk. I have been sedated because the surgeon knows that my screams of "call my husband" have resounded in his clinic unchecked for an hour. Khadim's phone has the fake Arabic message on it and there is no answer. The call to Fatima Zohra resulted in a callous message, stating that she has no relationship to me. When I am told this, I feel as though I have died and somehow landed in hell.

The second after the surgery, I know exactly what I have to do. Lying in bed in the clinic with my right arm in a sling and drifting in and out of painkillers, antibiotics, and other medication, I make one telephone call. It is to the largest shipping company in Casablanca. I tell them that I wish the contents of my apartment and my car shipped back to Canada at the end of the week when I am discharged by the clinic. The terror of physical injury has compelled me to make a decision that should have been made the day after the fake wedding. Home is Canada and I cannot get there fast enough.

Nine days later, I am seated in a wheelchair at Marrakech airport. The right arm is in a sling with a loose bandage around it. I have the medical files with me and the stitches will be removed in Toronto and not Marrakech. I have never looked at the arm even when the dressing was changed by the surgeon in Marrakech. When he informed me that I now have two steel plates in my arm, I still refuse to accept that he is talking about my arm. I float in a haze of antibiotics, painkillers, and anti-inflammatory medications. My mind is blank and I am convinced that my heart stopped beating days ago. The contents of my apartment and car are in a container at Casablanca waiting to be loaded on a ship that will reach Canada in four weeks. My flight stops at Paris where I will rest for a night and the next day I will fly home to Toronto. This is my first injury and all I want is the comfort of known surroundings and the doctors I am familiar with.

MY FUR COAT RESTS ACROSS my shoulders. I hold my handbag on my lap with my left arm. The wheelchair is pushed through the glass doors and I see Evanthia's shocked face bending over me.

"Welcome home." She kisses me gently.

"I am getting up," I respond, rising from the wheelchair.

I peer through the curtains of the hotel room that dark February evening in Toronto. Homeless, once again, I glance at my watch only to see if it is time to take my medication. The right arm lies in the sling close to my body and I ignore it as I have done for days. My thoughts are completely blank and I am oblivious to my entire surroundings. The wedding ring is still on my left finger but I am disassociated with my existence. In a space of nine months, I have returned defeated by both a country and a man who has betrayed my love. As this is an act of survival, I have buried the sinister cauldron of emotions. I have done this with calculation, as I believe that my entire state is altered. The snowflakes spiralling down from the sky blanket the entire street in minutes. The golden sun of Marrakech and the rose-tinted masonry disappear, as does a mirage, when I swallow two pills and turn the lights off.

CHAPTER 22

🏵 Marrakech, October 2007

NINE MONTHS LATER, MY LIFE has picked up a rhythm of its own. My arm has healed completely; I am settled in an apartment in Toronto and reconnected with a familiar life. I have also written two-thirds of my book. However, I have decided to complete the book elsewhere, and do not reveal my plans to anyone I know. Instead, I book a flight and return to Morocco. It is my desire to change my life script. The fabled city of Marrakech will not remain as a site of failure and tragedy. I will finish my book there and transform it into a place symbolic of victory rather than defeat. I had wanted to complete a book a year and a half ago when I was distracted by a doomed love affair. I will reverse my destiny.

When I land in Marrakech and stay with old friends, I tell them I am here simply to work for six weeks. The next morning a taxi drops me at the medina and I walk straight ahead. The scene in front of me is unchanged. The sensation is as though I am slipping into a worn bathrobe and know exactly how it will fall on my body. The sky of Marrakech is overcast and Djemaa el Fna, its great square, is quiet. The handful of people visible, are swathed in protective garments preparing for rain. I am walking into the heart of the square where the monkeys still sleep in their wooden boxes and the snake charmers keep the lids of their baskets shut.

The veiled women who apply henna to the palms of tourists doze on their stools under black umbrellas. The juice-dispensing carts stacked with conical mounds of glistering oranges are not operating and the entrance to the souks is shrouded by protective curtains of rough tapestry. There is a curious flatness to the entire environment. Every trace of its dynamic flavour subdued in chasing away the dregs of my association with it. My judgment is unclouded and I turn away knowing that I will not return.

I follow the path towards the outer edges of the square, halting to gaze at the Koutoubia tower across the street.

I am also a book, I beam to the minaret silently. You are built on the ground of ancient booksellers. So I have returned to complete myself.

I walk towards Rue Fatima Zahra and head for the arched gateway called Bab Laksour. The narrow terracotta laneway faces me and I enter it slowly. Walking down the street, I see the familiar faces of shopkeepers opening up. However, now they greet me with guarded expressions sometimes turning their eyes away. I bump into a man whose furniture store I often visited but never made a purchase from.

"Madame! You have returned?" Mohcin's eyes cloud with disbelief.

"Yes," I reply.

"You will stay?"

"For a while."

"You are welcome," he responds automatically, although his eyes reveal that he knows something else as well.

I continue down the path and turn left at the little square towards Café Arabe. The familiar blue urns and potted palms flank the doorway and I enter the covered courtyard where the blue wall with a fountain, three blooming orange trees, and the circular recessed seating evoke a nostalgia that I cannot seem to control. Paolo, the Italian owner rushes to greet me.

"Hello! Hello! What happened? You left Marrakech," he asks.

"I had an accident so I went home. I am here to do some work. I am scouting for a place to write. You know I can't remember the terrace, because when I saw it first, it was raining."

He leads me to the second floor with gleaming faux marble walls of rose tedlek, a paint that resembles marble, wall niches accented by graceful ceramic urns, and windows that offer a view to the courtyard below. His Milanese background reflects in the sleek ambience he has recently created. The opulent excesses of Moroccan décor items pared down to a minimum. We climb the winding stairs leading to the terrace and he pushes open the wooden door.

The terrace sprawls on the entire roof of the three-storey café where long divans and armchairs cluster in groups. A black marble bar stretches across the far wall with a kitchen tucked behind it. White strips of cloth form canopies over the seating areas except one raised pavilion with a conical wooden roof. The silent rooftops of the entire medina of Marrakech encircle the terrace. In the heart of the old city where life teems unseen below, the terrace is bathed only in sunlight and silence.

I smile at Paolo and tell him that I have found what I am looking for. I gesture to the pavilion with the roof.

I START MY DAYS BY going to Café Solaris, connecting to the Internet by wireless, and having the first cup of coffee. Then I hail a taxi and am driven to the medina where I am deposited at the familiar gate from where I walk to Café Arabe. It is an eight-minute walk and I pass by the same faces each morning. For the time being I have also become a part of the medina, and like my silent observers I have also become a silent recording organism. My laptop and papers are concealed in the blue leather bag I hold in one hand, and my purse is slung over the other shoulder. It is as though I have come to shop in the medina.

I write on the terrace and take a break for lunch at the marble bar while the computer recharges its battery. I write in silence gazing at the rooftops, thankful for the absence of all visual distraction. Most days I finish by six in the evening and then I leave. The shopkeepers greet me daily, and keep their eyes on me until I disappear from sight. I never halt to look at their lavishly displayed wares, and am aware that they are confused by my daily appearance. As they cannot look inside the blue bag, they are unaware of my activities. In the evenings, I spend time at two neighbourhood haunts frequented by foreign tourists. Often I will eat here and then go home to watch the two English channels on television and fall asleep.

At the end of the second week, I am confident that I will finish my work in another month. The narrative has released itself and I am surefooted. I function in the city on my own terms and am separating two sets of personal histories. The city that brought me to my knees will now have a different point of reference. As far as I am concerned, I could be anywhere in the world.

Often I have the sensation that I am being watched but I am not overly concerned by it. After all, I have positioned myself right in the middle of the once magical realm of "Khadim streets" where rainbows appeared on cue and the interior of the small shops glittering with hammered metal lamps and the vibrant shriek of multi-hued ceramic were an endless source of fascination. The winding lanes leading in from the arched gateway are full of observers who are in fact a conduit of information. These shopkeepers lounge outside their tiny shops and are the best spies in the medina. I am familiar with the system and have decided to use it myself.

One afternoon I make a bold move, and cultivate an informant. He has an air of pensive refinement and speaks English fluently. I feed him selected information. I tell him that although I have no contact with Khadim I would like a message delivered to him that I want my journal returned, preferably through an intermediary.

The informant approaches me after two days as I head to Café Arabe one morning. Over a cup of mint tea, he tells me that Khadim denies having it. Noting my expression, he adds that Khadim regularly passes by his store with tourists. In fact, he is seen in this area late in the evenings heading towards the legendary carpet store Palais des Moravides, a stone's throw from Café Arabe where I write everyday.

I take this alliance one step further and agree to meet him at the bar of the graceful Es Saadi Hotel in my neighbourhood a few days later. Hotel La Mamounia is undergoing a vast refurbishing exercise and has remained closed for more than a year. He orders a bottle of cheap wine and is in a garrulous mood. He finishes half the bottle quickly and then leans forward with a conspiratorial air. I am ready for this moment.

"The carpet shop hires a full-time pimp," he says unexpectedly.

"Really," I murmur, concealing my distaste.

"Upstairs where the entrance is blocked by hanging carpets there are many rooms. They bring prostitutes for the night."

"Ah! Is that so?" I indulge him.

"Wait. I have met the girl. She said instead of giving her money, a man paid her with a red silk nightgown. It was foreign, very beautiful."

I look at him silently thinking of my lingerie disappearing from the clothesline at Khadim's home a year ago. My hand trembles as I light a cigarette.

"There is more, Madame. She says the man would not sleep at night, he read from a small book. She saw it and said it was not Arabic but some foreign language. It was not a printed book, but written by hand. The ink was a deep purple."

He gazes at me expectantly and I return his gaze impassively. Smiling, he pours another glass of wine.

"I must leave. I am tired." I motion to the waiter to bring the bill to me.

"You must remember, this is Marrakech, you can buy the services of anyone," he adds slyly. "You can buy a man."

"I have no need to do that. Good night," I halt him, gather my purse, and rise.

He gets up as well. "The family who own this carpet shop is very powerful. They even have seats in parliament. They are criminals. It is a cooperative and they buy carpets at cheap prices from the poor Berbers and sell them at very high prices."

"All this is of no interest to me," I start moving away.

"It should be. Your man, Khadim, they own him. Like a soccer team. He is one of their players. He owes them a lot of money."

I see a curtain falling on an old vintage film studded with villains and dark alleys. I also see my shadow on unpaved stones and the roses lining the boulevards of Marrakech dripping blood. Cauldrons of indigo dye spilling over sand dunes. It is the thumbprint of Africa positioned squarely over my existence threatening to make the world unrecognizable. It will not succeed, as I know it well now.

I am now engaged in two exercises. I write by day confidently, watching the pile of manuscript pages rise and examines the shadowy world of the medina in the evening. This examination is conducted only in a speculative fashion. However, my stolen journal and its retrieval still prey on my mind. It still constitutes a violation of my privacy and, in an archival sense, my words belong in my world and not in the sordid confines of a brothel in Marrakech. The journal recorded my first impressions of Marrakech and meeting Khadim after fourteen years. Has he retained the journal as some sort of bargaining chip or a salve for his ego without realizing that the stroke of a pen can alter an entire perspective?

THE NEXT MORNING I FIND an email waiting for me when I am seated at Café Solaris.

FLYING INTO CASABLANCA ON FRIDAY ... BOOKED RENTAL CAR WILL DRIVE TO MARRAKECH ... THREE DAYS WITH YOU. BRINGING FILMING EQUIPMENT AND TRUMPET ... HEFF.

I telephone him in New York. He asks me about my journal and I tell him it is gone forever. He notes that I am quite excited and I inform him that I have only three more chapters left to write. I will take the weekend off for him.

"What if I call him and ask him for the journal?" he says.

"It's a dead telephone number. I have tried it. It is never answered. Besides I have been here for a month and have never bumped into him."

"Be creative, think of something."

"Be careful driving. I don't want a call from a Moroccan police station," I say, knowing full well that he will reach me wherever I am.

I bump into the informant the next morning when I am walking to Café Arabe. He insists on pressing a glass of mint tea on me. It is a standard Moroccan courtesy and I accept it, thinking about Jonathan's suggestion of being creative. So I tell him that an American filmmaker is coming to film an interview with me and is willing to pay money to get the journal. I casually mention a sum of money in U.S. funds, making it outrageously extravagant. I let this kernel of information float between us easily without any ceremony and note the flicker of interest in his eyes.

My mobile phone rings three days later.

"I am at the Atlas Hotel. The car is a stick shift and I have never driven one before but I was picked up by police on the highway for speeding. You are right; this is Africa."

I race out of the apartment where I am staying and head to the hotel less than a block away. Heff is standing outside the entrance with his hair flying in every direction and his trumpet case in his hand.

He sweeps me into a hug and I laugh asking if he has really brought the trumpet.

"Actually it's a pair of Heff pistolas. I am going to blow the guy away and get back your journal," he growls in mock ferocity.

Sheets of rain descend on us when we get out of the car next morning. Heff's arms are laden with his film equipment in waterproof cases and I am holding an umbrella over both of us. We walk through rivulets of water on the narrow lanes. The winding streets are dark and shadowy with the absence of sunshine. A chill rises from the cobblestones and the thick stucco walls. Our cumbersome progress is marked by the avid curiosity of all the shopkeepers. The news spreads like wildfire that I am here today with a man who will make a film.

They all assume that somehow they will make money from the absurd foreigners. Their faces turn sullen when we do not halt until we reach Café Arabe. Paolo gives us shelter from the rain, and we film the first interview against his terracotta walls on the second floor.

Marrakech hides its sun all afternoon and when we finish and walk through the darkened lanes towards the small square where the car is parked, there is a clearance and more light than in the winding lanes. I get into the driver's seat, as I am more adept at driving a stick shift. Heff sits next to me with his movie camera on his knees. He pans the surroundings. The car is parked illegally inside the gate of Bab Laksour, close to a little T-junction.

I struggle with the reverse gear and when I raise my head, I spot Khadim's head in the distance. His appearance is unmistakable. Wearing a beige jacket and a peaked olive-green baseball cap, eyes concealed by small dark glasses, he strides taller than the men around him.

"There he is!" I shout.

"Who?" Heff turns.

"Khadim." I see him move closer on the path to the side of the car.

"Which one? For God's sake! I have film rolling." Heff is moving his camera.

"Baseball cap, dark glasses," I whisper, conscious of my heart hammering wildly.

He reaches the space near the car, moving rapidly and as he glides by. I shout his name. He halts and slowly approaches the window. A column of darkness approaches us. The only visible part of him is his mouth where the lips are clamped together.

"Hi," he says slowly, face expressionless and the lenses of his dark glasses pools of grey.

"Meet Heff," flies out of my mouth.

The camera slips from Heff's knees as he sticks his hand across me towards the window. Khadim touches it briefly and turns, moving rapidly towards the lane.

"Hey!" I shout.

I stall the gearshift, open the door, and jump out.

He looks behind me as he jogs, and then halts and stands tucked into an abutting wall. When I race to it, he has disappeared. I stop in confusion and he reappears and moves towards me. I step into an empty store and he follows me. We are now standing before each other. There is not a trace of movement that either one of us makes toward each other. In ten months, the vivid history between us is chased away as an earthquake swallows a city.

"I want my journal back." I recover first, chilled by the quiet menace that flows from the still form of the man I have called beloved.

"I'll call you," he responds and steps out of the store and runs down the street.

"You should have let me handle it." Heff has reached my side. He peers at me anxiously. "Are you all right?"

"Yes, I am fine. Let's go home."

"I've shot something. I have his back running down the street," he says.

"It's all right, we will never see him again," I tell him.

"No, you are wrong. He wants something from you. I don't trust him," replies Heff.

"Fear not," I say, "he will never get anything from me."

I am sitting on a stool in the centre of the great square the next morning wearing an indigo caftan. I am following the tradition of the storytellers of the square who draw crowds around them. It is an old tradition. The language I use to read in is not understood by the people in the square. I read from the pages lying in my lap sitting in a pool of sunlight facing a movie camera fifteen feet away from me. People gather around in a circle pressed closer by curiosity, unaware that I am describing this location using the rhythm of language and the passion of my convictions to define their world with images of beauty and hints of mystery. The Arabic word "Katiba," meaning writer, floats in the air. This is what Heff calls his second interview. I shall do a reading and he will film me.

Now we are off to our third and final interview, as Heff calls the filming he is doing. So in the early afternoon we enter the carpet shop. The tall man in the vestibule greets us courteously and gives us permission to film. There is a sense that we are expected. I also sense that behind the walls of hanging carpets there are many unseen eyes watching us. They spread an orange carpet in the middle of the atrium. I sit on the carpet with my blue caftan billowing around me and read a section of the book set in this atrium.

I see Cesar's ghost seated on the wooden bench smiling at me in encouragement and wonder if another vision will also appear.

The skeins of wool in the carpets displayed all around pick out the tapestries of the lives of the carpet weavers. In complete harmony, I present the tapestry of my life woven simply in language. When we finish, Heff lets the eye of his camera roam through the spaces of carpets shrouding the upper floor rooms of the atrium. He does this with a deceptive nonchalance and I can hear the drumbeat of his valiant heart intent on capturing more than just a story.

We leave and stop at a shop along the way for him to pick up a gift before he flies out the next morning. I am waiting outside the shop keeping an eye on his camera equipment.

Khadim suddenly appears in the distance. Motionless. As always the body partially obscured by a curving section of the street. The baseball cap is missing but the eyes are shrouded by the dark glasses.

"He is back," I say to Heff, quickly sticking my head in the shop.

Heff steps out and before our eyes, Khadim disappears. We walk quickly down the thirty feet separating us only to lose him. There is only one dyer's shop with large vats of colour here. There is no other place where someone could hide. Yet Khadim has disappeared like a ghost.

"It's his signature," says Heff. "He likes to creep up behind you. He wants something. He will appear again."

We have started walking towards the car and Heff stops at another shop. I wait outside and sense Khadim's presence. I turn around and see him standing in front me. I study his face silently. It has the appearance of a death mask. Vertical lines of dissipation and patches of dry skin resembling the sun-baked earth of Morocco. The face expressionless, as the eyes remain masked.

"You can keep what you have stolen," I tell him and walk away.

When I wave goodbye to Heff early the next morning I tell him of the reappearance. "He came to make a deal. He thought I would buy the journal back. I told him to keep it." I kiss him goodbye. "So I have ended it."

"I want you to be careful. I don't trust him." His eyes cloud over.

"I have taken his power away, Heff. I am a writer; I can recreate anything."

I never return to the terrace in the medina to write again. Café Millennium, which sweeps two corners of the wide boulevard where I live, offers me a shaded spot. Here the city sparkles with modernity. Sleek cars glide by and the ambience is almost European. Men and women in Western clothing sip coffee and lunch on European food. Roses and fountains line the centre of the boulevard once called Avenue de France and the snow-covered peaks of the Atlas Mountains are etched against the sky.

It could almost be a setting closer to the home I will return to in a few days. I sit on a plush velvet circular armchair under a yellow and orange striped awning, and detach from the script of a particular life. The folds of the hood of a djellaba, the calèches of Marrakech and the shadowy labyrinth of the medina are a loose bundle of kindling. My fingertips pressing the keyboard of the computer are a thousand matches tossed into the kindling. The flames rise to scorch all vestiges of pain and betrayal and usher in a new consciousness.

The day I finish writing the book, I remember what I have blocked out for two days. It was the night of the full moon when Khadim made his appearance in the medina in the early evening. He had chosen that evening because he relied on the patterns and habits that marked most of my life. There were countless nights when he had seen me rapturous over a full moon, transformed and willing to push the limits on all sensorial pleasure. But I had walked through the ring of fire he had created out of our association and he was singularly unaware that I had mastered this ability. Perhaps he had accomplished this as well but we would never know this from each other again.

Hours later, Heff had raised his trumpet at midnight and serenaded the moon hanging over Marrakech. I raised my camera and aimed it upwards, deleting consciously, from the small aperture, the illuminated city and all the mythology I had imbued it with.

The next day I send an email to Margaret telling her that I had, of course, disobeyed her and returned to Marrakech, but had finished my book.

CHAPTER 23

TORONTO, 2009

SOMETIMES THE ENDING OF A book or that defining moment in which a narrative reaches its ordained conclusion becomes elusive. Or there may be a sudden derailment. In my case, this very fine line that exists between fiction and non-fiction disappears as both astonishment and speculation arise unexpectedly. The storyteller within me whispers of an opportunity that hints at the possibility of further extending a narrative. Then inevitable self-doubt also casts its shadow as I question whether the typhoon that tossed me from one continent to another as I chose to love two men has not rendered me as surefooted as I thought I was.

"It will take you at least two years to get over this experience," Driss, the Moroccan psychiatrist and cherished friend had said to me on the phone when I had returned three years ago.

Yet I proved him wrong. I had returned, regrouped, worked on a book, and endured. I had found my bearings all over again. I see movement in my life as I have both the desire and imagination to write other books and I have finally dismissed my losses as being largely material. I am alive, healthy, and have created a wonderful home for myself close to all the things in the city that I am fond of. I have regained stability.

Now, as I sit at my writing desk gazing at the red-gold splendour of a Toronto fall pressed against this window, I am acutely conscious of something sitting on a small table behind me. It is a notebook with a maroon spine. The pages in half of this notebook are covered in a plum-coloured ink and the rest are blank. I am now compelled to view this notebook as a metaphor for life. The notion that I cannot simply choose to reveal only one version of an event becomes an irritant. It is this act that I know instinctively will hint at half a wisdom gained. I am also intrigued by the realization that stories simply do not end because characters have been examined and sketched out or given their appropriate places. A villain must remain a villain until the end!

This summer I ventured on a vacation. I had decided that I needed to travel without a computer and book outlines, or chapters or promises made to my literary agent. My birthday also appeared in this period and I had never given myself a birthday present. I packed my paints and brushes instead. The Sunday painter had somehow perished in the past few years. My destination was Europe but I had also received an invitation to spend a week at a stunning beachfront villa at Cabo Negro on the Mediterranean coast of Morocco just near Tangier. The trip was more than what I had planned and I even revisited Marrakech. On my return in July, when I boarded a flight from Marrakech to Casablanca and onwards to Paris to fly home to Toronto, my luggage was lost. A delayed flight in Marrakech resulted in my reaching home to Toronto forty-eight hours later without my luggage. When it arrived, I only unpacked one bag. After a few days, I unpacked the other and lifted both flat, soft-sided canvas bags to place them in an overhead storage space. The bag on the top fell down and when I lifted it and pressed it flat again, I felt something hard in the outer long-zipped flap. I had never used this flap. I unzipped it and pulled out my lost notebook. It had found its way back to me after two and a half years.

"Sam, I found my notebook."

"The notebook! Oh, God this is so exciting! Wait till your publisher hears about this; maybe it can be used in the book," replied my literary agent without missing a beat.

But he had missed all the beats. This was no random accidental discovery. The notebook had been placed in the outer flap by the only man who claimed he could make things appear and disappear. He had waited two and a half years for an opportunity to present itself. I had been observed in the small city of Marrakech by many as I painted outdoors on the balcony of the little apartment where I stayed briefly. In the country where the right amount of cash can unlock any door, however secure one is deluded in believing it is. An unnoticeable place had been chosen in my luggage, which I did not have when I knew Khadim.

I regarded the notebook as a message. Yet to decipher Khadim's motives became another journey into myself. The pages recorded my riveting love affair with him where in the throes of enchantment I bestowed a status upon him. He was singularly aware that he played a part in the sixteen-year-old manuscript. Was he in some way protecting the integrity of a real experience? Or had he simply photocopied the pages, as he had secretly done to a part of my manuscript three years ago? Did he imagine that a day would come when a book would find its way to him and he would compare what was written?

Could this also be an act of contrition orchestrated faultlessly so he would ensure my goodwill eternally? Are redemptive acts often misleading? For I know that Khadim's mission at all times was to dupe me. This was his only known expertise. Cesar by contrast, had only duped himself by believing that he could deny the existence of a serious mental illness. This memoir was hidden under the guise of fiction for years as I had trained myself to hide as well. I had enough skill simply to skip away from a life. I could wave a magic wand and say look at these people and the lives they lead. All I could leave my reader with would be the seductive powers of a drama-riddled story. But as fate changes its course and growth hammers relentlessly at the gates of well-laid plans, then truthfulness is the only course of action.

The notebook lies buried in a wicker chest in my study. It is a lifeless stack of pages pressed down between its covers. I have transferred the life it once held into the pages spread before your eyes.

ACKNOWLEDGEMENTS

THE WRITING OF THIS BOOK exacted a toll that I felt was unendurable at times. The rhythm of my writing life followed no set prescription. It was as though the book had a life of its own independent of my life. There were prophecies that revealed themselves, a continuing sense of déjà vu, and terrifying physical hazard. My laptop computer and sections of the manuscript travelled back and forth between Canada and Morocco. At one point, a hundred pages of the manuscript were stolen by a thief in Marrakech and recovered. I wrote in the pristine order of my study in Toronto, pavement cafés of Yorkville, the rooftops of Marrakech in Morocco, and sometimes in the back seat of cars. I fractured both bones of my right forearm at my health club in Marrakech, lost all my files on my computer, and had a six-tiered glass bookshelf come crashing down in the night as I slept close to it. Completely unaware, I was also the victim of the *magie noire* practice prevalent in Marrakech and continually robbed and stalked. A few people observed this travail from close and far, coming very near to exhaustion by the drama that accompanied me and the writing process. Yet they simply refused to leave my side.

I acknowledge that without the startling challenge presented by my lively agent Sam Hiyate the book may not have emerged in this genre. I thank him for his suggestions, support, and the confidence he displays in representing me. I also remain dazzled by the editorial wizardry of Marc Côté, Publisher of Cormorant books. I am also deeply touched by the assistance of the Writers' Trust of Canada for allocating an emergency Woodcock Fund for me and the Writers' Reserve grants of the Ontario Arts Council.

I thank Malka Green for never leaving my side; Margaret Atwood for wise counsel and slaps on the wrist; Dr. Jonathan Bashinsky for his overwhelming affection and support; Atiya Mahmood for help during her diplomatic assignment to the Kingdom of Morocco; Mohammad Tanji, the Kingdom of Morocco's ambassador to Canada; the Bahra family of Marrakech; Turia, Achwak, Lamia, Malak, Yusuf, and Mehdi, for opening both their home and hearts to me; Chafiq Bahra for continuing to be my first friend in Marrakech and still caring; and Robert Mars and Stephen Scarman for establishing a British stronghold in Marrakech and being true chevaliers. Thanks also to the inhabitants of the village at Ras Mouka Oasis, Tiznit, Morocco, whose timely resistance saved me from a life catastrophe; to David Montgomery for being barman, banker, and boulevardier *par excellence*, I owe a debt of gratitude. The ever-present grace and hospitality of Ali and Zohra Ben Jelloun and Khalida Moussoui of Casablanca was indispensible. I respect the encouragement of a formidable *belle lettre* in Rabat, Fatema Mernissi. I thank Heff for joining me in Marrakech to shoot some footage at "the scene of the crime." I also thank Paolo, the proprietor of Café Arabe in the city of Marrakech for permitting me to complete the book in a magical environment, and the management at Hotel La Mamounia, Marrakech, who allowed me to write at the hotel in February of 2006, as well as bury a wedding ring and a Tiffany's silver hair brush in the olive gardens of the hotel and retrieve them three years later! Finally, I thank my valiant friend Khaild Usman whose protection and optimism is matchless.